IT CAME FROM THE CLOSET

QUEER REFLECTIONS ON HORROR

EDITED BY JOE VALLESE
WITH A FOREWORD BY KIRSTY LOGAN

Interior illustrations by Bishakh Som

Saraband

Published by Saraband,
3 Clairmont Gardens
Glasgow, G3 7LW
www.saraband.net

ISBN: 9781913393823
eISBN: 9781913393984

Printed and bound in Great Britain by Clays Ltd, Elcograf S.p.A.

3 5 7 9 10 8 6 4

PRAISE FOR *IT CAME FROM THE CLOSET*

"A book that should be read from cover to cover." *SNACK MAGAZINE*

"A brilliant display of expert criticism, wry humor, and original thinking. This is full of surprises." *PUBLISHERS WEEKLY* (**starred review**)

"A critical text on the intersections of film, queer studies, and pop culture." *BOOKLIST* (**starred review**)

"An essential look at how spooky movies so often offer solace through subversiveness." *ELECTRIC LITERATURE*

"An impressively diverse array of queer voices contributes their opinions on how and why particular horror movies made a personal and indelible impression on them." *BAY AREA REPORTER*

"A really terrific collection of essays by a great selection and variety of different authors ... about the intersection between queer studies and queer identity and horror movies." *GOTHAMIST*

"Wonderful and only somewhat disturbing ... (the subject is horror, after all). ... Horror, the anthology argues, while often full of misogyny and anti-trans, homophobic tropes, is also uniquely subversive and queer." *SHONDALAND*

"Weaving elegantly between passages on theory to first sexual encounters and wrenching experiences with a surrogate, the essays take surprising turns and don't look for easy answers. The movies they take on are as varied as the writing styles and traverse the queer spectrum." *BOMB*

"This book is perfect for exploring the queerness of horror through a kaleidoscopic lens." *THEM*

"A fantastic anthology of writing about horror, all from deliciously queer perspectives." *MS.*

"Unique and insightful." *DAILY DEAD*

"What is the monstrous and what does it mean to us? *It Came from the Closet* collects twenty-five takes on twenty-five horror films that make us cringe, crack up, turn away, and turn back again—each piece lavishly queer in its intelligence, vulnerability, and wit." **PAUL LISICKY, author of** *Later: My Life at the Edge of the World*

"Why do queers love horror? What a gift to read writers I love and admire offer so many different answers. *It Came from the Closet* is at times beautiful, at times funny, at times gorgeously weird and baroque, and always as off-kilter brilliant as the genre, and queerness, itself." **ALEX MARZANO-LESNEVICH, author of** *The Fact of a Body: A Murder and a Memoir*

"*It Came from the Closet* is the perfect gay bible for me. The navigations and dissections of some of my favorite slashers through various queer lenses are akin to any great horror film: mind-blowing, eye-popping, and heart-ripping. This book will see you and destroy you!" **DREW DROEGE, actor, writer, comedian**

"*It Came from the Closet* is a fantastic collection of diverse queer perspectives—an accessible, provocative, and much-welcomed addition to the growing body of queer horror analysis of our favorite films, new and old." **JESSICA PARANT, cocreator of Spinsters of Horror**

Contents

Part III. Fatal Attractions

Part IV. Whatever You Do, Don't Fall Asleep

Part V: Final Cuts

Foreword

KIRSTY LOGAN

I've spent a lot of time thinking about this foreword while going about my little queer life: building towers of blocks so my one-year-old can knock them down, reading *Goodnight Moon* for the five thousandth time, waking at 3:00 a.m. to coo "It's okay sweetie, just a bad dream, go back to sleep," watching films where women get hacked to death or sometimes hack others to death, writing books where I make people up just so they can experience terrible things I've also made up; you know, #JustQueerMumThings.

And I kept focusing on one word in the book's title.

Reflections.

The queer part and the horror part, I think we're all fine with. But: reflections. The thing about a reflection is that it's not the real thing. It's just a version. I don't know about you, but I've never felt that horror gives us LGBTQIA+ people accurate representation. The best we can have is a reflection: an image mirrored, turned backwards; an image in shifting water, wavering and distorted.

But is that so bad? Is it really so important to see your exact doppelgänger—and would that even be desirable? Or would it be, in its own way, horrifying?

Horror as a genre is thriving—it has been for a long time, but it seems more mainstream, accepted and respected than ever, even if there is a tendency to tack the word "elevated" on the front. The UK horror film scene in particular is an exciting place, with filmmakers like Rose Glass (*Saint Maud*), Remi Weekes (*His House*), Prano Bailey-Bond (*Censor*) and Rob Savage (*Host*) producing incredible and bold new work. I've seen so many recent horror films that I've loved, been freaked

1

out by, or been inspired by—and with British films, I do appreciate seeing architecture and hearing accents that are more familiar. I didn't choose a British film for my essay, because (like in many of the other essays in this book), I found that the themes I wanted to explore felt borderless, reflecting human nature rather than specific geographies.

Even with films made just up the road from my home, I've never seen myself or my life depicted on a screen. I doubt I ever will, and I don't think I want to.

But a reflection? A shifting, changing, backwards thing; an uncovering, a betrayal, a strange manifestation; something we can puzzle over, get right up close to—or ignore until it's hidden by dust, depending on how we feel?

Yes. Let's have that.

—Kirsty Logan
Glasgow, Scotland
February 2023

Introduction

JOE VALLESE

"WHAT ARE YOU, queer or somethin'?"

I'm eight years old and, though it's my first time hearing the word, the instant knot in my belly tells me it isn't something you want to be called. I'm watching *Sleepaway Camp*, the at once deeply transphobic and effusively homoerotic cult slasher, with my two teenage brothers. We're all stereotypes in our own right: they're cis, straight, sports-loving, girl-crazy wiseasses, and I'm the closeted baby brother—chubby, bookish, my brain struggling to simultaneously identify and bury any visible evidence of my lust for the beefy, crop-topped dolts on the screen. But, at the moment, we're just three kids from New Jersey, sitting too close to the television, gleefully awaiting the next gory kill.

It is Angela, the film's painfully shy fourteen-year-old protagonist, who has this accusation spat at her by Judy, a recently endowed bully who wields her breasts like a weapon. Judy's hatred of Angela stems from the latter being mousy, flat-chested, and seemingly uninterested in boys. Angela's late bloomer status is somehow a personal affront to Judy, whose face contorts with disgust every time she sees Angela not in a bikini, not swimming, not flirting. When Judy calls Angela "queer" in their crowded cabin, she's actively othering and attempt-ing to ostracize her. It's the early '80s, AIDS is fast making the queer community both victim and boogeyman, and Judy knows exactly what she's doing.

In a different circumstance, I'd steel myself for my brothers' inevi-table borrowing of a homophobic joke for my daily teasing (I learned early on to steer clear whenever I heard Andrew Dice Clay's voice booming through the bedroom door) but when we're watching a horror movie, it seems I most closely resemble the little brother they want me to be. They see my enthusiasm for the genre—my lack of fear watching Freddy Krueger invisibly slash a young woman to ribbons and drag her bloody body across a ceiling; the grin on my face while Jason Voorhees zips someone up in a sleeping bag and beats them to death against a tree; my effortless recitation of creepy dialogue from *Children of the Corn*—as a promising development. It means maybe I'm not as soft as I appear, that this perceived toughness might someday translate to me no longer flinching when they drive a football at my bespectacled face (spoiler alert: it won't). We share an insatiable love for these movies for very different reasons—they want to see tits and blood, while I want to see how the Final Girl outsmarts and overpowers the killer/monster/demon/whatever—but, for ninety-ish minutes, some of the distance between us is bridged.

Sleepaway Camp's infamous twist ending throws a wrench in things. Angela, we learn, is not only the killer but is also Peter, forced by his mentally ill aunt to live as a girl and sent off to summer camp (of all places!) with no contingency plan for how to deal with communal showers or his roiling hormones. The film's final shot—Angela, naked and bloody from a recent kill, growling like an animal—makes my brothers cackle, less out of shock or disgust than because it has the audacity to give us a distant, lingering view of full-frontal nudity (dicks, of course, are hilarious). They'll soon leave *Sleepaway Camp* behind and move onto a palate cleanser such as *Porky's* or *Bachelor Party*, while I'm left with questions I can't ask and a nagging sadness for Angela I can't shake.

Despite its bounty of queer themes, *Sleepaway Camp* is hardly a cinematic ally. It offers no grand social commentary or carefully architected subtext. Rather, queerness is used, even appropriated, as a plot device; at best, it's a sloppy framework for getting the film to its shocking finale, and at worst, it dangerously conflates mental illness, child abuse, and transness. In a society that prioritizes masculinity and increasingly endorses violence as a means to protect it, *of course* Angela would be driven to kill! Angela—er, Peter—isn't queer at all, he's just stepping back into his primal, God-given maleness. Or something . . . While *Sleepaway Camp* wasn't the first and certainly wouldn't be the last horror film to equate deviation from the gender binary as some nefarious act of masking (*Homicidal, Psycho, Terror Train, Dressed to Kill, The Silence of the Lambs*, and *Insidious 2*, for example, span multiple cinematic eras yet they all follow similarly exploitative blueprints) it is especially egregious in how simultaneously unresearched *and* confident it is. *Sleepaway Camp* is as invested in queerbaiting as it is in fearmongering, all seemingly in service to making a horror movie that ticks the requisite "surprise ending" box. Queerness is a means to an end and, boy, the ending of *Sleepaway Camp* sure is mean.

From this perch, it's hard to deny that horror movies can be, well, pretty fucked up. And yet, I and so many other queer people somehow can't help but find immense guiltless, unironic pleasure in them. We're titillated by the genre, even when it actively excludes us from the narrative—or, worse, includes us only to marginalize, villainize, or altogether neglect us. In 2011's *Scream 4*, the third sequel in Wes Craven's metahorror franchise, a character claims that "to survive a modern horror movie, you pretty much have to be gay." On the surface, it's a clever, progressive thesis, but, ultimately, it rings hollow: Does the novelty of queerness shield a character from danger because they are unconsidered and therefore underestimated, or is it simply that queer characters are so seldom found in horror films that their survival is a mere technicality? (Later, a character unsuccessfully attempts to save himself by telling Ghostface that he's "gay . . . if it helps.")

Notable efforts at integrating queer storylines into horror have had similarly mixed, even deleterious results: the brutal 2003 French slasher *High Tension (Haute tension)* undercuts its heroine's harrowing arc by revealing her to be a delusional, lesbian psychopath who has just murdered the object of her affection's entire family; Darren Aronofsky's ballerina nightmare *Black Swan*, campy and satisfying in so many ways, is guilty of reducing Nina (Natalie Portman) and Lily's (Mila Kunis) trippy sex scene into a figment of the former's imagination, whittling her down to a sexually repressed saddo; *Single White Female* unfairly hangs Hedy's (Jennifer Jason Leigh) terrifying break from reality and obsessive desire to merge her life with her roommate Allie's (Bridget Fonda) on unresolved sister issues that border on incestuous ideation; and Gus Van Sant's misguided *Psycho* remake places all of its queer eggs in the basket of Julianne Moore's interpretation of Lila Crane, attributing her no-time-to-flirt persistence to good old dykedom rather than a desire to find her missing sister (Van Sant digresses from the film's shot-by-shot rigidity just enough to allow Moore to get in a nice, butch kick to Norman Bates's face when she discovers him in Mother drag). It also isn't lost on me that these films' emphases on lesbianism reinforce the fact that queerness in mainstream horror is permissible as long as it's determined by and filtered through the male gaze.

So then, how are we to think about the complicated relationship between the queer community and the horror genre? How can we find such camaraderie in the very thing that so often slights us? As a still-closeted, still-horror-obsessed teenager in the late '90s and early '00s who did not yet know anyone who was out, I worried over this incongruity, fearing that somehow my wires were even more crossed than I knew. Was my affection for horror just some residual self-loathing, a sorry attempt at maintaining that bit of machismo I credited to myself while in my brothers' company? Did I need to shed my boyish bloodlust to make room in my brain and heart for more heady, urgent, queer pop culture? Worse still, did my chatty, encyclopedic, know-it-all-and-dying-to-share-it zeal for horror actually give my secret away? Thinking about this self-induced anxiety embarrasses me now, but when you're always hiding in plain sight, you second-guess every move you make, every word you utter, every passion you claim.

Introduction

It wasn't until I stumbled upon AOL chat rooms and Internet forums solely dedicated to horror that I discovered just how deep queer affinity for the genre runs. I was astounded by how many regular posters proudly identified (from behind avatars and witty handles) as LGBTQIA+, and was floored by how masterfully they explicated what they saw as queer coding in many of their favorite movies. My first true cyberbuddy, with whom I spent countless hours after school and on weekends AIMing about all things horror and, inevitably, queerness, worshipped Argento, Craven, and Madonna; I'd later find out, as we aged and moved onto more public forms of social media such as MySpace and Friendster, that he was none other than "Vogue Boy," who would eventually go viral by posting a video of himself at nine years old perfectly performing the song's iconic choreography against a green screen of a pre-9/11 NYC skyline. This is all to say: I eventually came to understand that, while I was busy fretting over whether being gay would displace me from connecting with the films I loved most, queer affection for horror was actively being claimed, recontextualized, and integrated into the culture and community—and, like most things touched by queerness, horror becomes more textured, more nuanced, and far more exciting when viewed through a queer lens.

Though the current horror landscape is slowly (*slooooowly*) telling more queer-centered and -adjacent stories, we largely remain tasked with *reading ourselves into* these films we love, to seek out characters and set pieces that speak to, mirror, and parallel the unique ways in which we encounter, navigate, and occupy the world. In this way, *It Came from the Closet* is very much the anthology of my cinephilic dreams: a collection of eclectic memoirs that use horror as the lens through which the writers consider and reflect upon queer identity, and vice versa. These essays don't draw easy lines between horror and queerness but rather convey a rich reciprocity, complicating and questioning as much as they clarify. The powerful and diverse voices in this collection reckon with trauma, shame, grief, loss, abuse, race, discrimination,

7

parenthood, familial structures, religion, disability, illness, art, love, and so much more. While these essays spotlight each writer's singular queer perspective, their respective representations and analyses of "the Horror Film" serve as a kind of universal connective tissue between them and their readers.

If current social media and podcast culture are any indication, the threads between queerness and horror have never been this tightly knit nor this expansive. *It Came from the Closet* holds space for its writers (and hopefully its readers) to engage in difficult, often surprising conversations with and about their films of focus. Most vitally, in these pages our queerness acts not as a barrier to connecting with these films but as an entry point. Like the best horror films, these essays will both satisfy and subvert expectations. And like any first-of-its-kind anthology, *It Came from the Closet* should not be read as definitive, which signifies a conclusion, but as a vibrant continuation of a dialogue that began long before I conceived of and curated this project—and will undoubtedly continue far beyond its pages.

Oh, and we're spoiling *everything*. Consider yourself warned.

—Joe Vallese
Palisades Park, New Jersey

A Demon-Girl's Guide to Life

S. TRIMBLE

The Exorcist

I'M SITTING ON a church pew covered in carpet the color of rust. It rises from the floor and wraps around the pews, musty and rough. The band has just finished playing us closer to Jesus, and one of the teens is testifying about his experience at a nearby revival service, where he was moved by the spirit to weeping and shaking. I don't like the sound of this. I'm struggling to be a believer, so I figure this won't happen to me. But part of me worries it might. And the notion of my inner life rising to the surface for others to see and hear is not good. I'm a twelve-year-old girl dreaming of other girls. I'm into one across the aisle and two rows up. And I'm pretty sure what's happening inside me needs to stay hidden.

It was the early 1990s. Gay was on the verge of going mainstream, but the culture wars were in full swing. In the face of the AIDS crisis, a newly empowered Christian right had squared off against queer communities in the name of faith, flag, and family. There were pronouncements of God's punishment and demands for mandatory testing and quarantine. By the time my family was trying on an evangelical shade of Anglicanism, Pat Buchanan was declaring a war for the soul of America and the Westboro Baptist Church was becoming infamous for anti-gay activism. In 1998, they picketed the funeral of Matthew Shepard, holding up signs declaring the young gay man who was tortured and left lashed to a fence was now burning in hell.

This was the cultural climate in which I grew into my queerness and discovered horror films. I watched them with my sister and cousin on summer afternoons, popping rentals into the VCR and metabolizing the mayhem. The feeling I remember most is glee. I cackled at Freddy

13

Krueger preparing death traps for teens like a demonic Wile E. Coyote. I loved Annie Wilkes from *Misery*, the deranged fan who commits heinous acts of violence but decries a potty mouth. I was entranced by the gender distortions on display. Freddy revels in being a badman, the slimy underside of the Father Knows Best ideal. And Annie does femininity so right she's wrong, exposing resentful, proprietary impulses beneath the caregiving surface. On some level I knew horror wasn't just about monsters doing bad things. It's also about doing gender badly. It's about the threat and the thrill of getting it wrong.

I brought all of this with me to *The Exorcist*. William Friedkin's 1973 horror classic is about a twelve-year-old girl who gets possessed by a foulmouthed demon and begins saying, doing, and knowing things she shouldn't. When medical science fails to explain what's wrong with Regan MacNeil (Linda Blair), her mother turns to a priest with psychiatric training for help. Father Karras (Jason Miller) is wrestling with some demons of his own, so the possessed girl forces him to find his faith again. Released in the midst of Vietnam and Watergate, a deepening economic crisis, and the ongoing energies of feminism, gay liberation, and Black Power, the film's depiction of a white girl corrupted by evil tapped into white American fears of nightmare futures. It also changed the cultural status of horror films for good. News outlets reported sold-out showings, endless lines, and viewers fainting, vomiting, and hyperventilating. Journalists staked out cinema lobbies, waiting for those who would stumble out of the theater partway through, shuddering and shaking their heads. Newspapers with gravitas suddenly had to take pop culture seriously. And horror, a genre previously maligned by critics and tastemakers, stole the show at the 1974 Academy Awards, when *The Exorcist* was nominated for ten Oscars, including Best Picture.

The *first* first time I watched *The Exorcist*, it was on TV, sliced up by commercial breaks, on one of those summer afternoons when I was twelve. I remember cracking up when we finally got to the head-twisting scene, shock and horror waylaid by a dozen pop-culture parodies I'd seen prior. The second time, in my late teens, it was a whole other film: the humor pitch black, the story creeping under my skin. I watched it alone, at night, with darkness pressing on the house. And it wasn't the cut-for-TV version, so I saw more of Regan's filthiness, including that moment when she crushes her mother's face into her bloodied vagina. I was older and becoming more attuned to the adult world and its violent separations of normal from not, saved from damned. I saw a revolting girl revolting against the little-girl box in which she was stuck—and I saw an army of men working to put her back in.

These two different viewing experiences taught me something about how selves and stories get tangled up together, how we remake ourselves through stories and see different things in those stories because of our ever-changing selves. As a child, I identified with Regan and aspired to her badassery, and the rest of the film fell away. When I was a teen, the context of her struggle came into focus and I was unnerved and outraged by all the men working to reform her. Now, as an overworked, harried professional, I find myself identifying with Father Karras as much as with the girl he's called on to save. *The Exorcist* is one of those films that keeps weaving into my personal mythology, offering shifting identifications as I age. Horror is good at this. The genre is all about slippery feelings and alliances. It's especially kaleidoscopic for those of us cast as real-life monsters. Once upon a time I saw myself reflected in a demon-girl, and she's been a fellow traveler ever since.

WE'RE IN THE atrium of a suburban shopping mall, sandwiched between the central staircase and the food court. Sunlight streams through skylights. Scents of french fries and teriyaki sauce waft toward me as I prepare for my big entrance. I'm wearing a white robe cinched at the waist. A crown of tangled twigs sits atop my head and my chin-length hair is tucked behind my ears. Someone positions a heavy wooden cross over my right shoulder as I find the stooped position I've been perfecting: burdened and determined. My sister and the other girls are moving through choreography on a makeshift stage, twirling pink ribbons as I weave toward them through the crowd. The band reaches a crescendo as I mount the stage, ready to die on this food court Golgotha. I understand I'm on a mission to proclaim the love of Christ to Easter shoppers laden with chocolate, but I'm distracted by the joy of performing martyred masculinity. I am handsome and tragic and the undisputed star of the show. Jesus was my one and only drag performance.

THE FIRST TIME I saw *The Exorcist* I had recently survived a serious bout of gender trouble. Like Regan, I became monstrous around the age of twelve, when I was dubbed Manwoman by my seventh-grade classmates and spent the year getting schooled on what girls are supposed to act, look, sound, and smell like. The experience filled me with shame. By then I knew I was queer, but I both craved and dreaded finding stories about people like me. Having suffered through an in-class viewing of *Ace Ventura: Pet Detective* alongside my bullies, I was convinced pop-culture pictures of queer and trans lives were doing me no favors. The trans "reveal" at the end of that film sent my peers into fits of laughter, their hysteria matched onscreen by Jim Carrey, who blubbers in the shower over the realization that he'd once kissed a freak.

But gender-bending has a different status in horror. There's a tradition of representing psychotic killers driven by what Carol Clover calls "gender distress."[1] From Norman Bates to Buffalo Bill, this trope has been both critiqued and reclaimed by queer fans and critics. There's also the figure of the castrating woman, the protagonist of rape-revenge

1. Carol Clover, *Men, Women, and Chain Saws: Gender in the Modern Horror Film* (Princeton, NJ: Princeton University Press, 1992), 27.

and slasher films who survives by unmanning her chainsaw-wielding oppressor. This figure belongs to the realm of what Barbara Creed refers to as the "monstrous-feminine,"[2] a cluster of representations of women in horror that are projections of masculine anxieties. The vampire, the witch, the breeding alien, the aging psychopath—they bleed and bite and ooze and shape-shift, queering the categories that preserve the patriarchal order of things. Regan MacNeil is one of them: the possessed girl who collapses the boundary between self and other and, like Eve before her, admits the devil into the world of men. Horror plays with white patriarchal nightmares and taps into our ambivalence about normality, which means the potential for radical storytelling is always there. We watch, awestruck, as the world we recognize comes apart at the seams. We love-hate our monsters and are repulsed-fascinated by the havoc they wreak.

As a kid watching horror movies on summer afternoons, I wasn't reading feminist film theory. But I sensed that gender played differently in the genre. Once, my younger cousin and horror-watching buddy treated me to a detailed (but fully clothed) reenactment of the climax of *Sleepaway Camp*, in which Angela is revealed as having a penis and being the killer all at once. Given my *Ace Ventura* experience, this could have been rough. But there was something irresistible about my cousin's performance. The capering, the cackling, the maniacal grin—it tapped into that quality I can only in hindsight name as "camp," the way horror winks at you while it screws with all the norms you live by. We had a similar reaction to John Waters's *Serial Mom*, in which Kathleen Turner is very June Cleaver until she drops the mask to prank call her neighbor. "Is this the Cocksucker residence?" she growls into the phone. We dissolved into laughter—three kids totally jazzed by the violence beneath the housewife veneer. This was storytelling I could work with.

2. Barbara Creed, *The Monstrous-Feminine: Film, Feminism, Psychoanalysis* (London: Routledge, 1993), 31–42.

I don't remember consciously identifying with Regan back then, but part of me must have registered our alikeness. We were both white girls around the same age. And while her metamorphosis is extreme, some of what makes her gross are qualities I understood my alter ego to possess. My peers had made it clear Manwoman was smelly and aggressive, and moved in all the wrong ways. And when they spoke for me, they pitched their voices low and growly. So, I would have noticed that one of the most unnerving things about Regan is that deep, guttural voice provided by the unseen star of the film, Mercedes McCambridge. Maybe I laughed my way through *The Exorcist* that first time to deflect some of the horror of recognizing myself in such a character. But I don't think so. Regan's mannish voice and foul language don't map onto the white-girl part she's supposed to play in society. Just when she's meant to solidify into a future wife and mother, she starts pissing on the carpet and spewing green stuff instead. But I wanted demon-Regan to survive the casting out of her demon. Her knowingness and shamelessness and fucked-up sense of humor were enticing. I was exhilarated by the sights and sounds of girlhood gone awry.

As a queer kid navigating a Canadian middle school in the 1990s, I had tried to be quiet and clean and very, very nice to convince my peers I was one of them. This strategy didn't do much to stave off social punishment. Luckily, horror opened me up to new possibilities for survival. Watching demon-Regan play mind games with the adults who wanted to save her, watching her topple furniture and grab her psychiatrist by the balls, I saw power in freakery and transgression and wondered if it could be mine. I was leaving childhood behind and starting to notice what the adult world does to those it casts as deviants and outsiders. Being quiet and nice wasn't going to cut it. So, like Regan, I started saying inappropriate things, especially at church. I turned youth meetings into debates on hot topics like abortion and feminism. I goaded adults into revealing their homophobic views and then gave them shit for it. I refused communion. But I could feel the stakes getting higher. My wrongness was bubbling to the surface in ways I couldn't control. My days of reveling in Jesus drag were over.

THE DAY THE Pastor announced that Laura was engaged to be married, I left the church for good. People had been whispering for a while about "Laura's problem." I'd seen her after services, on her knees surrounded by church leaders, all praying for the overcoming of her difficulty. Laura was in the church band. Once, she'd covered "(You Make Me Feel Like) A Natural Woman" after Sunday service was over, devastation on her face as she hit the chorus, desperate for it to be true. I'd been tracking all of this because I felt connected to her. When I first joined the church, we'd bonded over a shared love of guitars. I started to see myself reflected in the butchness she was determined to shed. By the time I came out to my mom and sister at fourteen, I understood I was witnessing a form of conversion therapy—that church leaders were praying Laura's gay away when they surrounded her after service, laying their hands on her back and shoulders, murmuring. And then came the happy news: Laura had been fixed up with a nice young man through the church and now, after a few months of dating, they were engaged. Praise be to God. That Sunday I went home and decided not to go back.

THE SECOND TIME I saw *The Exorcist*, I was an out queer teenager without a church. A healthy fear of Ouija boards aside, I'd never been a true believer, so leaving the church didn't feel like a spiritual loss. Instead, I lost the world I shared, however uneasily, with my dad. My mom quit the church before I did, alienated from the congregation first by her feminism and then by my queerness. But my dad was—is—devout. When I was younger, Sunday mornings often found him getting ready for church with *The Jimmy Swaggart Show* on in the background, his morning ritual accompanied by the sweating, spitting, speechifying televangelist. Swaggart was one of many who used evangelical Christianity to draw a new map of manhood in the 1980s and '90s, after the postwar liberation movements threatened to knock white men from their rightful place as kings of the humans. Within this more flexible framework, white men were both fathers and sons, patriarchs on earth and children of God for eternity. So evangelical masculinity was authoritarian but weirdly malleable, all loose limbs and speaking in tongues and crying out for godly guidance—especially when Satan got involved. Swaggart's tearful apologies for engaging the services of sex workers alerted me to the role of women in the stories and selves these men create. And Laura's engagement brought it too close to home.

I didn't know this when I sat down to watch the uncut version of *The Exorcist*, but demonic possession movies are the perfect vehicle for stories of men remaking themselves. Encoded in their depiction of a struggle over the body and soul of a young woman, there's usually the tale of a man in crisis. His is a conversion story in which he loosens his grip on science and reason and learns to believe in things unseen. Her body, his rebirth. Possession movies boomed in the 1970s and '80s, just as American evangelism began to cohere into a political and cultural force, reinvigorating white manhood as it went. Occult films dramatized this reinvention, throwing shade at white-coated doctors and siding with men in black robes, men tapped into a world of spiritualism and ritual, gods and monsters. We know from the opening ten minutes of *The Exorcist*, which take place in Iraq, that all of this is structured by the white imagination, that these are white men who have journeyed to places coded as mysterious, dark, and hotter than hell. The American man has faced evil, which always comes from elsewhere, and rediscovered his faith in the process. Now he's ready to restore the nation's beacon-on-a-hill image. And this work begins at home—with family values.

The Exorcist spoke to adult generations reeling from the '60s counterculture, convinced the kids are not all right. As Stephen King put it in

Danse Macabre,[3] the film addressed "all those parents who felt, in a kind of agony and terror, that they were losing their children and could not understand why or how it was happening." It's not much of a reach, really. From one perspective, the '60s movements had collapsed into the helter-skelter of the Manson Family. To those who were horrified and titillated by the 1970–71 trial of Charles Manson in LA, Regan's onscreen metamorphosis into a cussing, puking demon-girl might have reminded them of white girls who'd shaved themselves bald and carved bloody Xs into their foreheads, blowing kisses at their murderous messiah. Images of monstrous youth helped discredit the liberation movements of the 1960s, convincing many that an authoritarian correction was in order. Monstrous white girls, in particular, were bad omens. With apocalypse and paranoia in the air, *Rosemary's Baby* had already established that white women can become the carriers of nightmare futures. Which means white *girls* need to be kept on the straight and narrow.

So, there's a reading of *The Exorcist* that goes like this: the problem with Regan MacNeil is she doesn't have a daddy. She's being raised by a single mom with an androgynous name, potty mouth, and Hollywood life. This crack in the white family unit is how her demon, Captain Howdy, finds its way in, diverting the girl on the cusp of puberty from her path to an all-American future. Regan is supposed to grow up to marry a white man and have white children who will inherit his name, growing his family line and the property that goes with it and transmitting to future generations the worldview that makes white American families the image of goodness. But an absent dad exposes the girl to physical and spiritual corruption. The solution, then, must be a substitute father figure who can guide her back into the fold. We watch as men in white coats are followed by priests in black cassocks and the God who authorizes them. Patriarchal power layered on thick, correcting the girl who's gone astray.

3. Stephen King, *Danse Macabre* (New York: Gallery Books, 1981), 179.

The second time I watched *The Exorcist*, sitting alone in the dark, I wasn't laughing. I was reaching for a queer future, a life on my own terms, and all I could see were the forces arranging themselves around Regan to bring her back into line. Well before the exorcism was underway, I saw her observed, tested, and prodded. I saw her strapped to a gurney beneath harsh light, her throat exposed and a needle plunged into her carotid artery. I saw medical experts willfully unseeing what they couldn't explain, clinging to theories about brain lesions because without them they have nothing to say. Finally, I saw her drugged and strapped to her bed, physically and chemically incarcerated. After all that, it was almost a relief to see Regan spider-walking headfirst down the stairs. Awake and unleashed. I knew there was a drama playing out across the body of this wayward girl, that putting her right was somehow necessary to these men and their crumbling sense of normalcy. I knew because I'd seen it before: the prayers for a woman made unnatural by temptation and redeemed by Your grace, oh Lord; the benevolence with which she's guided into righteous married life. Amen.

IT'S THE MIDDLE of the night. Streetlights are lit. Inside a tiny house on a residential street on the outskirts of Toronto, the quiet is broken by a screaming child. A three-year-old races down the hallway from her bedroom and huddles beneath the dining table, breathing hard. She's asleep the whole time. Her parents have been told it's "night terrors" but aren't sure what this means. They've just started their own business—a 24-hours-a-day, 7-days-a-week operation—and there are two other children in the house, one of them an infant. The girl's parents are craving sleep and praying for a miracle. They're a churchgoing couple, but not overzealous. For them it's as much about community and aunties selling their knitting at church bazaars as it is about faith. But when their minister hears about the night terrors and offers to bless their house, they say, *Why not? What do we have to lose?* The girl isn't home when the kindly, gray-haired man arrives with holy water and heavenly vibes. He moves through the house, sprinkling drops and saying soothing words. Shortly after this visit, the girl stops screaming in the night.

I DON'T REMEMBER my night terrors. What's memory to my parents is myth to me. But I live with the knowledge that, once upon a time, an early version of me responded to things nobody else could see—as if another dimension mushroomed open inside our house with only me inside. Where did those experiences go? Where are they stored in me? Lately, I've been wondering the same thing about Regan MacNeil. "She doesn't remember any of it," her mother says at the end of the film. Regan's amnesia assures audiences that normalcy has returned, that the white girl has her innocence back. Where before she knew too much, now she knows nothing. But what happens next time Regan sees a bedroom curtain billowing in the wind? Or a doctor tries to touch her? What happens when what her body knows becomes too much for her mind to repress?

I'm always interested in the futures that come into view at the end of a horror film. From one perspective, the white girl who outlives the monster has been rewarded for her purity; her survival guarantees that white families will continue to make babies and have good futures. But what if her brush with monstrosity isn't so easily relegated to the past? What if she's changed forever, transformed by new desires and open to strange alliances? These questions first arose for me when I saw a little girl queered by demonic superpowers, and I wondered what might remain of that otherness when the demon is cast out. They felt even more pressing when I rewatched *The Exorcist* as an adult—when I noticed, for the first time, the queerness of Father Karras.

Father Damien Karras is the exhausted, guilt-stricken priest who Chris MacNeil (Ellen Burstyn) begs to save her child. He's kind and sad and deeply afraid he's no longer fit for his job of counseling priests who are struggling. Watching *The Exorcist* as a young person, I didn't know about the Hays Code that handcuffed Hollywood storytelling for decades, ensuring that queerness could only appear as subtext and that characters coded as gay wound up unhappy or dead at the end of the film. I was too young to notice that Father Karras's closest, most tender relationship is with Father Dyer (William O'Malley), the show tune–singing priest who gently slides his shoes off and puts him to bed when he's drunk. I didn't catch the innuendo when the homicide detective tells Karras he reminds him of the actor Sal Mineo. And I didn't really take in the depth of Father Dyer's devastation when he reads his friend the last rites at the end of the film. All I saw, back then, was yet another man in a lineup of men called on to cleanse a filthy girl. Now I see something more complicated: a queer man who sacrifices himself so the girl can survive. When Karras invites Regan's demon inside him and then throws himself out her bedroom window, is it a bury-your-gays moment? Or is there room to imagine a queer future beyond the final frame?

These days I like to see Karras and Regan as queer kin, the one giving up his future to ensure the other has one. We can assume Regan has been put right and will grow up to marry and be a good wife and mother, never recalling the priest who sacrificed himself to make it happen. Or we can assume, as I do, that Regan will never be the same after sharing her body with a lascivious, murderous monster; that doors have been opened that can't be shut tightly enough; that the alliance with Father Karras gave the girl a chance to become something interesting. It's what queer theorist Eve Kosofsky Sedgwick[4] would call a "reparative reading," which is a way of naming how marginalized audiences creatively engage with stories that aren't meant to sustain us. Horror was the playground where I learned to read this way, to send the entire story spinning off its axis by rooting for the monster. Horror helped me love my terrible truths, the things about me that disquieted others. Amid the mayhem and the viscera, signposts pointing to queer futures.

4. Eve Kosofsky Sedgwick, *Touching Feeling: Affect, Pedagogy, Performativity* (Durham, NC: Duke University Press, 2003), 123–51.

Both Ways

CARMEN MARIA MACHADO

Jennifer's Body

QUEER READER, let us take a moment for Jennifer's body. Not just the 2009 film—a once-panned, now-beloved feminist cult classic—but Jennifer's *body*. Megan Fox in knitted leg warmers and short-shorts, a puffy coat and red fishnets, a color guard uniform, an *Evil Dead* raglan tee and star-spangled underwear, a cropped hoodie and low-rise jeans, an Edwardian prom dress with long white opera gloves. A wet strand of hair drawn through her mouth. Swimming naked in a lake glassy with twilight. Blackening the tip of her tongue with a lighter. In hunger, wan and beautiful as a consumptive heroine. Levitating. Snarling. Doe eyes, full and glossed lips. Dropping onto a car like a wild cat. Projectile vomiting an unctuous, inky liquid onto her best friend. Teeth like a nurse shark. A distended, disarticulated jaw like a python. Jennifer's body on a sacrificial altar, sobbing. Jennifer's body moving eerily from a great distance; then too close, and from the wrong angle. Jennifer pulling a rod out of her shish-kebabbed torso, saying, through a mouth of blood, "Do you have a tampon?" Jennifer's body underlining the politics of *Jennifer's Body*; a sex symbol through a funhouse mirror. (The film's execs thought she'd be a draw for teenage boys, but teenage boys hated it. They didn't know they were coming to be eaten. Not like that.)

It's happened to me several times now: someone who doesn't know me very well asks me about my favorite horror movies. I am excited; I list this one among them. Sometimes they also love it; sometimes they've never heard of it, but once—well, more than once—they've scrunched up their nose. "*Jennifer's Body*? With Megan Fox? Isn't it ...?" Then they express a riff on a concept. Queerbaiting, gay for titillation, performatively lesbian; whatever they call it, it's always delivered in the tone of an unforgivable crime. In a way, I can hardly blame them; the film was marketed in precisely this fashion, highlighting Megan Fox's tongue dipping into Amanda Seyfried's mouth and, of course, this iconic exchange:

"I thought you only murdered boys."

"I go both ways."

But no, I explain, it's a great movie. A fucking classic. When indie-rock band Low Shoulder comes to perform in the tiny town of Devil's Kettle, Minnesota, two lifelong friends—Needy (Amanda Seyfried) and Jennifer (Fox), a "dork and a babe," respectively—end up at the local watering hole, watching them perform. Midshow the venue goes up in flames; the band disappears Jennifer in their van. She shows up later in Needy's kitchen, ravenous and beaten to hell and vomiting a mysterious black goo. As the community reels from the catastrophe of the fire and its fatalities, Jennifer is unfazed, and possibly even more beautiful than before.

But boys keep going missing and showing up in isolated areas, their bodies ravaged and cannibalized. (The phrase "lasagna with teeth" is used twice.) Needy eventually learns that Low Shoulder—attempting to curry favor with Satan by sacrificing a virgin for fame and fortune—sacrificed Jennifer, a nonvirgin, and she ended up with a demon inside of her. Only Needy knows what's really happening, and only Needy can end her reign of terror.

There are several showdowns in the film's climax and denouement: Needy interrupts Jennifer killing her boyfriend; later, she suits up and goes to Jennifer's bedroom, where the two of them wrestle, levitating in the air before Needy plunges a box cutter into her heart. Needy is sent to an institution; she escapes. As the credits roll, Needy hunts down the band, killing them gruesomely in their hotel room.

Though you'd never know it by reading the contemporaneous reviews, *Jennifer's Body* is terrifically smart and gut-bustlingly funny, gross and tender and nimble all at once, a punchy tribute to small-town survival and a sendup of the saccharine stupidity of post-tragedy rhetoric. (When Jennifer orders two "9/11 tribute shooters," she get them and pouts, "Ugh, Tower One isn't full enough.")

When the film celebrated its tenth anniversary, a new generation of critics and viewers got to experience its insight and prescience, especially in the shadow of #MeToo. The sexist coverage of the film (which in large part was due to the misogyny directed at Megan Fox) now seems unspeakably dated. But I cannot help but wonder about the charge of queerbaiting, which seems on some level to have survived, even intensified. What do we do with all this homoerotic energy? Where does it belong?

THERE ARE MANY themes moving through *Jennifer's Body*—the precarious insecurity of girlhood, the violence of male entitlement, the extreme badness of midaughts rock—but it's impossible to miss its queerness, though for a certain kind of worldview,[1] it's very easy to dismiss. Jennifer and Needy experience so many kinds of intimacy it's amazing we've retconned it into a kiss and a catchphrase. As children they are in love and already unequal: Needy brings her mouth to a cut on Jennifer's hand; Jennifer tells her not to tell. They exchange such long and devoted looks toward each other that a classmate calls them "lesbigay." Needy knows when Jennifer is near, even before the film turns supernatural. A ravenous, freshly turned Jennifer nearly bites Needy, though she resists. They eventually kiss, long and hard and sensuously, on Needy's bed before Needy bounces up, shrieking, "What the fuck are we doing?" Jennifer assures Needy she won't bite, then delivers silly, porny dialogue about "sharing a bed during sleepovers" and how they used to play "boyfriend-girlfriend" in the past. When Needy eventually

---

1. Which I think of as a mix of (understandably) hungry for queer media, (understandably) cynical about queer representation, and extremely sensitive to even a whiff of phoniness.

kills Jennifer, she does it facing her, straddling her; this is how Jennifer's mother finds them, compromised in Jennifer's canopy bed. Just before this, Jennifer breaks her promise and bites Needy in the shoulder, leaving a mark that transfers some of her powers to Needy permanently.

But one of the most interesting things about this film, one of the things that brings me back to it over and over again, is that it is not a film about lesbians, per se; it is not a generically queer perspective on wlw relationships. Instead, its energy is exceptionally specific: what it means to experience parallel sexualities with your best friend as you punch through the last vestiges of childhood; and, significantly, the central body of water that is bisexuality.

The moment in which Jennifer is lured into the band's van—and Needy watches the door close on Jennifer's vulnerable face—is one of rupture; from then on, they are staring at, and moving toward, different horizons. Queer Reader, set your gaze far away—imagine where they are going. Envision them as adults. Needy is a girl just learning she likes girls, sometimes, and loves Jennifer; Jennifer is a girl who, were her life uninterrupted by Satan, would have swung much harder into lesbianism.[2] (For all her talk about dicks and how "salty" boys are, Jennifer is remarkably obsessed with her best friend. Girl, same!) Just before the infamous making out scene, Needy has sex with her boyfriend while Jennifer devours an emo kid she lured to an empty house. Needy's bisexuality comes in fits and starts, serves her and fails her and confounds her; Jennifer dives teeth-first into hers.

WHEN I WAS in my early twenties, I followed a woman with whom I was deeply infatuated to her family's vacation home in Rehoboth Beach. One afternoon, she told me through tears of laughter that when

2. This impression is probably aided by the fact that Megan Fox is, herself, bisexual—she once told *Marie Claire* that Olivia Wilde was so sexy it made her want to "strangle a mountain ox with [her] bare hands"—and was famously extremely into the kissing scene.

I'd gone to take a shower, her mother had politely inquired if I was a lesbian. No, my friend said, Carmen is bisexual. "Oh!" her mother said, genuinely curious. "I've never met anyone who does both things before."

"But *which* things?!" I asked. My friend could not say. We spent the rest of the afternoon speculating on the precise nature of the two things, the way it suggested some massive paradigm shift while also being hilariously specific.

That evening, as we walked along the beach in the dark and while stepping around the clear bodies of hundreds of beached jellyfish, I asked her to be my girlfriend. I'd been waiting so long to ask her, and being surrounded by a landscape of stilled danger felt correct. She was silent for a long beat. "I think I'm straight," she said. "It's not you." Now it was my turn to be silent. "Are you upset with me?" she said. Eventually, I said no, but I was lying. I was heartbroken.

Did I mention we'd had sex? I'd hooked up with her and her boyfriend, back when she'd had one. That was our first encounter: I was a virgin, a unicorn who could only ride herself. Then, I was neither. After they broke up, we stayed in touch. She had a real job and would take me out to dinner; she always let me order extra food and dessert to take home. She started coming over to my house to watch TV and every time there was a commercial she'd kiss me, stopping when the show resumed. I don't even remember what we watched; whatever it was, I couldn't hear it over the sound of my thudding pulse. One time, she asked me if she could draw on me, and I took off my shirt and bra and she straddled me on my bed with a Sharpie in her hand and drew and drew. It felt beautiful, erotic, tingly, like how I imagined it felt to be tattooed, even though when I eventually saw the marks in the bathroom mirror, they were surprisingly imprecise and childish and I was embarrassed for both of us.

For a short and terrible time, I was so in love with her it hurt. But then she stood on that beach and told me she was straight, and I had nothing to say. I was already somewhere else.

I HAVE A real soft spot for stories on conflicted, spectral, transient bisexuality. I always have. While many of my peers turned their nose up at Britney and Madonna and Christina's kiss (staged for attention!) and Katy Perry's "I Kissed a Girl" (fake-gay titillation!) and a million other queer media fragments of my Millennial late adolescence and early adulthood, I always found them somewhere on the spectrum between harmless and delightful; an exercise in reading between the lines that I suspect José Esteban Muñoz would understand. (Plus, *the taste of her cherry ChapStick*" is just pure poetry.) I am sympathetic to the desire to name and shame queerbaiting—it is, after all, an attempt to protect queerness from dilution, from interlopers, from accusations of unseriousness—but every piece of present-day me bristles against it. Who established these terms? Why is it always bisexuals who seem to fall afoul of these rules? It always struck me as odd to think of public queerness in heterosexual terms, even for ostensibly progressive reasons.

I suspect that it's partially an issue of visibility. Bisexuality is slippery; it can appear to be other things, it can disguise itself in ways monosexuality can't, reveal itself against all knowledge and expectations. Bisexuals are coded as fickle, untrustworthy dilettantes. And like homosexuality, but unlike heterosexuality, bisexuality is temporally unmoored, unfixed from the sexual activity or desire of the current moment; a true teleological orientation.

In any case, I suppose you could call my skepticism of "queerbaiting" as a concept pure pragmatism: unless you're lucky enough to grow up in a world in which all forms of sexuality are totally understood, accepted, expressed, and contextualized from an early age as a default potential, many queer people are, at some point, conflicted bisexuals, or something akin to it.[3] Sometimes bisexuality suits you, and you stay; sometimes it doesn't and you keep moving; sometimes you return to it, surprised by your own capacity for mystery; but, at some point, you've crossed those waters. You think you know one thing until you know another. Aren't we all dilettantes, until we aren't anymore?

I went to college in 2004. I saw so many allegedly straight girls kissing each other at frat parties it would've made you want to burn down an Abercrombie & Fitch. Sometimes it was stiff and strange and sometimes it was organic, and yet far be it from me to say who really wanted what, or if the kiss itself wasn't a gateway, or if one of them (or both!) wouldn't be wrist-deep in a date in twelve years' time. People always talked cynically about this gesture as if men were the reason, but it felt like no one ever considered that men were the excuse.

"We can understand queerness itself as being filled with the intention to be lost," Muñoz wrote in *Cruising Utopia*. "To accept loss is to accept the way in which one's queerness will always render one lost to a world of heterosexual imperatives, codes, and laws ... [to] veer away from heterosexuality's path." A girl kissing her best friend—because she wants to see how it feels, because she's curious, because a boy is nearby, because she's in love, because she once bent her mouth to her best friend's bleeding hand in supplication and this just feels like the next logical step—is the acceptance of loss, the veering from the path. No matter where she goes afterward.

AFTER THAT NIGHT on the beach, I was furious at her, for all the reasons you might expect. My friends comforted me, assured me I'd been used, told their own stories of identity misfires and capricious lovers and *x*-sexuals-until-graduation they'd known. She started dating a new guy, and eventually married him. Even invited me to the wedding, though I declined to go. I have no idea if she's slept with women since then, if she ever thinks about it, if she identifies as something other than straight.

---

3. It is, understandably, considered gauche to describe bisexuality as transitory, almost as gauche as the word "bisexual" itself. Perhaps it would be better to think of bisexuality as queerly universal—stem cells potent with potential. As long as compulsive heteronormativity exists, queer people will pass through bisexuality at some point, however briefly. Some tear through it on a speedboat, heading for a more monosexual harbor, others circle, content, drinking aperitifs in the sun.

For a long time, I remembered that conversation on the beach—the nakedness and vulnerability of my want—with a dense and unctuous emotion you could probably call shame. I was determined to be angry.

But as the years have gone by, sympathy softened my resolve. How little we know of ourselves at any moment; how distinctly human that is. There is such little grace given to the perfect messiness of desire. Even queers feel pressure to homogenize the experience into catchy slogans. The "born this way" narrative, while politically expedient, has done untold damage to narratives of the queer experience, implying any number of horrible ideas: that you cannot move toward desire without some genetic component urging you to do so, that experimentation is inherently problematic, that you have to know your truest and deepest self to act on something. There were times in my adolescence where people asked me if I was gay and I said no, not out a sense of self-preservation but because I truly believed it to be so. You can be a stranger to yourself; you almost certainly will be, at some point or another. It is inevitable, as inevitable as the moment of rupture that sends you hurtling toward the self you were always going to be.

And so, Queer Reader, we return to *Jennifer's Body*, how the accusation of queerbaiting flattens, impotent, against its walls. Not just because the film is uniquely bisexual but because bisexuality itself is inherently resistant to heteronormative frameworks; because gatekeeping is shortsighted and unbecoming; because desire and understanding do not always go hand in hand. The project of identifying "false" or "performative" queerness is dead in the water. Do not trouble yourself to rescue it. Do not grieve at its graveside. Kiss someone, fuck someone, think about fucking someone while kissing someone else. Let sex be unknowable, warm, thrilling, funny, erotic, terrifying; let sexuality be all strange currents and eddies and unknown vistas and treasures and teeth. Because, Queer Reader, when Jennifer's body came for you—publicly, privately, neither, both—it was more than more than enough.

My Hand on the Glass

BRUCE OWENS GRIMM

Hereditary

What if resurrection is a concept dearer to life than to the afterlife?

—*Jessie Van Eerden*

A HAUNTING IS a repetition, which is what makes Ari Aster's *Hereditary* so frustrating, so scary, and ultimately a ghost story. The movie opens with a shot of a treehouse, as viewed through the window of Annie Graham's artist workshop. The camera's gaze mimics a first-person point of view, a ghost's gaze who will guide us into the story. Framed within this establishing shot: the white wooden window frame, which in turn frames a treehouse that seems to float among the trees. Frames within frames. A disorientation so subtle we might not fully understand why it unsettles us so. Camera-ghost steps back and pans through the studio, past Annie's diorama creations. The miniatures all depict scenes from Annie's life and will be featured in an art show, one that fate will ultimately not permit her to attend. The ghost settles on a miniature of the Graham house and tightens on an upstairs bedroom. A body sleeps in the bed, another miniature we assume, until Annie's husband, Steve, walks in to wake their son, Peter, to get ready for a funeral. We've suddenly been transported into the Grahams' actual house—a house haunted, we'll eventually learn, through the portal of the diorama. The characters are unaware that the story, the end of it, has already been fixed in place.

33

But who is the ghost? It will never be revealed. Is it Annie's ghost? Her mother's ghost? Or are we, the viewer, the ghost? We are in the position of a traditional ghost, present in the Grahams' lives but unseen, unable to stop what is about to happen.

I DO NOT create dioramas out of wood, plastic, and paint like Annie. I create mine with words. I create ghosts on the page. My camera-ghost gazes upon a miniature of a red brick church, windows framed with white molding, on the day of a different kind of ritual: a wedding. My wedding. My marriage's fate fixed in place, the end decided before it begins.

Floor-to-ceiling windows set inside white-and-gray walls run from the front door to the first pew. A red, yellow, and purple stained glass window behind the altar. Rows and rows of pine pews. The brightest sanctuary I've ever seen.

I'm twenty-four years old. I stand at the altar as Kaitlyn walks down the aisle. We smile at each other. The ceremony happens. Rings are exchanged. We are pronounced husband and wife. Deception is not my goal. My love for Kaitlyn is genuine. However, I'm not emotionally experienced enough to distinguish between platonic love and romantic love. And yet: the knowledge that I am gay is tucked between the creases of my brain.

We stand in a reception line as people congratulate us. My grandmother comes through the line. I bend down to kiss her on the cheek. She pulls me closer, whispers into my ear, "I can't wait for the real one." She is upset that we got married in a Presbyterian church instead of a Catholic one, so she doesn't consider our wedding legitimate. The rituals are similar, but not exactly correct. She pats me on the shoulder and walks away.

We gather with our wedding party to take pictures in front of the church. Melissa, the maid of honor, says to me, "I'm so surprised that you didn't cry."

Others chime in to agree. All of them had decided before the ceremony that I would be the one to cry. Jon, one of the groomsmen, doesn't join in on the conversation. He smiles at me.

"I'm just too happy." I look at Jon, unsure if I'm trying to convince him or myself.

We take a limo bus out to Squire's Castle for pictures. The castle's remains are in a park out in the more rural part of town. Scorch marks scar the concrete floor where people have started small fires to stay warm or, as rumor has it, where witches burn squirrels and other small animals from the woods as a sacrifice to the dark powers that inhabit the ruins.

The photographer directs the twelve of us into various poses inside and outside of the castle fragments. It's October, the leaves that are left on the trees blaze orange, red, and yellow. I hear snaps of branches off in the distance. No one is there. It has to be animals. Still, I can't shake the feeling of being watched by some force lurking behind the trees.

DENIAL IS POWERFUL for Annie throughout *Hereditary*, seen first when she goes to a "Losing a Loved One" support group meeting after her mother's death. There, she gives a rambling, disturbing family history, including how her schizophrenic brother committed suicide at sixteen. He left a note blaming their mother for "putting people inside him." We won't have the full context for this story Annie tells until the end of the film, when it is revealed that Annie's mother and her satanic congregation have set into motion a plan to cause Annie's daughter, Charlie's, death and, ultimately, offer Annie's sixteen-year-old son, Peter, as a human host to Paimon, one of the kings of hell. Retrospectively, it seems clear that part of Annie knows that her mother tried and failed at this plan once before; perhaps Annie uses her brother's schizophrenia as a shield so that she doesn't have to confront the reality of her mother's sinister actions—and her own inaction.

It's difficult for me to not consider the connection here to queer people, who so often do not have access to a life where they get to be themselves. Homophobia, especially internalized homophobia, demands we craft heteronormative versions of ourselves and erase any trace of our queerness. Other people are put inside of us. We're both there and not there.

OUR RECEPTION IS in a log cabin nested on the property of an apple orchard. Dinner, cake, drinking, dancing. It's hot inside. I need a moment away from the crowd, away from the commotion. I step out onto the deck that wraps around the reception hall building. The full October moon lights the golf course in the valley below in blue light.

The door behind me opens and clicks closed. Jon leans on the deck railing next to me. Condensation drips off his beer bottle and onto my hand. He is considered the attractive one in our friend group—muscular, lean, a cute, dorky face. His eyes squeeze shut whenever he laughs or smiles. There is an ease to him that makes me feel comfortable, comforted, when I'm around him.

Behind us the music from my wedding reception thumps. Kaitlyn and her friends' shouting and singing audible through the windows. There is a story about Jon, a rumor, that he had broken a bottle one night while drunk and had eaten the glass. I ask him if it's true.

"Do you think I would do something like that?" he says, turning his whole body toward me.

"Kind of," I say. His father had recently died in a motorcycle accident. I do believe his grief could make him eat glass.

He sets his bottle down on the railing, opens his arms. "Come here," he says.

I rest my bottle next to his, lean into his hug. Instead of patting my back as he usually does when we hug, he runs his hands across my back in small, slow circles. I pull away, but his embrace only allows me to lean back, our bodies pressed together.

Leaves rustle across the ground in the breeze as his mouth finds mine. Our lips rest against each other for a moment, then part and lock together. He runs his tongue against my top lip. We stop, but neither of us runs from the other. We are alone, but all someone has to do is look out from a window inside the cabin to see us.

We eventually go back inside. My wife shimmies toward me and pulls me out to the dance floor with her. Jon keeps drinking. I still feel the scratch of his stubble against my chin, my cheeks, as the wedding party dances as a group. Toward the end of the night, when most guests have already gone, Jon stands in front of the wedding party's table. He looks sad. He sways a little bit. I take the beer bottle out of his hand.

"You don't need anymore." I cradle his head in my hands and kiss him.

I don't care who sees. This is my last chance to kiss him, to kiss another man, and I don't want to pass it up. He tastes different than before. Stale beer, vomit. It doesn't matter. I want this despite all the sour. In a different timeline, I come out right then and there, tell Kaitlyn that I can't be married to her. *I love you, but not like that.* But that doesn't happen.

"That's enough," Kaitlyn says behind me, her voice stern. Jon and I part, and it is never spoken of again.

ONE OF MY family's favorite stories: my grandparents' belief that my uncle Ken "became" gay because he left Cleveland to go to college in Cincinnati, the few hours' drive in between creating enough distance for homosexuality to possess him. For this reason, my sister and I were told over and over, we had to pick a college in Cleveland if we expected our grandparents to help with our tuition. This is why I end up going to John Carroll University in Cleveland. A Jesuit school where my father and his younger brother had once enrolled. Neither would graduate for reasons no one talked about. "Don't disappoint us like they did," my grandfather would say at the beginning of each semester.

SIX YEARS AFTER graduation, Kaitlyn and I move from Cleveland to Urbana-Champaign so I can attend grad school, focus on my writing. We are there for two months before I can no longer ignore that I'm gay. The portal opened by a YouTube video of a fat man eating ice cream, rubbing his belly. I can't look away. I want to watch more. I click and I click and find there is a whole community of gay men who want to be fat, who want to be with other fat men. The community message board requires registration, an email, a username, a password—the technological equivalent of unlocking the spirits on the other side of the registration page.

"Don't," I say to the computer screen. However, I can't resist the pull, the men on the other side beckoning to me. I create a new, secret email account to register for the site, a username, a password, and I'm granted access.

"I'M GOING TO put my hand on the glass, but not apply pressure," Joan, a friend from the grief support group, instructs Annie at the beginning of a séance to contact Annie's daughter, Charlie, who has died in a freak accident.

Joan uses a plain water glass on a Ouija board, a familiar item placed upon a forbidden one. The juxtaposition is fitting, Annie's desire to learn how to make contact with Charlie overshadowed by fear as the glass moves across the board. Fear sends Annie into a panic so deep she runs out of Joan's apartment. Joan places a candle in Annie's hands, encourages her to continue this at home, to bring this force into her home.

Put your hand on the glass, but don't apply pressure. I could have easily said this to myself as I logged in to the message board for the first time. I set rules. I can look at pictures, read posts, but I cannot interact, cannot post pictures of myself. I can put my hand on the glass as long as I don't apply pressure.

But, eventually, the ghost moves the glass.

My Hand on the Glass

A whole new world, new possibilities emanate from the black frame of my computer screen. Guilt—a kind of fear—ultimately comes for me, sends me running out of the message boards. Kaitlyn and I share this computer, so I clear my browsing history five times to be sure it is all gone, sent to the shadows of the Internet. I close the laptop. I take a deep breath as if to shake my queerness off. One of the rules of a séance is to say goodbye at the end, an indication to the spirit world that you are done communicating with them. I close the tabs, erase my digital path. But I don't say goodbye.

OPENING HERSELF TO the spirit realm is part of what ultimately dooms the Graham family. Despite the part of her that knows she's allowing her mother's sinister plan to unfold, Annie finds a kind of relief in unlocking the part of herself she has been repressing. She has a coming out of sorts when she shouts, "Fuck! I'm a medium!" at her husband and Peter when trying to convince them she can call Charlie's spirit home. Joan provides Annie with the tools, the motivation to reach out to Charlie's ghost, thereby making Joan a sort of mediumship mentor for Annie. Now that she's learned how, she can't stop.

I wish I'd had some kind of gay mentor when coming out. I always think my Uncle Ken, who died a month before my wedding, would have been the right man for the job. I try to call to him during a writing workshop at the Fine Arts Work Center in Provincetown. The workshop leader asks us to bring a picture of a family member as part of a prompt about our connection to this ancestor. I take with me the only image I have of Ken, a picture of our family table at my cousin Arlene's wedding:

We are arranged around the table like we've been posed for a painting. Plates with half-eaten food. On one side, my grandmother looks at an empty chair, my aunt's arm is outstretched as she reaches for her glass, and my mother sits at the far end looking at the other side of the table, seemingly at Ken and his partner, Damion. She and Damion smile as if they're midjoke. Ken's head is turned away from everyone, one arm rested on the empty chair, his other hand rested on the edge of the table, and his gaze is off camera. He looks annoyed. Nine-year-old me stands behind him and Damion. We, the queers, all grouped together. I'm the only one looking at the camera.

I'm in Provincetown the same summer of *Hereditary*'s release. I've already seen it, which informs how I respond to the prompt. I try to write in Ken's voice. I hope this will encourage his ghost to take the pen from me, to start writing in my notebook the same way that Joan's dead grandson writes on a chalk tablet during her séance with Annie. I would have asked him what he wishes he'd known when he first came out. But my hand is the only one that moves the pen.

CORNFIELDS AND CEMETERIES frame the outskirts of Urbana-Champaign. One night, I go to the grocery store to pick up some onions and garlic for the chicken stir-fry Kaitlyn is cooking for dinner from a recipe she found in *Cooking Light*. This makes us heterosexual stereotypes, I know: the wife in the kitchen, the husband running an errand. In reality, she had wanted to go to the store herself, but I insisted that I go, careful not to show my eagerness, careful to not reveal how much I wanted, needed, to go without her.

"Relax. Watch some TV," the dutiful husband told her. "I'll be right back."

I buy the items she requested. I also buy a pint of chocolate milk. I had wanted a half-gallon, but I'm not fast enough at chugging. She will notice if I'm gone too long. I need to stretch my stomach out so I can eat more, so I can gain more. She doesn't know that I'm gaining weight on purpose, doesn't know that I've started chatting and exchanging belly pictures with guys who are also into gaining. I've told her my weight gain is from the stress of grad school. Her *Cooking Light* subscription is to help me keep my weight down. All this requires that the milk stay a secret. I'm the only car parked on the side of the store. The perfect hiding spot. I chug my milk and rub my belly with little risk of being seen by anyone.

ON MY THIRTY-THIRD birthday, Kaitlyn takes me out for breakfast before work. Our conversation is easy, filled with laughter as it has not been since we moved to Illinois, until a guy I've been chatting with online sits at a table near us. I point my face at the table to hide, hoping he doesn't recognize me. I go quiet because I fear he'll recognize my voice; then I remember he has never heard my voice. He is with a couple other people, and I recognize one of them as his roommate who was in a picture he sent to me. I relax a little. I realize this could be it. He could approach me and then I'd have to explain how I know him. My double life, over. The stress of it gone. I keep glancing over at him, but he doesn't notice me. Kaitlyn and I walk right past him on our way out. The rest of the day, I daydream about what might have happened if I'd reached out, placed my hand on his.

TWO DAYS AFTER my birthday, I'm in our apartment's second bedroom that I use as an office, my workshop where I write and create my other, secret life. Kaitlyn comes home from work and shouts hello through the house. She walks into the room as I type away at a story for my thesis.

She kisses me on the cheek. "What are you working on?"

"A story." I don't turn to her. I keep typing.

She backs up to the edge of the desk. I had always shared my work with her, what it was about, told her how drafts were going, but I'd stopped, cut her off from that part of me. She talks about her day. Such postwork chats had been a routine for most of our relationship. In most relationships. All I have to do is listen. Instead, I become annoyed.

"I have a lot of work to do."

Kaitlyn's silence is sharp, tells me she is angry. She walks out of the room without a word. Guilt fills the space between me and the computer screen. I can hear her on the other side of the wall opening drawers in the kitchen.

I go in there to apologize, but I stand at the end of the counter unsure how to begin. She stays focused on the vegetables she is chopping for dinner as I try to figure out how to open this conversation. She makes a joke. I don't laugh.

"You used to laugh at my jokes."

"Say something funny and I will," I snipe, in spite of myself.

"That's enough." She slams down the knife. "What is it? What's going on?"

The washing machine on the other side of the room rattles to a finish. I've practiced telling her so many times. I've whispered the words "I'm gay" when I'm alone, when she can't accidentally hear me. Many times we'd be in a room together and I'd wait for her to turn her head or walk into the other room; then I'd mouth it: "I'm gay." *Fuck it! I'm gay!* I imagine myself saying in the same exhausted way Annie tells her husband she's now a medium. But my coming out is much more subdued.

I take a deep breath and exhale, "I'm gay."

"That makes a lot of sense," Kaitlyn says, some of the tension between us banished.

ANNIE TRIES ONE last time to resist the inevitable by throwing Charlie's notebook of drawings and sketches into the fireplace. She thinks this will stop the demon spirit she's let into her house from terrorizing her family. As the pages start to burn, Annie's arm catches on fire. The flame slowly moves up her arm. It disappears once she rescues the book from the fire. Once Annie understands the full scope of what is happening, how it has been orchestrated, she is determined to burn Charlie's notebook. However, this time she asks Steve, her husband, to do it, thinking she will be the one to be sacrificed. He won't, so she grabs the notebook, throws it into the fire, and he goes up in flames instead.

Watching the movie again and again it seemed it had broken its own rules. Why does Steve catch on fire, instead of Annie? Annie's mistake, *my* mistake, was thinking there are rules where none exist. I thought I had missed some crucial knowledge about coming out, being queer, but there are no rules.

MY CHILDHOOD HOUSE has a sliding glass door in the kitchen that leads to a deck in the back. The locking mechanism broke at some point and was too expensive to replace, so we stuck a wooden pole, a broken-off broom handle, in the frame along the floor to create some approximation of a locked door.

One night, after Kaitlyn and I have started dating, I hear the glass door's heavy slide against the frame. I listen. I don't hear any footsteps. I go down to investigate, hugging the wall as I ease down the steps until I'm on the edge of the kitchen. The door is wide open. Only darkness on the other side. I flip on the lights, which make the kitchen super bright. This only increases the richness of the dark outside

"Hello," I say, like any foolish character in a horror movie. Of course, no response.

I think about going outside, into the unknown. Something beckons to me, but I don't know what it is, so it scares me. I slide the door shut and roll the broom handle into its place in the frame.

JASON IS FAT, wants to be fatter. I'm on a work trip in Vancouver, so we are able to finally meet in person after a few months of online courting. He walks over to my hotel to pick me up for dinner. Our conversation is instantly easy, comfortable as he looks at the view from my room, the city and him framed by the black lines of the window.

He has planned out a place for dinner and one for dessert.

"Assuming we still like each other after dinner," he says as he walks over to me.

He is much taller than me, so I tilt my head up to meet his eyes. "I actually have an escape route planned just in case."

"Good, good." He smiles and bumps my belly with his. I bump back.

A light snow begins to fall as we walk to the all-you-can-eat sushi restaurant Jason has picked out for us. Jason likes this place because the food is good, the people who work there are friendly, and the booth seats move so that your belly doesn't get smashed against the table as it expands as you eat. "People like us have to think about that," he says. We both laugh.

We order enough sushi for it to be served on a platter shaped like a boat. The waiter comments on how much we have ordered, but in a way meant to celebrate, not shame. We eat. Jason teases me for not being able to eat as much as him. "I'll get there," I say.

"You will," he says, smiling, before eating another piece of sushi. He leans back, the yellow and brown plaid fabric of his shirt straining across the width of his belly button.

He asks for the check. Pays. "Escape plan still on?"

"I can barely move so I think I'll stay," I smile.

"Dessert?"

I nod.

We go to Breka Bakery, which specializes in cakes. We find a table in the center of the bakery's seating area and consider the menu. I tell him I'm thinking about getting a slice of key lime cheesecake.

We start talking about previous relationships as we browse the selection. My stomach churns from my resurfaced nerves about telling him about Kaitlyn and his possible reaction. Jason tells me about his last relationship, with a guy who had moved from Florida to be with him in Vancouver. It hadn't ended well, and the guy returned to the US.

I take a deep breath. I have a choice: Do I tell him about my marriage or not? To not tell him about my marriage is not only to lie but to flip the repression I thought I had escaped. I tell him about Kaitlyn. Our marriage, how it ended. I wait for the night to go up in flames. "Didn't know you needed an escape plan, right?"

He raises an eyebrow. "Why would I need one?"

"It doesn't bother you?"

"Why would it?"

I tell him about the other men it did bother.

"They're stupid." He pauses for a moment before looking back at the menu.

Relief. I mention ordering cheesecake again.

Jason leans in. "Listen, I have no problem with you having been married, but you order cheesecake and I'm out of here." He smiles. My body relaxes.

My hotel is in the opposite direction of his apartment. He hails me a cab. He opens the door for me. "Goodnight," I say as I walk into the pocket of the open door. I turn around because I want to see his face one last time tonight.

He kisses me. I kiss back.

I get in the back seat. Jason shuts the door. As the cab pulls away, I look back at him standing on the corner. He is watching and waves and I wave back. Something has been set in motion. Something that is not manipulated by outside forces.

By the time I get back to the hotel, we have made plans to see each other the next night. Once in my room, I walk over to the window. I have no sense of orientation of where I am in relation to where we have been. I only know that I like both places.

The camera's ghostly gaze never explicitly appears beyond the opening scene in *Hereditary*. However, whether we are aware of it or not, it has been there the whole time. My ghost-camera cuts to a shot of me outside my room, framed by the window. I can still feel the tingle of Jason's lips. My memory's camera continues to pull out until I'm as small as a figurine in one of Annie's dioramas. Except it's not Annie's diorama. It's mine. I get to choose which scenes from my life I want to recreate, to linger in. Right now, it's this one.

From the point in time in which I write these words, I do know how things will end between Jason and me. This knowledge haunts ever so slightly between the sentences. But the ending, its inevitability, doesn't matter because every ghost is alive at the beginning of their story, ready to repeat itself, to try again.

The Girl, the Well, the Ring

ZEFYR LISOWSKI

The Ring; Pet Sematary

IN 2018, when my pain resurfaced, I thought of it as punishment.

I was working my coffee shop job where, after my shift, I'd bike home, write, and go out dancing. Nights I didn't go out dancing, I went on dates. Nights I didn't go on dates, I'd break into the big park at the outskirts of my neighborhood, scrambling over the fence and walking among hydrangeas bright and pale as the moon. My father had just died. I filled every second of my time with people, drawing goth circles around my eyes in eyeliner, daubing crimson lipstick, kissing strangers with abandon.

That summer I did my best to forget my previous history of sickness, an entire childhood in and out of hospitals. Which isn't to say I had become healthy then. I still passed out in bathrooms, massaged my aching wrists every night, handled fierce and frequent bacterial infections. But for a while, it all was manageable; I could tell myself these were anomalies. And when things got worse and every part of me hurt for months, I couldn't believe it. I feared becoming sick again for so long, the actual event was almost anticlimactic.

Fear never produces itself on its own. A young, sick child, I'd linger in the horror aisles at the local Blockbuster, picking up cassette after cassette. I was built by scary movies, and those scary movies built how I felt about myself. Girls were punished. The disabled were to be feared. Anything gender-nonconforming was out of the picture. What does it mean as a sick girl to learn again and again that sick girls deserve to be punished? What does it mean as a trans child to only see a film industry's bile spat back at you?

In the summer after my father died, I spent days unable to get out of bed. I had vivid nightmares of monstrous women lurching out of televisions or crammed into attics, bones cracking out of place. I had nightmares that I was monstrous too. I thought these dreams were further punishment, a reflection of who I had become. But now I wonder how much the things that scare us are always trying to form their own communities too.

If you first see yourself in a host of ghosts, what does it mean to live despite that? If you grow up disabled and only have hatred surrounding you in every bit of media you consume, what does it take to turn that into an act of love anyway?

I. GIRLS AND GHOSTS

As a child, no one talked about why *The Ring* was scary, just about it as a state of being. The autumn after that movie came out, all the girls with the same long thin legs as me walked down their streets extra quickly when they passed a tree too flaming-crimson. That Halloween, white water-stained dresses were everywhere.

In 2002, my body was a mess. I grew up *sick* in ways that didn't make sense at the time, each day a new physiological surprise. I'd convulse into seizures when I was least expecting it—on runs, in my gym class, at dance parties, at my uncle's funeral, once while urinating in the middle of the night. I had mood swings that would take over my entire day, crying violently through whole periods of school. My wrists and ankles would sprain themselves weekly. Maybe this is why it took me so long to see *The Ring*; the fear it held for otherness was too real for me still. When I did watch the movie, my father had just recovered from his first cancer scare and I was in the middle of several trips of my own into the hospital. It was 2005; I was in the sixth grade.

In the movie, the girl, Samara, had a father who called her evil and stomped around the house and a mother who talked endlessly about how much she loved the girl. In the movie, the girl was locked in a medical treatment facility away from home and then, once released, locked in a little room at the top of her family's barn. The girl stared unblinking at the closed circuit television in the medical facility she was in, and the girl stared unblinking at the bottom of the well.

When I say I felt seen by her, I'm not justifying her evil. It's just that when a movie tells you to hate a child again and again and again, there is something else it is telling you to ignore. In this movie, with all its animosity for people like me, I had found a second home.

A POINT *The Ring* makes inadvertently is how interconnected all monstrosities are. The young dead girl who's the villain is different and sick, so she becomes a recipient of violence. She becomes a recipient of violence, so she becomes an enactor of violence. Then, only then, do the deaths start.

This isn't the case with everyone. Some people, I'm sure, are more purely victims, and there are certainly types of violence that are worse than others. But in my own life, I've seen unforgivable acts beget themselves again and again. The girl in *The Ring* is domestically confined and abused, so she becomes a horror—a genre that always infects the domestic, wreaks its own violence on the bodies in closest proximity.

In sixth grade, I watched *The Ring* because it scared me, but also because it and its ilk taught me how to act. This is what horror movies do, send their coded moral messages to a whole generation. I took notes: the blond woman was mean to her ex-husband because he was bad, and we felt sympathetic. The girl at the bottom of the well looked scary so it didn't matter how badly she hurt. The stepfather was loud but ultimately not guilty and that made him redeemable. Anyone who looks dissimilar from the norm ultimately becomes a threat.

But in my friends' scramblings over tree stumps, pretending they were wells—long hair draped across the face—we ignored the *other* message buried throughout this whole film. Every time we see her, the girl in the well is clearly sick, and no one who purports to care about her cares about this at all. Unless it's used to stoke fear, the girl's sleep disorder, pale skin, dislocated bones, moods, deep sadnesses, are all completely ignored. Instead—living inside a well, twisting her body within a television—her proximity to the grave becomes her sole defining trait.

As a child, I shuffled from doctor to doctor, and each of them ignored me in a different way—because I was femme, because I was sick, because, to some doctors, I appeared healthy and had nothing to worry about. When I turned twelve, my father started training me to run, following along on his bicycle, telling me that if I became strong, I would stop getting ill so often.

This extended to boxing lessons in our garage, a small set of weights in my bedroom, a whole regimen to make my body both masculine and healthy, becoming less and less visible to doctors. Maybe this influences why I see the neglect that the girl herself faces—how it exists as part of the same continuum I am on, the desire to heal disability by hiding disability from view. Maybe it explains why her family was hiding the girl, too.

I've read dozens of books and articles on *The Ring*, trying to make sense of the film's message, and not a single scholar—mainly white and able-bodied and cis and in power—mentions the girl being sick or disabled. No one even mentions how she's *bad*, she's inhuman, because her body refuses to appear like everyone else's—in the well but refusing to *be* well. Even at the end of the movie, when we see Samara finally in full frame, decomposing and rotting with water, she's only presented as an object of mourning. She's never a girl by herself, only a body filtered through the horror or grief on others' faces—a self mediated by others' disgust, barely a girl at all, a cypher, a ghost, primarily—no, only—hated.

II. THE TREATMENT FACILITY,
THE PET SEMATARY

Of course, it's not just *The Ring* perpetuating these ideas of sickness as evil or as punishment. It's an entire blood-soaked society.

Pet Sematary, which I watched as my girlfriend fucked me drunk and upside down on Halloween 2015, features a woman with spinal meningitis terrorizing the beautiful blond main character. Her hair looks dirty, long, stringy, and copper; her skin is sallow and pale; her backbone, exposed and fossilized, pokes through a torn nightgown. I paused the movie and rolled my girlfriend off of me. It was 3:00 a.m. I was still drunk.

As a sick person who doesn't look sick, I see the revolt in this moment as something supposed to be aspirational. There's a hatred I should feel on behalf of the character who looks like me at the one who doesn't. For most people, according to IMDb reviews, the sister is far scarier than the cemetery that brings the dead back to life, or the spirits lurking within the cursed, colonized land.

Inevitably, the trappings of sickness are supposed to be "scary." Back in *The Ring*, our first glimpse of the dead girl's face is when she's under doctor's observation, and this is a sign she's bad. Her skin is anemic, with deep circles under the eyes; she constantly has electrodes taped under her hair. Even as a dead body floating in the well, the girl wears a dress the color of a hospital gown.

When I was in the seventh grade, I took an EEG test to find a source for my seizures—a test we got largely because my parents, recently settled into the white middle-class, could afford it. But I can't deny this was also a test administered because I didn't yet appear disabled. Instead, I was "otherwise normal"—a phrase that appears again and again on diagnostic sheets throughout my life, from appointments seeking to remedy joint troubles to chronic sinus infections to day-to-day mood irregularities to the autism diagnosis that, in the third grade, doctors decided not to record on my chart "to make my life easier."

The test I took was inconclusive, and we had a hard time scheduling a follow-up appointment after doctors realized the futility of finding one straightforward diagnosis for me. I've heard this story too; after resisting medical categorization, there are two piles people tend to be tossed into. I was discarded and dismissed and became invisible to those in power. In the movies, the dead girl and the sister were scorned, turned into objects of fear. I felt angry being ignored, but didn't even stop to think the alternative was much, much worse.

There are far worse precedents for this neglect. During the AIDS crisis, homophobic doctors would refuse to even touch their patients, afraid they would become contaminated. Now and always, Black patients in hospitals are disproportionately denied testing, blamed for their own ailments, ignored. It's a common statistic that women's pain, to say nothing of those whose gender is less readily legible, is regularly ignored by doctors. Hospitals are built on anti-sick architectures of thought, but not all sick people are equal in the eyes of the institution. Existing oppression proliferates.

When my father died, he was in the ICU. My whole body freckled with bruises from the twelve-hour bus ride to visit him. Twenty-four-hour care, the hospital told us, was a medical necessity; us checking him out and taking him home was impossible. By the end, my father had had multiple strokes. He was resuscitated twice. He was in withdrawal from acute alcoholism. When I visited, the combination of his bodily pain and my memories of the wreckage of my childhood led to us barely speaking all day.

During my time in the hospital, I'd ask for blankets to wrap around my body against the shattering AC, pillows to make sitting in the hard hospital chairs easier. I didn't get any of these things. I was angry at the circumstances we both found ourselves in—my inability to receive diagnosis at the time, the ventilator and medical staff he had access to immediately and the little good it did. As he was dying, we both seemed to be ignored. So many people have it worse than this.

This essay is, among other things, a defense of rage. It has to be. During my father's death and after, the anger of every one of these ghosts was the only thing that could stifle my grief. As we found out later, there was no reason my father couldn't have been released. Half the information we got from doctors—prognosis, chance of recovery, his illness's trajectory—was erroneous. My father was kept in the hospital because, for the doctors there, it was the easiest and most financially lucrative option. Could my father even agree to the level of sedation necessary to keep him near-unconscious and on a ventilator, tubes in his throat rendering him nearly voiceless? His own desires were completely disregarded.

"I was laughing when my sister finally died," the blond protagonist says in *Pet Sematary*, and everyone rushes to express empathy. "If you were," her husband adds, "I salute you for it. No one should have to deal with that *thing* in their life."

I can handle the neglect, but it's the cruelty of it all that tips me toward the monsters' side.

THE WOMAN IN *Pet Sematary* is actually a man (or is played by one), just like Samara in the original Japanese book is—one last irredeemable thing about these movies that glommed onto my own identity.

Medical transition, like disability, is viewed by the mainstream as a sensational departure from normalcy. But the two are not the same. I've been injecting hormones into the fat of my leg for years, and every time the needle draws a little tip of blood, I feel faint again. I'm trying to reconcile the complexity of my body, but these movies aren't concerned with how my hormonal needs and my larger health exist out of whack. By their calculus, what's bubbling through my joints and what's beneath my pants are both equally repugnant.

Here is my life. I was born, according to some, defective. Because my family had the privilege to do so, we had tests done, which initiated a long and incomplete corrective process. I went to physical and speech therapy. I went to doctor after doctor. By the time I hit undergrad, my defects were all but invisible. Even now that they've resurfaced, I still can go day-to-day without displaying a sign of a single one. The surprise on people's faces—but *oh*, how you don't *look* disabled at all. I would have *never* known. I came out as trans in the middle of this, and became acclimated to a different sort of passing as well.

As I write this, I'm weary of the endless bromides of those adjacent to power that their own powerlessness has been incorrectly recognized. But at the same time, I have to know that at every moment I pass, even as it makes my life easier, I have chosen to define myself by a system of rules operating to enclose and restrict. I put on makeup and shut my trap, and disappear from record. I write "F" on the intake form at an urgent care facility and have to fabricate an entire history of menses to the nurse practitioner in order to even make my appointment. As long as I don't show signs of being disabled or trans, I'm safe.

There's a whole canon of literature determined to talk about the redemptive qualities of horror as a mode of truth-telling—the feminist or subversive ways they can be a home for marginalized viewers. That's not what I'm interested in discussing. These movies hurt me and I kept watching them, and there's nothing redemptive about that. They were all I had.

Before I knew what I was, I built a life out of them. And so I'm stuck with it all. I have to believe that if we stare closely enough at what hates us, somehow we can make our own love as well.

III. EVERYONE'S COLD

I watch most things through a scrim of rage, and horror movies are no exception. Each film I see—and there are many many more I haven't mentioned—draws a line in the sand. On one side, the heroes, able-bodied and quivering at becoming different. On the other, disabled people, shunned and cast away by dominant systems of support. These films render chronic illness and physical difference only in terms of their capacity to shock and disrupt.

When my father died, I thought the way to respond to *The Ring, Pet Sematary*, and other films was through their own frameworks. Here is a negative representation, so I will show you why it's wrong. Here's an evil girl, so I will show you how she's the hero instead. But this cause-and-effect thinking is a problem by itself, still adhering to the same rotten goalposts. There I was, like a doctor. I set a problem, diagnosed it, and attempted to vanish it. My father was still dead. I was still disabled. Nothing had changed.

So maybe instead the solution is refusing to answer the question asked in the first place.

When you live on an island and catch a cold, a doctor in *The Ring* says, *it's everyone's cold*. The doctor says this to excuse her complicity in the girl's murder. She believes the murder serves the good of "everyone." She believes sick people are the vector of infection themselves. I'm bored by the doctor's casual cruelty, but what happens if we ignore her prompt and start sharing space with ourselves instead, the infected?

The poet and activist Leah Lakshmi Piepzna-Samarasinha calls disabled people caring for one another together "revolutionary love without charity" in their brilliant book *Care Work*. I love how this is an argument by extension not against these films' narrow representation but in a different plane entirely. If there isn't a supremacist culture to view things through, does monstrosity even exist? Certainly, my own life got immeasurably easier once I stopped hiding every affliction, and instead began resting with friends. Taking care of ourselves, we reject the abled gaze.[1]

So instead of challenging these films, maybe the way forward is to acknowledge the gift they give, oblivious in their own framing. What does it mean to "share a cold" instead of shutting it away? I'm inspired by all the small dominions we, the disabled, have, how much has been shared already. Money. GoFundMes. Personal care assistants. Lists of accessible events spaces. Virtual dance parties. Knowledge, shared openly online and in group texts and over encrypted chats and through webs of in-person and digitized gossip. Disabled people have created a whole wellspring of culture and activism and vitality—and that buried truth is part of what makes us scary to the abled mainstream. My girlfriend herself has chronic pain, and as we fucked over *Pet Sematary* that Halloween in 2015, it struck me that this, too, was an act of defiance, of connection. I believe sick bodies doing what they do, refusing to be stifled—together—is one of the most radical things there is.

When I realized I was sick again after my father's death, I didn't get better. I didn't stumble across a cure. I didn't emerge from the other side in a burst of triumph. Instead, I just resumed the treatments I was engaged in earlier. I started wearing wrist braces to sleep in, took herbal supplements. I booked more appointments with massage therapists, medical workers, pilates instructors. I joined support groups and surrounded myself with the brilliant knowledge of those like me. And gradually, I altered my field of comparison, avoiding the trap of thinking I was grotesque or an other. Slowly, I built a community out of a life.

I'm grateful for what I've made. I'm grateful for the anger that

---

1. Some of those friends, whose work influences my own: Jesse Rice-Evans, Cyrée Jarelle Johnson, Joselia Hughes. And those who I have not shared friendship with but see the work through nonetheless: Eli Clare, Anne Boyer, Johanna Hedva, Harriet Washington. And innumerous others. (I speak in a footnote because it's the clearest way I know to not speak alone.)

propelled this making in the first place. But even still, I have to wonder what my life would be like had I never been exposed to these supremacist messages in the first place. Without the culture I responded to, would I even need to find myself in these wrathful ghosts?

Here's one last little story.

In *The Ring*, when the girl climbs up the well, her bones cracking out of place, bending behind herself, this is supposed to be a sign she's to be feared and pitied and isn't even human.

When I discovered, suddenly as a child, that I could do the same thing, joints twisting out of place and then aching, aching afterwards— when I discovered that myself, oh, it felt like freedom.

This essay originally appeared, in slightly different form, in The Offing, July 23, 2020.

Imprint

JOE VALLESE

Grace

ELIO'S BOTTOM TEETH, two rice-white shards freshly cut through swollen gums, graze my pinky until they find the cuticle. He clamps down with such ferocity and purpose that I yelp at a pitch that would be embarrassing if we weren't alone. I snatch my hand away, which sends him into a fit of belly-shaking laughter. Elio insistently reaches for my finger again, guides it back into his mouth, and I let him, bracing myself for the next bite. He knows it will feel good, I know it will hurt, and neither of us can resist.

THE FINAL SHOT of Paul Solet's *Grace* is a mutilated, bloodied breast, hunks of flesh chewed out, the nipple disappeared. Madeline, mother to the titular undead infant who feeds on human blood instead of milk, has gone to harrowing lengths to properly nourish Grace.

"She needs more now," Madeline tells a horrified Patricia, her midwife, lover, and now accomplice. "She's *teething.*"

Following a requisite spree of murder and mayhem to keep Grace fed, they've absconded in an RV and given themselves pixie cuts and dye jobs, resolved to live as a queer family on the lam. Grace has rapidly graduated to flesh, and if she's to live, to grow, they'll need to amass more victims—or, Madeline will have to sacrifice every last inch of her body for her miracle baby, who died in utero but warmed to life in Madeline's arms, went from corpse blue to newborn pink at the first suckle of her mother's breast. The film ends here but, based on the preceding eighty minutes, it's clear that she's prepared to allow Grace to consume her entirely. Madeline seems to have entered a state of ecstasy in the most biblical sense, her limp, blood-depleted stoicism suggesting she's already given herself over to the horror of it all. The last thing we see: the baby's open mouth moving to latch back onto Madeline's gored, fly-speckled bosom, an unsubtle reminder that for the devout every meal commences by saying "Grace."

EARLY IN THE film, Madeline alludes to two previous losses, which would make Grace her "rainbow baby," a term coined by a late-term abortion advocate who believed that babies born following the interruption of a nonviable pregnancy were an especially welcome and healing presence. The term has since been mainstreamed to represent any healthy pregnancy after miscarriage at any stage, and the pregnancy-industrial complex has responded accordingly. Type in "rainbow baby" into the Amazon search box and you'll be assaulted with a picture book from the celestial POV of a spirit baby waiting to hitch a ride on the wings of a stork; affirmative keychain charms, because who doesn't need love and light when they're unlocking the backdoor or starting the car; onesies crowded with far too much text for the average newborn torso: *After every storm, there's a rainbow of hope. Here I am!*

Some have referred to Elio as my husband Alex's and my rainbow baby. Schmaltzy, sure, but, as gay dads, we get to squeeze a bit more juice out of the metaphor. As a general rule, we refrain from snark (our queer birthright) and gladly accept their goodwill. Elio is indeed miraculous to us, but not thanks to some invisible hand; on the contrary, we were privy to every step of his conception and birth and, before his arrival, we endured a series of losses that both hardened us and cracked us wide open. Our particular storm lasted four years, the frustration and grief increasingly torrential.

In surrogacy jargon, the process from making embryos to a live birth, and all of the disappointments and devastations in between, is referred to as a "journey," which cloaks it in a kind of adventurous allure. In reality, it's less a journey than a descent into the deepest recesses of queer anxieties and insecurities. Nothing more aggressively reminds you of nature's refusal to accommodate life outside of cishet procreation than sitting in a windowless conference room on the Upper West Side with a hundred other hopeful men, watching a lawyer give a PowerPoint about the necessity of immediate post-birth adoption so, in some wildly unlikely but still possible scenario, you aren't charged with kidnapping your own baby. Surrogacy offers the illusion of control, promises a path to circumventing the limitations of what queer bodies can do together. And for a while, you buy it, because you have literally paid for science to provide what biology cannot, to make real the fantasy of fatherhood by taking a little of yourself and borrowing the rest from the bodies of women. Once your contributions are complete—some time alone in a room on a leather loveseat with a plastic collection cup and a few DVDs you probably won't bother with since there isn't really anything in there for you anyway, followed by HIV blood work administered by an apologetic nurse who understands how offensive this part is—it's all out of your hands, so to speak.

WHEN WE FIRST meet Madeline, she's having almost comically perfunctory sex with her husband, Michael. She lies beneath him, her face contorting with impatience; he's deeply invested, his face buried in a pillow as he thrusts. As soon as Michael climaxes and rolls off of her, Madeline brings her knees to her chest, encouraging conception. Her eyes close and her face relaxes in meditation, maybe prayer.

In the next scene, she's in her third trimester, a staunch vegan (a grim program showing the brutality of the meat industry perpetually plays on the kitchen TV, as if conditioning herself against the craving), and resolute in her decision to have a natural water birth under midwife

Patricia's care. Michael tries to steer Madeline toward a more conventional hospital birth overseen by a family doctor, but Madeline resists; she'll fry the occasional piece of liver for him, but her birth experience isn't up for discussion or negotiation. Madeline seeks to exert control over a body that has twice betrayed her, scrutinizing everything that goes into it, preparing for its great work ahead. But this is still a horror movie, and a quiet dread underscores Madeline's every gesture. She tiptoes through space with a tentative confidence, the fear (or, perhaps, expectation) that something will go wrong trailing her like a shadow.

AMANDA AND I like to joke that I actually met her breast before I met her.

I had just started a new job as an administrator and faculty for a program that grants liberal arts degrees to incarcerated students and, after a day of meetings, the entire staff went to a local restaurant for pizza and wine. I sat down beside Amanda and introduced myself, but didn't extend my hand since hers were full, propping her one-year-old son Jacoby up on her lap. Jacoby, impressive in his motor skills, plunged an arm deep into Amanda's blouse and helped himself to her breast, lifting it out with two steady hands. I waited to blush, to be overcome with that unpredictable awkwardness that either glues your eyes to the ground or makes it impossible to look away, but there was something hypnotic in the rhythm of Jacoby's blissful squeaking as he fed. That, coupled with Amanda's ability to simultaneously eat her pizza and ask me all the right questions about myself, neutralized any of my hang-ups before they even had time to register. I soon found myself blathering on about my and Alex's desire to be parents, how we'd recently begun researching and exploring our options, how they all seemed impossible in their own ways.

"Well, you never know," Amanda said coolly, offering Jacoby her pizza crust. "If we become besties or something, maybe I'll carry your baby for you." I don't remember my response—laughter, probably—but I do remember believing her.

THOUGH THE FILM adaptation of our story would feature an upbeat montage of our budding friendship and cut to our cheerful first embryo transfer, a lot of life happened in those intervening two years: Amanda became pregnant with and birthed a blond, blue-eyed clone she named Emmeline; our husbands finally met, and mocked my and Amanda's near-constant texting about work drama as a way to break the ice; Alex and I became engaged, saved for, planned, and had a big fat Italian wedding minus the church mass and the bride; and, soon after, Amanda officially announced her decision to be our gestational surrogate. Over a teary conversation after the kids had gone to sleep and wine had been poured, Amanda confessed that carrying a baby for someone else was a fantasy she'd harbored since her teen years, though back then she imagined more of a Lifetime movie scenario, doing it for a barren sister or a dying friend. Amanda's younger self also accurately predicted that she would feel most alive, most in control, during pregnancy. She and Kevin had decided to put a moratorium on having more children of their own, but an urgency thrummed within Amanda to make use of her body's gifts while she had the youth and the strength to safely do so. Our collective belief that a kind of serendipity was unfurling before us dimmed any fear of the risks—to Amanda's body, to her and Kevin's marriage, to our friendship. She felt powerful, and we felt protected.

THE FIRST MISCARRIAGE happened at eight weeks. It blindsided us all, particularly Amanda, who had never before experienced pregnancy loss. She'd planned carefully for Jacoby and Emmeline, conceiving just as she intended, and delivering them full-term exactly how she envisioned:

at home, without drugs, her midwives Susan and Birdie guiding her through days of searing labor that concluded in peaceful water births.

"It doesn't make any sense," she lamented after she'd begun spotting and cramping.

We'd been in the honeymoon phase, feeling elated, and maybe a bit arrogant, that we'd be the lucky ones for whom this process worked out seamlessly the first time. A call to the fertility clinic offered a momentary glimmer of hope that it might be implantation bleeding. "That embryo is just *so* strong he's burrowing in extra deep," said a chipper nurse we all hated. "I guarantee that's what it is."

The sudden gush of blood that soaked through Amanda's underwear told us there would be no guarantees.

THE SECOND TIME we made it a few weeks further, even got to hear a heartbeat. The gray, pulsating lump on the monitor was a thing of calming beauty. I began sleeping with a copy of the sonogram under my pillow, kissing it before bed and greeting it in the morning. Alex was taken aback the first time he caught me doing it, surprised by this superstitious streak I'd managed to keep hidden from him. I told him it made me feel less anxious and that I didn't intend to stop.

A few days later, after a morning of teaching at a women's correctional facility, I got into my car, retrieved my cell phone from the center console, and saw that I had a swarm of text messages from Amanda, from Alex, from Amanda *and* Alex. Before I could swipe to read them, a call from Alex broadcast over the car speakers. Through thick, aching sobs, he told me that he was on his way to the clinic to meet Amanda, who was ostensibly miscarrying once again. She'd been leading a discussion about *12 Angry Men* when one of her students interrupted to tell her that she was bleeding through her white capri pants. Another student hurried out of the classroom to alert an officer, who escorted Amanda out of the prison and tried to comfort her with stories of his own wife's many losses. "We'll have to buy her new pants," Alex said, a welcome bit of pragmatism breaking through the panic.

They waited for me to get to the clinic before the doctor performed an internal ultrasound. Alex and I each held one of Amanda's hands and clasped one another's as we watched the monitor, waiting for confirmation of the worst. To our surprise, the baby's heartbeat remained intact. The doctor offered a non-answer ("Sometimes bleeding is a sign the pregnancy is failing, and sometimes it doesn't mean anything at all") and sent us home, with instructions for Amanda to be on bed rest for a few days, drink plenty of water, and return the following Monday.

But Amanda was unconvinced we'd make it until then. "There's just *so* much blood."

ONE NIGHT OVER dinner, Madeline begins to experience intense chest pains. Michael rushes her to the ER, where the family doctor, the one Madeline had previously chosen not to see, hastily diagnoses her with preeclampsia and orders an immediate induction. It's a truly frightening scene, multiple men—the nurses are male too—holding Madeline down, trying to sedate her against her will. Patricia, mercifully, arrives at the hospital and intervenes, arguing that Madeline likely only has a gallstone and that baselessly rushing an induction at just thirty-one weeks would be nothing short of malpractice. This dressing down of male authority works, Patricia's hunch proves correct, and Madeline and Michael are released from the hospital later that night. Their car ride home is tense: Michael seems frustrated, perhaps even a bit emasculated by his inability to step in as forcefully as Patricia had; Madeline is visibly rattled by how quickly she lost control, how all of the meticulous care she's taken of her body and her baby was nearly undone on the whims of some man who assumed he knew better. Suddenly, an aggressive driver appears from behind, nearly running them off the road. Madeline suggests Michael pull over to get them out of harm's way, but he refuses. Once the car passes and blazes into the distance, the airbags release, Michael loses control of the wheel, and they veer off the road. There's a quick, silent cut before a police officer happens upon the scene and finds Michael dead in the overturned car. Soon, Madeline, too, comes into view, sitting up against a tree, bleeding from the head, hemorrhaging between the legs. A watch dangles from her shaking hand, the other on her belly as she tries desperately to track Grace's fast-vanishing movements.

IN THE WEEKS leading up to our third loss, a baby girl we named D—, a mockingbird began dive-bombing me. The first time it happened, I was walking our dog Bridget in the movie theater parking lot behind our apartment building when the mockingbird flew down from its perch and held right above my head, its wings furiously fluttering. As Bridget pulled me farther down the sidewalk to investigate a scent, the mockingbird followed, still hovering, but low enough now that I could feel the wind generated by its wings separating the curls on my head. I yanked Bridget back and hurried us in the direction of home, the mockingbird soaring parallel to us the entire way.

The next morning I took Bridget out, never imagining that the freak occurrence might repeat itself, but when I reached the front of the theater the mockingbird swooped down from the tree, landed on my neck, and began pecking. I lost my breath, genuinely terrified, and tightened Bridget's leash, interrupting her midstream. Back inside, Alex laughed in disbelief as I recounted the ordeal. I let him take Bridget back out to finish her business while I researched mockingbirds. The information wasn't especially encouraging; mockingbirds have highly developed memories and won't stop dive-bombing a perceived threat until they believe it's gone. Most commonly, a mockingbird attacks when its nest is threatened, but, despite racking my brain for any memory of when and how I might have accidentally done so, I came up empty. That evening, I reluctantly joined Alex and Bridget on a walk and, within seconds, the mockingbird's caustic trills echoed through the parking lot. Soon the mockingbird descended and Alex nearly choked on his laughter as I covered my head and bolted for the garage entrance of our building.

Alex took over Bridget-walking duties for the time being, though a few times I experimented, unsuccessfully, with leaving from the building's front entrance (within seconds, the mockingbird's shriek rang overhead as it landed on top of the corner stop sign and dared me to take another step), with wearing a baseball cap (futile, since it seems mockingbirds remember faces, not heads), with wearing sunglasses and pulling the cords of my hoodie as tightly as possible (the mockingbird took notice and pecked at the cords, seeking to undo them). It didn't take long for my lapsed Catholic, Italian American superstitious tendencies to take over and convince me that this couldn't be anything other than a terrible omen. I reasoned that if I kept vigilant, if I avoided the mockingbird and continued sleeping with and greeting baby D—'s sonogram every night and every morning, if I could send some psychic signal into Amanda's womb that she was so wanted and so loved, I could save her from whatever fate might befall her. I deleted every somber song from my Spotify playlists so I wouldn't accidentally stumble upon some lyric that evoked death or grief. I was careful not to watch any film, television show, or reality show that portrayed miscarriage, always on high alert to change the channel if the mood shifted or there was even a suggestion of pregnancy loss.

And for a while, it seemed to work: we sailed through our thirteen-week scan, ruling out any chromosomal abnormalities, and heard a strong, determined sixteen-week heartbeat at Susan and Birdie's office. I was still hesitant to begin telling people, but Alex was excited to finally share some good news with our parents, and, after multiple pregnancies, Amanda's body couldn't play along with the charade any longer, no matter how baggy her clothes. So, we enlarged copies of the latest sonograms and presented them to our families and friends. Alex spoke with human resources about taking bonding leave that spring. Amanda and I announced the pregnancy at a staff meeting, stunning our colleagues who were unaware that we'd even gotten close enough to hatch such a plan. D—'s due date was around Easter that year, so Jacoby and Emmeline began calling her Chickie.

One morning, a few days before our scheduled anatomy scan, I pulled the sonogram out from under my pillow and saw that it was wrinkled and faded beyond recognition. It was an early weeks image anyway, so I placed it in the drawer of my nightstand where I kept all the previous sonograms, put on the coffee, and decided to attempt Bridget's morning walk. To my relief, there was no mockingbird in sight or earshot. Bridget and I took an extra lap around the parking lot, hitting every spot where the mockingbird had come for me. I looked up from beneath the tree, the only sound the rustling of a few dead November leaves that hadn't yet fallen to the ground. I exhaled and, for the first time in months, felt my entire body relax. The mockingbird had retreated. We were halfway there.

We still lost her.

BEFORE *GRACE CAN* realize its schlocky, zombie-vampire-baby, B-movie destiny, it has to reckon with its most sincere depiction of body horror: Madeline delivering her stillborn daughter. Following the accident, Madeline refuses medical intervention to extract Grace, waiting instead for her body to naturally go into preterm labor. She may be denied the experience of mothering Grace but she won't be denied the experience of birthing her. And so, Madeline's labor unfolds mostly as she intended—in a birthing tub, Patricia at her side, cheering her on with every push—but with the solemn knowledge that after all this pain there will be no baby to take home, no baby to feed.

"Do you know how much I want you to stay?" Madeline whispers to Grace when she finally gets to cradle her delicate, lifeless body. *"Please stay."*

Patricia, increasingly concerned for Madeline's state of mind, gingerly tries to remind her that a dead baby cannot be willed back to life. But before she can finish the thought, Grace is suddenly reanimated, nursing hungrily at Madeline's breast. Patricia gasps in disbelief; Madeline smirks—satisfied, contented—because she always believed.

IT TOOK US a few seconds to realize she wasn't moving. Amanda, reclined in an oversized chair, her shirt rolled up and her belly slick with ultrasound jelly, groped for my shoulder and choked down a sob. Alex blinked and blinked at the large monitor above us, unsure of what he was seeing or not seeing. I kept waiting for the sound of a heartbeat to fill the room, but all we heard were the fuzzy bass notes of Amanda's still womb. In the corner of the screen: D—, curled up, her little limbs folded over themselves, her profile beautifully, cruelly defined. The technician, an awkward young woman whose hands trembled as she stood from her seat, told us she was so sorry and stepped out of the room.

Jacoby, now a precocious five-year-old who had begged to come to the appointment so he could see Chickie, stood in the corner, his face flush with confusion. He looked to Amanda for clarification. "Mama?"

She locked eyes with him. "Oh, it's sad news, sweetie."

"But I already *loved* her!" Jacoby cried.

As soon as those words left his mouth, I doubled over and began convulsing with grief. It was as if something had entered my body and was throttling me from within. A pained barking sound I never knew myself capable of making shot up out of my throat, matching the frightening rhythm of my body. Alex rushed to my side and leaned his weight against me. Amanda jumped from the chair and came up behind me, rubbing my back, offering a motherly "shshshshshsh." I looped an arm around her waist and pressed my head to her stomach. "My baby, my baby, my baby," I sputtered, my eyes glued to the monitor, wondering if maybe just this once, life could be like the movies, wondering if she'd stir.

A FEW DAYS later, a birth. Not the birth any of us had imagined, but a birth nevertheless. Amanda insisted we induce as quickly as possible, because she couldn't imagine carrying D— around for much longer, because every morning that Jacoby and Emmeline saw her still-there belly, they needed to be told all over again that, though Chickie was inside her, she was no longer alive.

"I'm terrified that it's *me*," Amanda confided, rocking from side to side on a large yoga ball on the hospital room floor, trying to instigate labor. "What if I was lucky to even have my babies in the first place? What if my body is killing your babies?"

What if, what if, what if. As we sat and listened to Amanda's fears and doubts about a body she had once so confidently believed in, my skull throbbed with guilt. After all she'd done for us—the needles, the hormones, the blood, *so much blood*—and everything she still had to do for us, we were managing to take yet another thing away from her.

IT TOOK SEVERAL hours for the Cytotec, an induction medication, to finally kick in. Amanda, who had never even taken a Tylenol during her previous pregnancies, seemed panicked by the sudden, unnatural shift in what her body was doing, as though she'd been spun around in circles in the dark, then told to find the light switch. Amanda had often jokingly warned us what she would be like during labor—sarcastic, potty-mouthed, impatient—but now she kneeled on the bed, deliriously sobbing from both the physical exhaustion and the emotional anguish of our journey ending this way.

Kevin sat somberly in the chair beside her, while Cee and Suzie, two local "loss doulas" who saw Amanda's post on a mommy group and decided we all needed as much support as possible, massaged Amanda and softly reminded her of her body's strength. Cee and Suzie's sudden appearance that morning felt like something out of a movie—two wise, compassionate strangers who seemingly came out of nowhere with bags full of blankets and snacks. Amanda had immediately warmed to their presence, allowing herself to crumble before them, these mothers who had come out of the virtual woodwork to take care of another mother, in a way she hadn't—couldn't—in front of us. The longer the process went on, the more voyeuristic, even intrusive it felt for Alex and me to be there. The baby was ours, but the pregnancy had always been Amanda's and now, in this terrible context, what was unfolding in that room had little to do with us. Suzie, sensing our increasing discomfort, walked over to us, enveloped us both in a deep hug, then opened the door for us to exit.

On the drive to the hospital that morning, Alex and I agreed that we did not want to see D—. We'd instruct the hospital staff to have her immediately taken to pathology so they could diagnose what had gone so terribly wrong inside her little body. It was the only way to move forward, we decided. Seeing her could only serve as confirmation that we were in fact being denied fatherhood by some malevolent outside force, that we had recklessly tempted fate and here was the result. But the longer we sat alone in the bright, sterile hospital room next to Amanda's awaiting word that it was over, the more our resolve began to fracture. For Alex, it was the thought of everyone but us getting to see her: "She's our baby," he wept. "*Our* baby." An intense anxiety that I'd forever be haunted by her image sat stubbornly on my chest, but when Amanda eventually appeared in the doorway and I saw the swell of pregnancy nearly gone beneath her sweatshirt, that same out-of-body wailing from days earlier poured out of me. I knew then that there was no choice, that I needed to see her for myself, this being we'd made but could not keep.

Before D— was brought into the room, Cee came in and prepared us for how she'd look. "More like a baby than you'd think," she said, "but also less like one than you might hope."

"But she's perfect," Amanda promised. "You'll see."

A nurse knocked on the open door, wheeling a small cart in front of her. She asked if we were ready for her to come in. Alex and I locked hands and silently read each other's faces, to make sure the other was sure. As baby D—, draped in a pink blanket and impossibly small, slowly came into view, Amanda quietly slipped out of the room.

WHAT MADELINE DOESN'T know, at least not at first, is that it isn't her fortitude or the strength of her love that returns Grace to her; rather, in her inability to let Grace go, she invites in something far darker and more destructive. *Please stay*. Her plea is heard and answered, but not by Grace. Something unseen and unholy has been feeding off Madeline's grief, and now it will feed off her body until there's nothing left to take. Alex and I, too, held our baby girl and told her how much we wanted her to stay, but we did not ask her to. Instead, we felt the scant weight of her in our hands, touched her translucent skin with the tips of our fingers, and inhaled her scent as deeply as we could, desperate to imprint her on our senses, on our memories. Then, we gave her back.

ELIO AND I are at an impasse. He's staring right into my face, tugging at his ears, a ribbon of drool plunging down his chin. I search my hands for a finger that isn't already dotted with teeth marks and frown at how cracked my knuckles and scratchy my palms have become from round-the-clock washing and sanitizing. Elio is not only our rainbow baby but he also has the distinction of being a pandemic baby, born four months into the COVID-19 crisis. With a virus raging outside, our time together inside is both more precious and more concentrated. Elio's shifting routines give our blurred days some semblance of structure, his whims keep us on our toes.

In the early weeks after his birth, when Alex and I would lie shirtless with him on our chests for skin-to-skin contact, he'd inevitably roll his head toward our nipples and try to latch on. We'd let him attempt it for a few seconds before correcting him, trembling with laughter because it tickled and because it was absurd; when he eventually discovered the pleasures of jamming our fingers into his mouth, we were loath to deny him what meager substitute for breasts we could provide. Soon, I found myself also depending on the hit of dopamine I got from his lips fastening around my thumb or gumming at my pinky as he drifted to sleep. To give of my body in such a simple and tangible way healed something I couldn't name but could feel coursing through me, like a revitalizing shock to the heart, with every bite.

But now: teeth are involved. We'll have to break the habit before Elio breaks skin. He extends his arms, babbles a pained whimper against which I have no willpower. I present my hands to him and he shrieks with delight, placing both over his face—an impromptu game of *peekaboo!* I laugh with him, glad for the reprieve, grateful that he is here.

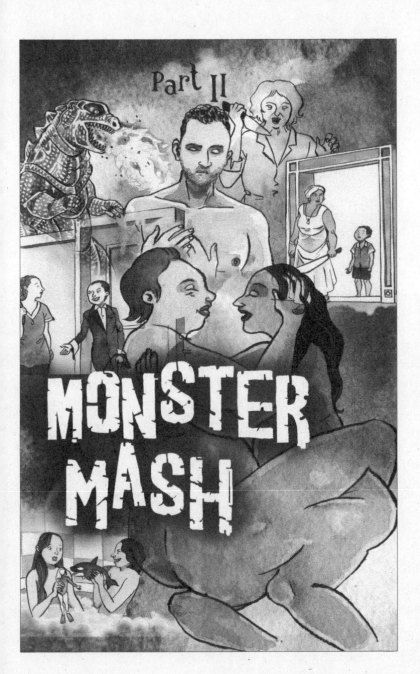

Indescribable

CARROW NARBY

The Blob; Society

BY THE TIME I staggered into the ER, it felt like my insides were liquefying. As if, at any moment, I would erupt: gallons of hot, pink froth would spew out of every orifice, even from my ears and eye sockets. The nurses would scream, my body would collapse into a pool of steaming goo, and it would finally be over.

This was not supposed to be an essay about the COVID-19 crisis. And it still isn't. But I am writing some of it from a hospital room, in the spring of 2020, in the midst of the global pandemic. This is the second time in a week that I have been admitted to the hospital, and it is my third ER visit in the past two weeks.

The rampant coronavirus is not the reason that I've been hospitalized. Like many people, I have gallstones: some of the bile in my gallbladder has coalesced and hardened into small, pebble-like deposits. Bile is a compound that is composed primarily of water, lipids (fats), and salt. It is produced in the liver, and stored in and excreted into the intestines by the gallbladder. Bile makes it possible for humans to break down and absorb fats by acting as an emulsifier. It allows the otherwise hydrophobic lipid molecules to be suspended in the water-based solutions that squelch through the intricate plumbing and ducts of the digestive system. Soap, basically.

For the past few years, I have suffered every now and then from a condition called *biliary colic*. To me, the moniker sounds infantilizing, and perhaps even dehumanizing; I have only otherwise heard the word *colic* in reference to babies and to horses. What a ludicrous dichotomy, come to think of it. A colicky infant is uncomfortable and fussy, while a horse with colic can rapidly die from the underlying cause.

I am somewhere in between baby and beast, I suppose. Hypothetically, my condition could become life-threatening. My gallbladder, or one of the neighboring organs, could become infected or even necrotic. That has not happened (yet) and I have not been in any immediate danger so far. But to say that I have been "uncomfortable" would be a staggering understatement. The pain that I am experiencing is indescribable.

Despite the impossible agony of the ordeal, my insides were not being dissolved by some alien acid. Rather, a tiny stone had been squeezed out of my gallbladder into the common bile duct. Both the liver and pancreas are connected to this common duct, and both of those organs had also become irritated. The pain chewing through my guts was the result of severe pancreatitis. I made it to the ER, collapsed into a wheelchair, and was whisked along the corridors, vomiting all the way. Nothing came out but little pats of yellowish foam. Because of the pain, I had not eaten in a few days, so there was nothing to eject. I wasn't really dissolving; my internal plumbing had backed up, and the delicate system of pumps and enzymes had been thrown into chaos.

I could not speak or move until a nurse administered hydromorphone, a powerful narcotic. "It's stronger than morphine but not as strong as fentanyl," she explained. It sent me instantly into a euphoric haze from which I was able to respond to the providers and follow their instructions. I did not emerge from this foggy state until I found myself in the basement of the small suburban hospital, crammed tightly into an old MRI machine. As I grew creepingly overwhelmed by claustrophobia, my surroundings and physical sensations snapped into focus. The MRI was installed in what seemed to be a converted loading bay. I was almost too fat for the machine, and my body pressed against the sides of the coffin-like tube. I listened to the rhythm of my breathing and the soft gurgling of my mutinous guts. I wasn't in pain anymore, but I was intensely aware of how the elastic hair tie at the nape of my neck was digging into my head and pulling at my scalp. I thought about how greasy and unkempt my hair was, how my legs were unshaven (because I am not in the habit of shaving them) and how my sparse goatee was starting to show (because I had no access to a razor while I was in the hospital). When I was finally released from the machine, I realized that the concrete space around it was crammed with old oxygen tanks. These must not have been ferrous; otherwise I might have suffered a very ugly accident. I had read about such a thing happening. I could not recall the details, but once, somewhere, a patient died when his head was struck by a gas canister that had been turned into a missile by the powerful magnet. I shivered in my bed after the MRI, plagued for some time by visions of my skull being crushed.

Writhing in savage agony and then getting shoved into tubes, enduring jabs and proddings, wrestling with stiff hospital sheets, fumbling back and forth from the toilet, bleeding onto the floor when a clumsy nurse struggled to put in my IV port—the whole experience made me keenly aware of myself as a *thing*. An aggregate of soft, slimy parts, any of which could suddenly leak or rupture or rebel. The providers and hospital staff, though, necessarily had to interpret and address me as a person. Whatever other prejudices might be at play, they saw me at least taxonomically as a fellow human being.

I do hate when people look at me, though; when they can *see* me. I cannot bear it. With every cell in my body I despise the very thought of being observed, of my body being scrutinized, interpreted, and judged. As much as I can, I hide from or try to ignore strangers' gazes. In the hospital it was unavoidable, of course. I was constantly seen. Naturally! I had to be! Yet it is hateful to me, even now, to think about what the nurses and physicians saw, to imagine whom they thought they were talking to. A frumpy, fat little woman. Maybe a lesbian, with those hairy legs and unfeminine bearing. Maybe someone soft in the head, slightly dim or deranged.

I cannot explain what bothers me so intensely about this utterly mundane and necessary process of observation and interpretation. I can only say that it feels like a grave intrusion. Perhaps it is simply the indignity of it, the unwelcome reminder that I am whatever it is that I am. As ludicrous as it is, I resent that anyone could presume to observe and taxonomize me without my permission or consent, without at least consulting me first. What's more, the impudent observer might be *wrong* about what they see. For one thing, I am not a woman. I wouldn't know how to correct anyone about this, though, because I am not a man either. I am not something in-between, or in some third-gender category like nonbinary. My gender identity does not have a name, because I do not have a gender identity. My gender is void, the null set, nothing. But it is impossible for anyone to look at me and see *nothing*. I cannot make myself unseen.

The nature of society is that we necessarily observe each other through certain prescribed lenses. Gender is one such lens. Not just a lens but, in its way, the entire telescope, observatory, research institution, and epistemology through which any and all observations are gathered, logged, and interpreted. Gender is inescapable. So, someone like me, however much I might insist that I "identify as agender,"[1] can never actually *be* genderless. The best that I can hope for is what I usually get: I must be some kind of gender clown.[2] A living parody—though a parody of what, exactly, no one can quite be sure. I might read as something like a woman, as a mannish, if not quite butch, lesbian. Or else I am curiously effeminate, a clumsy imitation of male femininity. An embarrassing distortion of womanhood or a wan pastiche of manhood—ridiculous, either way.

---

1. Which I do as infrequently as possible, because it is an oxymoron. To me, the entire point of genderlessness is the absence of a "gender identity."
2. But doctor, I am Pagliacci . . .

Indescribable

IT SEEMS OBVIOUS, even silly, to point out the importance of monsters to queer people and queer cultural expression. So much has been made in cultural criticism of the monster's relationship to the Other, and to othered sexualities and gender identities in particular. Vampires, for example, might be understood as an allegory for the fear of homosexuality as a social contagion.[3] In queer culture, in the media and stories produced by queer people about ourselves, monsters represent our fears, traumas, aspirations, and desires. Mermaids, werewolves, cryptids, and witches all make regular appearances in work produced by queer storytellers. Because the monster embodies so much meaning at once, it remains a contradictory figure. It is our distorted mirror image, our secret self. We are as ambivalent toward the monster as we are toward ourselves.

Of all the "classic" monsters from folklore and film, the iconic blob monster never seems to get much attention as a queer figure, in scholarship or in popular media. I've found next to nothing by way of queer analyses or interpretations of blob monsters in particular. In an essay about teaching with and about monsters,[4] art history professor Asa Simon Mittman is even dismissive of the idea that blobs could have any queer potential:[5]

> The valuably destabilizing role of monsters, the queering work that they can do for cultures, is to a degree predicated on their difference not being *quite* absolute. I suspect that blob monsters are not

---

3. Richard Primuth, "Vampires Are Us," *The Gay & Lesbian Review*, 108 (March–April 2014).

4. Asa Simon Mittman, "Teaching Monsters from Medieval to Modern: Embracing the Abnormal," in *Monsters in the Classroom: Essays on Teaching What Scares Us*, eds. Adam Golub and Heather Richardson Hayton (McFarland & Company, Inc., 2017), 19–34.

5. This essay is otherwise perfectly good, and Mittman has produced a large body of work on the subject of monsters and monster theory. I just have a quibble with this one point.

especially popular because, while they threaten bodily integrity, they do not threaten societal norms in as potent ways as more human-oid horrors would. The original poster and trailer for the 1958 film version of *The Blob*,[6] starring Steve McQueen in his debut role, tells us that the blob is "INDESCRIBABLE." This is not, of course, literally true—the blob is a carnivorous, animated, shape-shifting, glistening, semi-transparent red gelatinous mass. I *can* describe it, but I cannot much relate to it.

I, for one, find blobs to be eminently relatable. I also have to confess, sheepishly, that I have never seen the original 1958 version of *The Blob*. While the special effects look like they're great, at least by B movie standards, the plot doesn't exactly sound thrilling: the titular monster is a literal red menace that is ultimately defeated by an equally unsub-tle analogue of the Cold War. I am, however, very much a fan of the 1988 remake,[7] a fairly sophisticated and decidedly cynical take on Cold War anxiety. By comparison, the original seems like mere propaganda.

In the 1988 version, the blob is not red but vibrant pink. It descends on a picturesque slice of Americana: a small town where high school football is the center of public life and a folksy local diner serves up homemade pies. It immediately begins to upend the entire social order. The film is unsubtly metatextual, playing with the viewer's own biases and expectations to build suspense. We might expect the goofy jock and resourceful cheerleader to be our romantic leads. We certainly anticipate that Brian, the leather-jacket-wearing, motorcycle-rid-ing, beer-drinking delinquent, will be an inexplicably sociopathic yet otherwise featureless villain. But it is the delinquent who is constantly bullied, and the jock who turns out to be cruel.

Early in the second act, the football player, our presumed hero, is

6. *The Blob*, directed by Irvin Yeaworth (1958; Hollywood, CA: Paramount Pictures).
7. *The Blob*, directed by Chuck Russell (1988; Burbank, CA: TriStar Pictures).

suddenly and gruesomely killed by the blob, and from that point on no one is safe. The motherly proprietress of the diner who is kind even to Brian? The gruff but well-intentioned sheriff who worries over the townsfolk like a concerned father? Both are devoured by the blob. Even the manner of their deaths might subvert the viewer's expectations. The sheriff seems, at first, destined for heroic self-sacrifice, but he is unceremoniously dispatched offscreen; we only see the aftermath, his half-digested corpse swirling inside the blob's gelatinous mass. The diner owner dies during a special effects–heavy set piece. It is the kind of spectacular and horrifying death that one might expect to be inflicted on a minor villain or an unlucky bystander, not on someone whom the viewer knows and is supposed to like.

Near the end of the film, the blob snatches up and digests a little blond boy, and its assault on heterosexuality is complete. It ruptures the romantic tension that we might have expected to be the driving force of the narrative. It dissolves the nurturing mother and the authoritarian father. It devours even the most enduringly sacred figure of all, the child. I don't know what could be more queer than being narratively positioned as a threat to family values, particularly to children.[8]

"I'M IN THE mood for some body horror," I cheerfully announced to my now-fiancée, early in our relationship. We both enjoy horror films, and monster movies in particular, so we eagerly cuddled together on her couch and I put on Brian Yuzna's 1989 magnum opus *Society*. My girlfriend had never seen it. As the movie played, she gradually inched farther and farther away from me.

Society is a cult film notorious for the sheer amount and outrageousness of the body horror crammed into its graphic, outlandish climax.

8. We stan a pink menace.

I sincerely like it. It is a fun movie, and I think that everyone who isn't too squeamish should watch it at least once. The film presents itself, in part, as a heavy-handed commentary on class. The collective villain is Beverly Hills high society: old money tycoons, politicians, and debutantes. It turns out that the rich people are in fact not people at all, or at least not human. They are blob monsters, and they feed both economically and literally upon the proletarian masses.

As unsubtle as *Society*'s representation of class exploitation is, this dimension of the film is nonetheless overshadowed by its near-hysterical fixation on sex and sexual deviance. The social elite aren't just blob monsters, they're *sex-crazed* blob monsters. There is something rather more fascistic than Marxist about the film's equation of affluence with sexual decadence and depravity. At the very least, it is deeply, almost quaintly, conservative. *All* sex is portrayed as repellant and threatening, but certain kinds of intimacy are beyond the pale. The blob creatures gleefully indulge in group sex, incest, and homosexuality. They stage ritualistic orgies wherein their bodies swell and twist and merge into a single grotesque mass.

The attempted social commentary is further muddled by the world-building, and the fantastic world suggested by the film is the very thing that I find compelling about it. The villains are not human, but we are meant to be disgusted because they flout human social norms. Is there a compelling reason why a society of blob creatures—who may not even reproduce sexually, and whose physiology is obviously very different from humans'—should have an incest taboo in the first place? And what would a homo/heterosexual dichotomy (or gender, for that matter) even mean for creatures who can physically merge with their sexual partners and manipulate the shape of their own bodies at will? What is it like to experience such absolute intimacy? Is it exquisite?

Violation of the body's boundaries, structure, and function is the very essence of body horror, and body horror is every great blob's stock in trade. What makes *Society* so distinctive, and so infamous, is how bluntly the film portrays that violation as sexual. Like all blob monsters, the creatures devour their victims. But they begin this process by kissing them. At the height of the feast, the de facto leader of the creatures rams his entire body (fist-first, of course) into the victim's rectum. When Bill is compelled by the monsters to physically spar with his nemesis, a smug bully named Ted, the latter at first overpowers Bill and asserts his dominance with a passionate kiss. Bill ultimately uses the creatures' pliable physiology to his advantage and triumphs by literally fisting Ted to death. He rams his arm so far up Ted's asshole that he is able to pull his rival inside-out by the back of his face.

So now, in making my point, I have described some of the most shocking images in *Society*. And yet I contend that the film and its imagery are ultimately indescribable. Its essence remains elusive. I cannot reproduce, through mere description, the experience of actually watching those images on screen. That is what *indescribable* really means. Not that a thing literally cannot be described in terms of its physical properties or observed behavior but that it exists so far outside the observer's or the listener's frame of reference that mere description—and perhaps even direct observation—cannot render it comprehensible. The phenomenon remains inscrutable; it resists legibility.[9]

In the course of *Society*'s simultaneously thin and overwrought narrative, Bill becomes romantically involved with a sexy and mysterious blob-girl named Clarissa Carlyn. The portrayal of Clarissa and her relationship to the other monsters is the most fascinating thing about the film to me. Even though she always appears in the form of a beautiful young woman, Clarissa is, in some crucial ways, the quintessential blob. You see, regardless of how inhuman it might

---

9. This concept of *unknowability* is a key feature of cosmic horror, another subgenre that, like body horror, is replete with blobs.

(usually) look, the blob's otherness is *not* absolute.[10] For one thing, blob monsters are defined as much by their appetites as by their amorphousness. At the very least they eat (and, in *Society*, fuck) and there probably isn't any sensation more universally relatable than hunger. What makes the blob so terrifying is that, precisely because of its uncontainable appetite, it threatens to absorb us into itself. At any moment we could become (part of) the blob, and it could even become us. The very distinction between Self and Other—a fundamental distinction that we rely on in order to make any sense of ourselves and our world—could collapse.

Like the other blob monsters that populate the nightmarish world of *Society*, Clarissa mimics human form and social behavior. But she does so imperfectly. She doesn't bother to conceal her sexual urges; she can't *quite* seem to follow the flow of a "normal" conversation. Her imperfect disguise, her slightly "off" behavior, belies her alien nature.[11] For both Bill and the viewer, Clarissa exists right on the alluring cusp of legibility. She is clearly some kind of person: she has interiority, in the sense that she experiences desire, emotions, and agency. But she cannot *quite* be interpreted or understood using the same metrics that one might use to decide if another human is intelligent or trustworthy or kind. She isn't the same sort of person as Bill, or me, or you.

The other monsters seem to hate Clarissa. They treat her with open scorn and contempt. And whatever it is that sets Clarissa apart seems to run in her family. "Have you seen her mother?" one of Bill's classmates exclaims when Bill expresses interest in Clarissa at a party.

---

10. I think that it might be impossible to describe, represent, or even perceive *absolute* otherness, and that the Other, by definition, always holds a dim or fragmented mirror to the Self, but don't quote me on that or anything. I only skimmed the Lacan and Derrida that I was assigned to read in grad school.

11. I think it is worth noting that the monsters in *Society* are very adamant that they are not literally extraterrestrials.

Indescribable

Clarissa's mother, it turns out, is a monster that is barely able to hide her monstrousness. Ms. Carlyn doesn't fit into Beverly Hills society at all. Her makeup and outfits are outrageous to the point of parody or camp. She shambles around the neighborhood, vocalizing only in grunts. She is like a shoggoth trying to impersonate Divine.[12]

Clarissa and her mother, as blobs who look like and are sympathetic to humans, but who cannot help acting like what they are, do not fit into the society of inhuman overlords nor into regular human society. This is endlessly compelling to me. They are monstrous to everyone, even and perhaps especially to their fellow monsters. By failing to perform the facade of glamour and etiquette—of "good breeding"—that the other monsters put on, perhaps Clarissa and her mother remind them of what they really are: mere creatures, motivated as all creatures are by the impulses to eat, fight, and fuck. They remain trapped between the rejection and contempt of their own kind and a fundamental incompatibility with actual humans.

This conundrum is never resolved. Bill never stops being afraid of Clarissa, or more specifically of having sex with her, but he drags her off into the sunset anyway. Thematically, it seems as though the film is making a bleak statement about heterosexuality: all sex is frightening and repulsive, but the uneasiness of straight sex is at least preferable to the terror of homosexuality. Thinking about the characters and their fates, I am just left with nagging questions. Is it even possible for Clarissa to have sex with Bill without harming him? Certainly she cannot be *fully* intimate with him in the extreme way that her species experiences intimacy. Is she really willing to do that for him, to deny herself the possibility of intimacy? Even if she wants to do that, *can* she? Does she have the willpower? Or will loneliness eventually compel her to devour him?

12. In short: iconic.

THERE IS A particularly delightful meme that pops up now and again in my Twitter feed. It usually takes the form of a comic or a similar sequence of images, captioned with some variation on "If you want the rewards of being loved, you must submit to the mortifying ordeal of being known."[13] This phrase is lifted from the final line of "I Know What You Think of Me," a 2013 *New York Times* opinion piece by writer and cartoonist Tim Kreider.[14] In the essay, Kreider expounds upon the necessary agonies of being seen and interpellated by other people, particularly but not exclusively in our current age of instant mass communication. "It is simply not pleasant to be objectively observed," Kreider writes. "It's proof that we are visible to others, that we are seen, in all our naked silliness and stupidity."[15]

One of the clearest memories that I have of my first relationship is lying in bed with my then-girlfriend, our bodies intertwined and pressed together as closely as possible. In that moment, my most fervent desire was that she and I could somehow be even *closer*. That we could exist physically together without any boundary or separation. I still feel that familiar pang sometimes: the hunger for impossible intimacy, a desire to be known completely *without* first having to be seen and scrutinized. As I have come to know myself better, this fantasy of perfect intimacy has revealed itself to be inextricably intertwined with the problem of gender. Gender, among its other applications, is the

---

13. It turns out that Internet memes are not funny when you try to describe them. You should look it up, though.

14. Tim Kreider, "I Know What You Think of Me," *New York Times*, June 15, 2013, https://opinionator.blogs.nytimes.com/2013/06/15/i-know-what-you-think-of-me/.

15. I am all the more endeared to Kreider's essay because the incident that inspired the piece was not itself endearing. It was genuinely stupid: Kreider was accidentally cc'd on an email in which a friend gently mocked him for *renting a herd of goats*. Kreider's reasons for doing so "aren't relevant" to his thesis. Renting a herd of goats is very silly, and spiraling into anxiety because someone else acknowledged your silliness is embarrassing. And that's the point. To be loved we must be known, and to be truly known we must allow others to see the parts of ourselves that are genuinely mortifying.

primary framework through which desire and romantic intimacy are understood. We are gay or straight or bisexual or pansexual or asexual: we desire men, or women, or all genders, or no one at all. But if I am nothing, if I am without gender, how can I ever be desired? Is intimacy possible—that is, is it legible *as* intimacy—without *some* kind of interplay between femininity and masculinity?

Blobs are not queer incidentally. They are not queer simply because, through narrative contrivance, they might be associated with the destruction of heterosexual order, as in *The Blob*, or with the terror of homosexual intimacy, as in *Society*. The blob's relationship to queerness is a product of its basic symbolic function. The blob dissolves boundaries. It embodies what Julia Kristeva identifies, in her seminal work *The Powers of Horror*, as *the abject*.[16] The abject is that which violates corporeal, social, and conceptual boundaries by collapsing mutually exclusive, and thus mutually constitutive, categories. We know what *woman* is because, in any given context where *man* and *woman* are conceptualized, we can define the boundary of what is and is not *man*. We can name *homosexuality* because we can contrast it with *heterosexuality*. We develop a sense of self because we can recognize that which is outside of or apart from ourselves. But what if those distinctions were permeable? What if they collapsed entirely?

Where, psychoanalytically speaking, the *object* facilitates meaning-making and order by functioning as a foil or complement to the *subject*, "what is *abject*, on the contrary, the jettisoned object, is radically excluded and draws me toward the place where meaning collapses."[17] Neither subject nor object, neither Self nor Other, the abject threatens meaning itself, and we react to it with visceral horror and revulsion as well as fascination.

16. Julia Kristeva, *The Powers of Horror: An Essay on Abjection* (New York: Columbia University Press, 1982).
17. Kristeva, *Powers of Horror*, 2.

An all-consuming blob is about the most literal representation of the collapse of meaning that I can imagine. In the blob, Self and Other dissolve and merge into a single undifferentiated mass. Psychoanalysts and film theorists are inclined to associate this monstrous union with a fear of, and an Oedipal urge to merge with, the archetypal or archaic mother.[18] I don't think *everything* has to be so narrowly Freudian, however. What the blob represents is a total union or oneness that is simply impossible because of human physiology, and because of the ways in which humans relate to the world and to each other through meaning-making and language. The blob represents an absolute and unattainable intimacy. Not necessarily, or not only, intimacy with the mother but intimacy with anyone and anything, with *everyone* and *everything*.

For me, this is precisely the allure of the blob. It isn't just that I recognize "the soft animal of my body"[19] in the blob's ungainly mass and uncomplicated appetites. It isn't just that the blob's assault on the social and symbolic order reflects my own desire to reject gender. The blob, by threatening to merge the subject and the object of desire into a single being, promises the "rewards of being loved" without submission to "the mortifying ordeal of being known." I want what she has! Who doesn't? There is no need to make myself vulnerable to scrutiny, interpretation, and judgment by another if I, and said other, are already one and the same. What the blob offers is intimacy without legibility. Not the eternal separation of annihilation but just the opposite: the end of solitude.

HAVING A VOID where one's gender is supposed to be is lonely enough. But it does not compare to the desolation of brute physical pain. The cure for my recurrent gallbladder trouble should be

18. Barbara Creed, *The Monstrous-Feminine: Film, Feminism, Psychoanalysis* (London: Routledge, 1993).

19. Mary Oliver, *Wild Geese* (Northumberland: Bloodaxe, 1986), 13–14.

straightforward: In the absence of complicating factors like inflammation or infection, gallbladder removal, or cholecystectomy, is a simple operation. Under normal circumstances, I would undergo surgery shortly after my latest hospital stay, as soon as my pancreas returns to normal (in the hospital, a very intense surgeon informed me that operating while the organs are inflamed is "like trying to work with very tacky glue"). But, as I write this, the COVID-19 crisis has been ongoing for months. Hospitals are stretched beyond their capacity, and surgeons are not performing any operations that are deemed "elective." For the foreseeable future, I cannot be cured unless or until my condition becomes imminently life-threatening.

So, I am left in a curious state. I live now with a constant hyper-awareness of my body *as* a body, of myself as a living thing. I have to be vigilant about my diet, wary of every little twinge and spasm. On one hand, I feel more bloblike than ever: Forced to scrutinize and name *myself*, I find that I really am just a big soft, slimy thing that eats and shits and eats again. Everything else that I pretend to be is a charade. And it is also just terribly lonely, to live with pain and fear so intense that I cannot describe them.

Of course, the incomprehensible intimacy promised or threatened by the blob is just a fantasy. Each of us is ultimately alone: a discrete little being with access only to our own senses and sensations, our own thoughts, and our own fragile body. Left to fumble for meaning in our constant pursuit of imperfect intimacies. We submit ourselves endlessly to that mortifying ordeal of knowing each other, just for the chance to be alone together. Language might be the best thing that we have to bridge the void between ourselves, but it will never be enough.

A Working Definition of the Monstrous

RYAN DZELZKALNS

Godzilla

LET'S SAY I have to go to a wedding. Let's say I don't want to go. The only mask I can think of to protect myself with is Godzilla: unafraid, hyperbolic, unapologetic in his wreckage. He'll spend the whole night dancing with the grandmas, dangerously festive. He'll smile back when spoken to. He'll be a natural. The people won't help but love him.

I knew I was different for a long time. Whenever the boys at sleepovers would clack, *who do you have a crush on?* I always answered, *no one.* This was not a lie. I had no girl crushes and I had no boy crushes. Even after I started masturbating and using my teammates in excruciating detail, I was not, strictly speaking, attracted to them. Their bodies were simply those with which I had become the most acquainted. Self-deception can be a monstrous thing, especially when nothing about yourself remains recognizable. It was no coincidence that I wasn't attracted to a man until I left home.

In the 1954 film, we begin to know Godzilla by the destruction he leaves behind. Coming in like a storm, he replaces houses with his footprint, disappears entire ships in a flash of light. When we finally get to see him, it's only ever in pieces. That first time on Odo Island, he rears up over the cliff exposing his head and upper chest, his two arms braced against the horizon, a reptilian colossus. Throughout the entire movie his silhouette is constantly being broken by the frame of the camera, the cityscape, the surface of the ocean. Godzilla is simply too large to be taken in all at once.

Anne Carson's *Autobiography of Red* follows Geryon, who is both a boy and a monster. He describes himself as having six arms and six legs, wings, and—like everything else worth recounting—as being red. In this retelling of Herakles's tenth labor, Geryon is heartbroken instead of murdered, violence given a different outlet. The lyricism that Anne Carson imbues in the text is arresting, transfiguring strangeness into beauty. In my early twenties, this was the only balm for the weak thoughts, the first time I recognized myself in art. There *are* other boys who think they are a monster!

What does it mean to be a monster? To fail in the predictable ways? It is a queer light that comes from the burning city, underwriting Godzilla's power. His capacity for destruction lies just as ably within as without.

Godzilla has always been figurative, construed as an allegory for Japan-US relations, a reframing of the atomic bombs. Or Godzilla, nature's manifesto against the excesses of mankind writ in prehistoric flesh. Either he knows what he's doing, or he doesn't. Either he's a force of nature, or a tool used to destroy. Whom will I invoke at Cousin's wedding? Will I hurt, or will I do the hurting?

It was a shock to realize that people wanted to have sex with me. So much of my life had been dampened and circumspect that I never considered flirting a possibility. What sad epiphany: not the specifics of sexuality but its mere existence at all.

In the beginning there was Godzilla. He appeared and then he died. But due to popular demand, the production company resurrected him for the sequel, creating new and fabulous enemies for him to interact with.

According to the figures, people like me make up the majority of new incidences of HIV each year. This is called "MSM," *men who have sex with men.* It makes me uncomfortable to be flattened automatically into statistics or stereotypes, into a "high risk category." "Riskiness" makes it seem like *if only* you were more vigilant you could've saved yourself, as if you've gotten *only* what you deserve. But the virus can be transmitted via semen and blood and breast milk. It's a good reminder that those who contract HIV are innocent too.

PrEP stands for Pre-Exposure Prophylaxis, and, if you're straight, is the biggest breakthrough in preventative medicine you've never heard of. It is a daily course of medication that, when taken routinely, builds resistance to contracting the human immunodeficiency virus. The pill is blue and anecdotally oneirotropic. The first time I was on it, it gave me nightmares—the dream where Mom killed the both of us in a murder-suicide. The second time, I didn't notice any change in my sleep, except the anticipated loosening of my night habits.

Being on PrEP has made me realize that I am afraid of sex. The threat of this virus shames my blood, slips guilt like a needle under my skin. What I'm trying to say is there are facts and there's what we're taught happens to people like us. While there is danger here, a knife can cut anyone. I didn't know how forcefully I clung to my fear, until it was gone.

A Working Definition of the Monstrous

On his second tramp through Tokyo, Godzilla discovers an aviary in the city, some fancy thing in the Ginza. The birds are crazed and flitting about from perch to perch. Godzilla seems almost to speak to them, growling in quick succession. Does Godzilla know what he's doing? The will to communicate indicates some sense of self-awareness. But then again, he does the same thing to the bell tower before he tears it down.

I started writing poems about Godzilla when I lived in Minneapolis. Perhaps not so much "about" but rather "through." This began before marriage equality, either on the federal or the state level. I still recall that summer sitting on my Christian friend's couch and listening to the Minnesota Public Radio broadcast of each state representative giving their speech as they cast their vote. I had a beer and cried as Minnesota became the twelfth state to legalize same-sex marriage. My first Godzilla poems were all about sex but slowly crept to include marriage and family. All the various forms of love wrought so uneasily between us.

> *Godzilla stares at the sun*
> *and thinks of his mother.*

With a slide projector, the famed paleontologist Dr. Yamane gives his theory on the origins of Godzilla to the Diet. *It was probably hidden away in a deep sea cave, providing for its own survival, and perhaps others like it. However, repeated underwater H-bomb tests have completely destroyed its natural habitat. To put it simply, hydrogen-bomb testing has driven it from its sanctuary.* All of this because he found a single radioactive trilobite in Godzilla's footprint.

It's funny imagining Godzilla living in a cave eating trilobites like popcorn. It's funny imagining Godzilla eating anything at all, his life so large it's completely unsustainable. The original reveal of him on Odo Island had him carrying a dead cow in his jaws. This, of course, was removed because it's ridiculous.

I didn't want to go to Cousin's wedding because I was troubled by the thought of being his best man. I did not want to be complicit with an institution that, at the time, excluded me. This is a political explanation. Even more, I was worried it might break me.

It quickly became apparent that I had made a terrible miscalculation. Certain thresholds cannot be uncrossed. Once I sent the email explaining that I wouldn't be coming, I couldn't unsend it. And as my family so kindly reminded me, *not everything is about me*. At that point, every action became hateful in its outcome.

A working definition of the monstrous: (1) behaviors, appearances, or appetites that are unrecognizably different from one's own; (2) some invisible force that keeps one apart from others, or some otherness that marks one as though by an invisible force; and (3) someone you would watch die.

At the end of the movie, Dr. Serizawa kills Godzilla with his Oxygen Destroyer, an invention with no practical application except as a weapon. He sneaks up on Godzilla, who is drowsing on the seafloor and lazily glances over his shoulder as he notices the intruder. But it's too late. The device is triggered and both Godzilla and the good doctor (along with all other living things in Tokyo Bay) are liquidated. At least Dr. Serizawa is afforded some sense of dignity. We have to watch as Godzilla's flesh disappears, his bones ripped clean. And to our chagrin, even his bare skeleton disintegrates before our very eyes. Such betrayal of intimacy.

When I do turn up at Cousin's wedding, I can feel the invisible force of my presence straining against my family. I had said I didn't want to be there and then I let myself be convinced. After all their *persuasive* argumentation, everyone has to pretend that they want me here. The bride's sister makes a speech about marriage equality. Someone boos softly in the background. It's startling to lose so resoundingly, both to yourself and to others.

In the end, there is nothing remarkable about any of this. I am just a queer white boy from the Midwest. The rough lesson between being tolerated and being loved, between what you want and what you need.

For Godzilla, even death promises no end.

Every city I've lived in has been on the water; every city has been one city, the buildings rubbing up against the end of the land. Rivers, too, serve as a conduit to the unknown, boundary for the dead. Tokyo, New York, Minneapolis—all places where I had made a home, pretended that no part of my life would crawl from where it had been hidden, be spit from the seafloor to remind everyone I am not what I am.

Godzilla is a tool. He allows a reflection with which to grapple, a body to explain away. Godzilla is my shadow, my delicate monster.

In *Godzilla*, the invisible threat of radiation can be construed as queerness. Godzilla's pear-shaped body is the vessel through which desire flows. The order of the city so easily upset by one fabulous step. What's the difference between a weapon and a tool? Even if it's useful, a weapon can't help but kill.

We are all dosed yearly from ambient sources of ionizing radiation. These particles are strong enough to pierce your cells and knock on your DNA—and are completely normal. The average exposure to ionizing radiation comes in at right around 5 millisieverts per year. This is largely from cosmic background radiation that sneaks through Earth's magnetic field and from radioactive elements that escape the ground, like radon or radium.

Similarly, "the love that dare not speak its name" has existed from time immemorial, with same-sex behaviors observed in over 450 different species. "Homosexuality" was invented in 1869, the term coined in defense of an individual's privacy from the state. It was quickly co-opted by the burgeoning psychology of Sigmund Freud and Havelock Ellis, and in the 1900s deployed through the various technologies of diagnosis and confession to help buttress normality with the abnormal. That which was heretofore natural, became an aberration, dangerous— the beast driven from its cave, given a name. It wasn't until 1987 that homosexuality was completely dropped from the list of mental disorders in the American Psychiatric Association's *Diagnostic and Statistical Manual of Mental Disorders*, coincidentally, the year I was born.

A Working Definition of the Monstrous

A new theory: What if love necessitates monstrosity, creates this terrible flesh by laying one's wanting bare? Monstrosity both in the confession and the desire; in the vulnerability and the hunger. You let this happen. How strange to grow up envious of what everyone else has and to be afraid of it for yourself. Ah! Here, our desire has become unstable, but that means we're getting somewhere.

Who are these people that feel unmonstrous in their love? As though the world was made for them to exist in it, as though they want not to tip their head back, take the whole damn thing in their throat.

The Wolf in the Room

PRINCE SHAKUR

Good Manners / As boas maneiras

"YOU WILL NEVER tell anyone about this," my mother ordered from the front seat of the car, a machete in her hand.

The day before, we'd come home to find our house ransacked. Before the police arrived, my mother searched the house wildly, crying and ranting in a rage as my brother tried to stop her from tampering with things the police might use as evidence. When the police did arrive, they nodded, scribbled uselessly into their notebooks, and left. The next day we piled into the car and drove to confront my recently arrested stepfather Dennis's family, who my mother knew had been the ones who robbed us at our most vulnerable.

My mother marched us to the front door, banged on the door, and as soon as it opened, she walked in, instructing us to wait for her on the front stoop. My older brother stood beside me with his face in his hands, afraid, ashamed. But as I heard my mother cuss in patois and threaten the people in the house, I felt a sense of pride. The world was falling apart around us, but I felt protected.

THE PROMISE OF a queer family—and a future—is at heart of the Brazilian werewolf film *Good Manners (As boas maneiras)*. This hope, however, is quickly dashed when Clara, a woman hired to be a live-in nanny to the affluent Ana and her not-yet-born child, discovers that Ana has carnivorous cravings on full moon nights. Clara learns from folklore that the painful cramps that Ana is experiencing are not due to her pregnancy, of course, but rather a much darker cause: a one-night stand with a man-turned-wolf who Ana subsequently shot a bullet at and never saw again.

To complicate matters, Ana and Clara have fallen for each other. As their romance blooms, the sinister nature of Ana's conception becomes a much more visible weight on Ana, who pretends to be okay but seems to inherently know the burden she carries will ultimately destroy the intimacy and semblance of family she and Clara have created. Ana's attempt at normalcy comes to an abrupt end when she is violently ripped open during childbirth. When Clara finds Ana's eviscerated body, she plants one last kiss on her lover's lips, a somber mutilation of *Sleeping Beauty*. Clara, in a state of shock, locates a gun and readies herself to murder the monster. On the floor, a wailing baby covered in fur and blood.

Lost in her unimaginable grief, Clara leaves the wolf-child near a river. As she walks away, the full moon bright in the sky behind her, the baby's cries call her back. Clara stops, recovers the baby, and sobs on a train as she carries with her the only remaining piece of her almost-family with Ana.

The second half of *Good Manners* occurs seven years after the tearful scene on the train. It opens with a depiction of a loving relationship between Joel, the wolf-boy, and Clara, dancing together in the mornings, just as Ana did while she was pregnant. This love compels Clara to craft elaborate routines to stave off Joel's need for blood: cooking him only vegetables, not allowing him to go to a local dance during a full moon, constructing a hidden room for him to be locked into when he begins to change form. After a full moon transformation, Clara shaves away Joel's hair and tells him the fairy tale–like story of how she was walking home from work and found a baby boy crying by the river. The story Clara has constructed for Joel's safety, however, falls apart when Joel finds a box of photos of his mother that Clara has been keeping secret.

CLARA'S APPROACH TO protecting and loving Joel echoes the kind of love I look for as a queer viewer in a world that so often tells me that people like me shouldn't exist. I also see so much of my own mother in Clara's ability to wade between chilliness and warmth, her resourcefulness, and her unexpected bouts of affection. When Clara fidgets through her initial job interview, the classist tension thick as she takes in Ana's impossibly regal apartment, I see my mother as a fifteen-year-old Jamaican immigrant facing the taunts of her white classmates while enduring desegregation bussing in the late 1970s. The many hours on her feet at work, the many things gone wrong at home, and unexpected ferocity with which children and lovers demand affection. How she scrubbed our teeth diligently with baking soda in the mornings before preschool. How my brother and I learned early to detect how her slight downward gaze meant she was disappointed, how it always took a few seconds for her shoulders to soften into our hugs.

Today, I see my mother wielding the machete as a double-sided analogy that so many black parents impart when they have children. In a hungry and violent world, our parents must be both our protectors and enforcers when we stray outside the lines. Their means of affection, at turns abundant and withheld, become the walls around us, meant to keep out the world of monsters outside. But what happens when we, the children, become the monsters, the very things meant to be cast out?

SHORTLY AFTER DENNIS'S arrest, puberty struck. My body unspooled into something lanky and wiry. Dark sprouted around my groin. My mother complained of the strange smells that came with two teenage boys at home. I spent days secretly leering at boys in my class in Catholic school and my nights sweating in bed as I prayed to God to change me before lust imploded my world. My frantic online searches for porn guided me to the terrible truth. I couldn't rid my brain of all the memories of my mother telling me "not to shake my head like that when you talk" or my family's homophobic murmurs when they saw a gay person out in public. The monster grew inside of me, and I continued to feed it.

ONE NIGHT, after an argument in the kitchen, my mother slapped me. I made the mistake of pushing her away. Her face, which could sometimes be a maze of stress, opened to a new rage.

"You're gonna be a woman-beater, just like *your father*," she roared. "And I hope the men get you in prison, like they probably got him."

THE DEEPER TRUTH about the stories that our parents tell us to protect us is that there is seldom an actual plan for how to reveal the truth intentionally. It is almost always a frantic search in the night, an inadvertent reveal of an elephant—or a wolf—in the room.

Early one morning, when I was fifteen, my mother shook me awake. The room was so dark I could barely make out her face, but I felt her weight at the edge of my bed.

"Is it true?" she asked, through tears.

As my eyes adjusted, I could see the outline of my journal in her hands.

"Are you gay?"

I wished the darkness would swallow her.

EVENTUALLY, Joel begins to rebel against Clara. He thirsts for both human flesh and a deeper understanding of who and what he is. A desperation to ratify his own identity, whatever hurt that might bring, to others, to her, to himself.

It Came From the Closet

NOT LONG AFTER she'd discovered my journal, two letters arrived home from my brother, sent from the camp where he was in military training. My mother and I stood in the dining room only a foot away from each other as we read our own letters. Chills moved through my shoulders as I took in the feverish scrawl of a brother who once held me in headlocks for full episodes of cartoons and now wrote phrases such as "always admired you" and "couldn't tell the truth about who I was before" and "I'm sorry I treated you like a nobody."

When my mother finished her letter, her nose red, she sat on her knees in the middle of our living room, spitting, "Why me, God? Please take this burden away. Oh God, why?"

ON MANY OF my early viewings of *Good Manners*, I hungered for Clara's version of motherhood instead of the version I'd been raised with: the Jamaican mother who survived abuse that sometimes closed her off from her children, who sometimes told me as child that I had taught her "how to love," and sometimes could only see in me my father's worst parts, and who had tried so hard to change me. Jennifer Lewis, in her *Werewolves: A Three-Dimensional Content Analysis of Films from 1980–2014*, tells us that "monsters encompass the good and bad parts of society in a physical state making them hybrid, showcasing polarities of society." But monsters do not only expose the good and bad parts of society; they also expose the character of those that come into contact with them. The things that we do because we are afraid also tend to be the very things that define us. I have learned that we can make monsters out of people, but it is only when we live in a world where being a monster is not the end, a world where good manners can't save us from inevitably disappointing others, that sacrifice need not be intrinsically tied to love.

The Wolf in the Room

WHEN MY MOTHER moved me in to my college dorm my freshman year, she sat me down and said, "Don't be gay while you're here."

I hugged her goodbye but promised nothing.

A rewarding, queer, and confusing life, it turned out, would be my rebellion against my mother's omens. I went to college. I read sometimes good poetry at open mic nights, had my first kiss in a dorm room, made friends with the queer, DIY music kids, and chugged malt liquor in bathrooms at parties. Drunkenly, beneath backyard starlight, I'd sometimes kneel in desperation and pray for a different past.

AS A CHILD, I simply saw myself as a black boy with a murdered father and a stepfather. Any questions I had about my biological father were brushed off with platitudes or admonishments "to appreciate the father I had." Yes, Dennis let me stay in his truck and read books while he ran errands or visited friends around the city. Yes, he was the one who carried me from the backseat to my bed after night rides home, the one who told me fantastic stories about being born on a boat, which meant he belonged to no nation.

But while in Jamaica earlier this year, I went to Bogue Cemetery in Montego Bay and searched through the dirt and broken tombstones to try and find the man who had done monstrous things to the woman who brought me into the world. I couldn't find my father's grave but, despite the warm wind howling at my ears and the sun blurring my view, I kept on hunting.

Three Men on a Boat

JEN CORRIGAN

Jaws

I'VE KNOWN THAT I like women since my Sporty Spice obsession at age six, but the feeling was one I'd mostly ignored until I watched *Jaws*. My dad had given me a Target gift card for my twelfth birthday, and while shopping for my own present, I was immediately attracted to the blue, metallic sheen of the double-VHS 25th Anniversary Collector's Edition. The cover depicted the classic image: a blond woman swimming naked, an enormous mouth of teeth reaching up from the depths, the name of the film above in blaring red letters. It seemed scary, dangerous, and a bit sexy. I bought it and watched it perched on the edge of my bed. I was entranced, enamored with the elusiveness of the shark, how you couldn't always see it, but you knew it was there by the camera angles and the pulsing thrum of John Williams's iconic score. I laughed at the jokes and tensed up at the scary parts, shrieking when Ben Gardner's head rolled out of the broken hull of his boat. I was filled with so many feelings that my young body almost couldn't handle it. One of those feelings was a sexy feeling, a breathless tingle that squirmed around in my abdomen, a trembling that excited me as I watched Brody, Hooper, and Quint together on the boat.

We don't talk about *Jaws* as a queer film, but it is. At least, I like to read it as one. Is there really anything gayer than three men on a boat? The thing about *Jaws* is that it's only queer if you're looking for it. To mainstream audiences, queerness is most easily tolerated when masked with straight performance, or an appearance that *could be* coded as straight. Queer films like *Fried Green Tomatoes* are widely enjoyed even by more conservative viewers, in part because they can be read as straight should the audience prefer that safer reading. On the flip side, *Jaws* is a straight film that can be read as queer, which is the reading that I choose.

People don't read me as queer either. I have never come out to my family. At least, not to everyone. My brother knows, and when I told my father when I was a teenager, he said, "Okay," and we never spoke of it again. Coming out to my grandmother, now dead, was always out of the question. She told me this more than a decade ago; I don't remember what triggered it, but she phrased it casually while I drove her home from grocery shopping, the backseat brimming with food. The whoosh of the air conditioning flapped the plastic bags, *fwip fwip fwip*. The lettuce wilted in the heat, and the ice cream carton sweat icy droplets.

"Being gay is fine. A person can't help that. But being bisexual is gross. Just pick one! You shouldn't double-dip." She said this brazenly, definitively. I imagined myself as a broccoli floret, dunked twice into a tub of French onion dip at a party.

"Why is that gross?" I asked. I pressed the accelerator, and my grandmother grabbed the door instinctively. The car hugged the curves of the highway.

"Would you want to have sex with a man who has had sex with another *man?*"

I didn't answer. I couldn't answer. At that age, I had begun to see queerness everywhere, in myself and in others, in real life, in books, in movies. Even when it wasn't there, I searched for it, as if finding it would help me decode the puzzle of my own sexuality. And sometimes I found it in places where most people didn't look for it, like in hyper-masculine monster movies like *Jaws*.

I never came out to my grandmother, but I didn't need to. All my partners who stuck around long enough to be invited to Thanksgiving dinner have so far been cis men. I'm able to hide my queerness, a privilege that is convenient and gives me a safeness that some other queer identities don't have. Yet, there is a guilt nestled underneath that relief, a sense that I am not really participating. By not coming out and declaring myself, I have the clinging feeling that I'm not being queer enough.

I used to present more queer. When I was in junior high, I had a shag haircut and wore an oversized pink-and-purple-plaid flannel every other day. A friend at the time, who was never very nice, told me I looked like a lesbian lumberjack. I knew it was supposed to be an insult, but I didn't know which part was supposed to be the insulting bit. I'm not sure what I said back, or if I said anything. I wore my flannel a few more times, then shoved it far back in my closet. I let my hair grow out.

Around this same time, I went clothes shopping with my grandmother, an activity I loathed. We walked past a bunch of elaborate formal dresses on display for the prom season. I touched one, seafoam green and voluminous, the bodice bedazzled with beads that glinted like glass shards. The fake jewels itched against my skin.

"Gross," I said. I was self-righteous in that way most thirteen-year-olds are. "When I go to prom, I'm not going to wear a dress. I'm going to wear a sensible tuxedo."

"You want everyone to think you're a lesbian?" my grandmother sneered. "Because that's what they'll think." She said this as if it was the worst possible thing anyone could think of me. Being a lesbian was not a sin, but looking like one was.

The joy of *Jaws* is that it's still queer even though the men don't look queer to an outside eye. But I see it when I observe their interactions. My queer reading stems from two aspects of covert communication: the gaze and innocuous touch, both classic indicators of desire. Historically, queer interactions were dangerous, and, really, still are. The looks and touches between the men signal an intimacy that is easy to overlook, particularly when the touches occur in jest; in the midst of arguing with Mayor Vaughn about the seriousness of the situation, Hooper places his hands on Brody's stomach and pats him to punctuate his irritation. It's easy to orchestrate these touches so they seem natural, because the characters are often standing in close proximity to one another. Director Steven Spielberg frames the water and the characters in the same way, very close. The technique results in their whole bodies and faces taking up the screen. The distance between them seems negligible and the possibilities endless.

Touching with hands has a significance in queer intimacy. It is a touch that is both erotic and personal yet can easily be perceived as casual. Upon meeting for the first time, Quint says to Hooper, "Let me see your hands." He takes Hooper's hands in his and pulls Hooper toward him as if they are about to embrace. The contrast between Quint's hands and Hooper's hands is an analysis of class—Quint claims Hooper has "city hands" and it's obvious from his hands he's "had money all [his] life"—but it is also a touch that is personal. By examining Hooper's hands, Quint is examining Hooper and his history.

Closeness between the men's bodies becomes even more pronounced when they embark on the *Orca*, Quint's fishing boat aptly (or ironically) named for the shark's only natural predator. The close quarters and the great nothingness of the sea requires that the men occupy physical spaces close to each other. The greatest moment of intimacy occurs at night when the work has stopped, and they are drinking inside the boat. Hooper and Quint compare scars, trying to outdo one another. Quint shows a fake tooth and then leans across the table so Hooper can touch a lump on his head. Hooper responds by displaying a jagged scar on his arm from a moray eel. Quint rolls up his sleeve to show Hooper he can't extend his bicep all the way. The touch and bodily proximity increase as Hooper scoots along the booth closer to Quint, rolls up his pant leg, and stretches his leg out to display a scar on his calf. As he displays his leg, he places it on Quint's hand, and Quint turns to Brody off-screen and grins. Quint rubs Hooper's leg playfully and then moves closer, rolling up his own pant leg and placing it over Hooper's to present a scar from a thresher's tail. Brody, standing off to the side, asks, "Thresher?" and Hooper explains in an annoyed tone that a thresher's a shark, demonstrating that Brody is being excluded. There is a brief moment where Quint and Hooper look at each other and smile, and it's an inviting look that I cannot read as anything other than erotic. Quint asks Hooper if he wants to drink, and Hooper says they'll drink to each other's legs. As they cackle and down their drinks , Brody lifts up his shirt to show his own scar. He pauses, as if he's considering inserting himself into the intimate exchange, and ultimately decides against it.

The one-upping of scars is a safe form of touch. While the game embraces playful touch and a revealing of each other's respective pasts, it can appear as a competition in which the men are continually trying to out-tough one another. Rather, it's a test of boundaries, both physical and emotional, and the climax of this intimacy between the three men is Quint's famous monologue where he describes the horrific experience of surviving the greatest US naval disaster in history. The root cause behind Quint's obsessive sharking is revealed as he describes waiting three days in the water, dehydrated and starving, warding away the frenzied sharks that dragged the sailors away one by one. This moment of vulnerability is the climax to the explorations of their bodies, because even homoerotic touch is less intimate than the baring of Quint's trauma.

I'd always want to play and touch my girlfriends. In first grade, when staying over at my best friend's house, her mother stuck us in the bath together, an experience that filled me with an excitement that had a bodily sensation but no name. We played in the bathtub, dipping her Ocean Friends Barbie (and the Orca toy that came with) down under the water and then up, splashing, the droplets dappling our bodies.

Playful touch was a safe way that I could explore my relationship to other girls and the feelings that came with it, but only if it did not cross a line, a line that I didn't always see. My grandmother came to pick me up from soccer practice when I was in the first grade. She waited in her car next to the field. A girl named Jessie and I ran across the grass, spanking each other and laughing hysterically at our game. When I reached my grandmother's car I said goodbye to Jessie and climbed in.

"What the hell were you doing?" my grandmother hissed between clenched teeth. "Running around spanking each other like that. What will Jessie's mother think of you?"

I sat silently in the back seat and tried not to cry, letting the shame wash over me, shame that I hadn't even known I should have.

VIEWERS MAY BE tempted to write off, or never even consider, the queer intimacy between Brody, Hooper, and Quint because of their relationship history. Brody is married to a woman and has two children, and Hooper makes a passing joke about an ex-girlfriend. Some might point to these details as evidence of their straightness, as if there's only gay or straight, and nothing outside of that dichotomy.

Using sexual history as the sole indicator of orientation is detrimental and damaging, and it's why I struggle with my pansexuality, often feeling guilty for calling myself queer while not being *more* queer. I've not been with many women, trans or cis, nor many nonbinary people, and for some, this is an indication that my queerness is not valid. People, mostly straight men, have made comments like, "You're not bisexual, you're just bi-curious," or, "You just kiss girls because it makes guys interested in you." I've also been told that I am like a piece of spaghetti: straight until wet, my orientation whittled down to a joke. Or that I wasn't really bisexual, but was probably just horny and wanted to fuck everyone. I am, in other words, straight until proven gay. These are all small things when they are looked at in isolation, but when examined together, they become a series of moments that attempt to delegitimize my identity.

It's true that queer representation in media has become more nuanced (if not fully revolutionary) in recent years, with different kinds of gender and sexual expression highlighted in shows like *Pose* and *Sex*

Education, where the narrative environment does not position straightness or cisness as the "norm" from which all other identities deviate. Even so, no medium will ever be perfect, and there's the temptation of leaning back into expected tropes (*Sex Education*, while charming, employs the gay best friend trope, and the tired narrative twist of a bully character coming out as queer). These are steps forward, for certain, but we are just a decade or so removed from some of the flattest or most haphazard representations of queer characters on TV. The farther we go back in time, the less nuance we find when it comes to queer characters. We are no longer living in an either/or cultural climate, even if that is what most of us were taught growing up in a time where you might only find the queer characters you were looking for if you read straight texts through a queer lens. As a kid, people in my microcosm of experience only talked about two orientations: Straight or Gay, or, Straight and Not Straight. It was easy to contrast homosexuality with heterosexuality as if they are mutually exclusive, as if any deviation from straightness is a polar opposition. Our vocabulary limited us. The adults around us treated non-heterosexual relationships as not only deviations but reactionary responses when heterosexuality (the default) didn't work out. I remember hearing hypotheses suggesting lesbians date women because they hate men or because they experienced trauma at the hands of men and can now only feel safe with women. And only a few weeks ago, I heard an acquaintance make an unfunny joke about prison rape, equating it with gayness, the implication being that gay sex is not a self-contained act but a violent result of an environment where women are not readily available. Still, despite the improved representation, too many parts of Western society continue to work to delegitimize queerness, to rationalize away the gay. In the context of *Jaws*, the homoeroticism can flourish because women are taken out of the equation, but it's not positioned as a reaction to the lack of women present. It's not that the men are sexually drawn to each other *because* there's not women, and therefore no other option (Hooper and Brody have undeniable chemistry throughout the film, even at the dinner table with Brody's wife), but rather eroticism is given room to grow, because the experience is not continually contrasted with straightness. They're isolated from expectation, from the civilization that is Amity Island, and all that exists is themselves.

Still, paradoxically, juxtaposing homosexuality with heterosexuality can be a safety net. Many of my sexual experiences with women as a young adult were within threesomes with a man in the mix. While it disgusts me now to think about my queer desire as fuel for a straight man's fantasy, threesomes provided a "safe" way of exploring my love of women in an act normalized and fetishized by the patriarchal rural Midwest community where I grew up. There was a security in pretending that making love to a woman was really just me catering to what the man wanted, and I negated myself of any responsibility I had to be "good" at lesbian sex.

In college, I had a difficult time with my body and boundaries. Sex made people (mostly men) think I was fun, and it made them pay attention to me, even if it was only for a little while. Kinkiness and promiscuity were covers for other things, a way of distracting other people and myself. Performing lesbian sex in a group sex setting provided me with the space in which to explore my sensuality with another woman. One night, drunk, I went down on a female coworker at a party in my apartment. I pushed her up against the wall and licked and tore at her body while the men watched, some of them turned on, some just uncomfortable. Her shoulder bumped the thermostat each time I thrust her upwards with the pressure of my hand. Over the course of the night, the apartment grew hot and humid like a greenhouse, and it took us a second to figure out how the thermostat had been cranked to 84 degrees. Our sensuality was a sort of performance art: although we were there, making love in front of our male friends, the sensations I felt with her were intimate and invisible.

In queer intimacy, the presence of a person of the opposite sex does not negate the sexual experience between the queer lovers. Likewise, having a wife or girlfriend in the case of Brody or Hooper does not make the characters straight. Categories are helpful to humans, evolutionarily beneficial. They make the world easier to navigate quickly, and having markers to help us make decisions is a technique we instinctually employ. However, this two-category system does not apply to all complexities of ourselves, particularly when it comes to sexuality and desire. While we might wish to place Brody, Hooper, and Quint into neat categories, the on-screen evidence of the gaze, of touching, of standing so close together, points to a queer intimacy that refuses to be contained within the binary. The fact that there are three men instead of two is a subtle dismantling of the binary view of sexual orientation. There is a sexual power in threes in general, such as with the predominance of love triangles in narratives, and *Jaws* is no different, even if the love triangle is implicit.

SO MUCH HAS been written about the physical dangers of the pussy, particularly the mythical fanged pussy, that it's become a cliche. The *vagina dentata*, a popular image in numerous folklores, now runs rampant in horror films: the extraterrestrial monster in *Alien*, Audrey II in *Little Shop of Horrors*, the whole premise of *Teeth*. *Jaws* is another example that viewers may argue embodies this monstrous feminine presence. Like a mouth, the vagina is an organ that devours. I remember flipping through *The Joy of Sex* as a kid and reading a paragraph that offered a frightening description of the vagina, because it accepts the strong, masculine penis and then regurgitates it once the penis is limp and inert.

The vagina and the mouth bear similarities. Both can experience hunger and want, both can experience sensation, pleasure. Consuming food, having sex, chewing gum, masturbating, picking teeth with a toothpick, all of these are responses elicited by the desires of the body. When I watch *Jaws* and see the beast's dorsal fin pierce the water, I see the drive of desire, not the monstrous feminine. When the shark breaches the surface and grins its terrible grin as Brody chums the water, I feel exhilarated by its hunger. It's a similar feeling to the one I have when Hooper offers his leg to Quint or when Quint brushes up against Hooper in the narrow quarters of the boat. To me, the mouth is not a feminine symbol come to destroy male camaraderie. Instead, the mouth is a reminder of the ever-present hum of desires, of wanting, of pursuing things that might potentially harm or undo us entirely. The mouth is a symbol of expression. When I think about my own mouth, I think about impulse and resistance. I think about what foods I allow myself to eat and how much and how often, and whether this is in line with the wants of my body or with the wants of others outside my body. I think about my opinionated nature, and what I let my mouth say and to whom and in what context, whether this expression will serve to help me or hurt me, or perhaps both. To view the mouth and by extension the vagina as a vehicle for straight male destruction is an error, because it once again places the straight male at the center of the narrative. Instead, when I see the shark's gaping maw, I think about the embrace of queer desire and the retribution that comes from the revolutionary act of expression.

What I like about the sexuality in *Jaws* is the ambiguity, the implicit attraction between the men, revealed only by touch and gaze. There's an in-betweenness there that I am drawn to, in which the men are not gay nor straight but are instead neither or both, however one wishes to define it. My place on the spectrum of sexual orientation doesn't seem to stay in one spot. Sometimes I'm more attracted to men, sometimes I'm more attracted to women. Sometimes I'm more attracted to people outside the binary. Sometimes I'm attracted to nobody. Sometimes I'm attracted to all genders equally. Many days, I feel like I am not queer enough, and there is a self-shame in that. It is an annoying habit I am trying to break from. But I feel comforted while watching *Jaws* and seeing characters that defy these labels, as much as I find myself wanting to use those labels that I know are false or incomplete.

I'm easily bored, but *Jaws* is a film I can watch on repeat, especially when I feel sad or insecure. There's a moment in particular that almost brings me to tears each time. After Brody's son goes into shock after witnessing the shark tear apart a fellow boater, Brody sits up and looks out at the water. The camera pauses on that shot, the strings of the musical score singing high-pitched, as the great expanse of the ocean opens up in front of the viewer. The ocean is not just one thing. It is both the livelihood of the island and the destruction of it. It is both beautiful and terrifying. It is knowable and unknown. As Brody gazes out into forever, I think about how the sea is not just one thing, and neither am I.

This essay originally appeared, in slightly different form, as "Jaws Is a Film Full of Queer Intimacy You Never Noticed," in Electric Literature, August 9, 2018.

The Wolf Man's Daughter

TOSHA R. TAYLOR

The Wolf Man

THE VHS TAPES waited inside a small pull-out cabinet. Thin adhesive panels on the cabinet's sides gave the chipboard the appearance of polished, solid wood. The heavy inner drawer rolled smoothly on its track to reveal the row of tapes, each with a hand-lettered label—some in my mother's careful italics but many in the large block letters of my father's hand. As a long-haul truck driver in the pre-GPS early '90s, my father was responsible for manually logging his trips in an oversize ledger when he got home. Those block letters spelled out maps like secret codes: *I-77 S PICK UP, 460 E, I 77 N DETROIT*. But his writing on these tapes looked very different: *FRANKENSTEIN. DRACULA. THE MUMMY. THE WOLF MAN.*

All of these movies had been recorded off Syfy. Early '90s Sci-Fi Channel, as it was then spelled, was a television treasure. It was dark, it was scary, and to my child's mind it seemed to reveal the hidden world of unspeakable truths I felt sure existed. Even the channel itself was a secret. Growing up in a working-class family in rural Appalachia, we didn't always have easy access to nonlocal channels. I can't describe the technical process by which we got Sci-Fi without a subscription because I never actually knew it; all I did know was that it involved a dish we pretended didn't work and a big silver box connected to a TV that was already vintage. The numbers on that box passed through channel after channel of static or, in some cases, heavily distorted pictures with intact sound. But it picked up Sci-Fi with perfect clarity, which suited my father, a horror-loving child of the '60s, just fine. One year my parents decided to use our illicit access to the Sci-Fi

Channel to tape as many of the Universal Monsters classics as they could, and thus the cabinet of VHS tapes came to be.

My home, like the community around it, was a deeply conservative and religious one. Long before I knew what they thought of queerness, I knew that many in our community, including some of my own family members, believed horror movies were of the devil. The act of watching one opened the viewer up to demonic entities, even Satan himself. That belief makes some warped sense back home, where geographic connections to heaven and hell seem possible. The skies in the mountains are like none I've ever seen elsewhere. Looking out in the morning or after a storm, you can see smoke-thick fog rising out of the trees in long plumes to touch the clouds. Valleys and hollows are deep enough, but deeper still are the abandoned mines and runoff lakes that we used to use as playgrounds, both of which have poisoned the dirt and water around them. *Pet Sematary* doesn't sound all that unrealistic there. Christian fears of witchcraft coexist with regional folk magic. Phenomena that can only be described as Weird Shit happen all the time, and even many local skeptics believe they've personally experienced something that conventional science can't explain. Sights of unholy form and violence might seem just as likely to open up supernatural contact as staring too long down into one of those howling sulfur-smelling mine shafts.

My father was an anomaly. While he did believe that contemporary, gory horror was wicked, the classics were safe. His only child was allowed to rummage through those tapes freely, and the only movie I was forbidden to watch was, for reasons I never understood, *Christine*, John Carpenter's 1983 adaptation of Stephen King's novel about a killer car.

As a small child, I loved all of the old Universal movies, but it was *The Wolf Man*, director George Waggner and writer Curt Siodmak's take on the werewolf, that most captured my heart. The fog rolling over the Welsh countryside in the film reminded me of the fog that embraced our hills. The danger of being caught out at night in the woods where dangerous creatures roam was deliciously familiar. Larry Talbot was kind of an oaf, but he seemed *predestined* to do wrong, and I pitied him as his life spiraled out of control and he became the monster of the town's nightmares.

Werewolves have always fascinated me. They combine two of my favorite elements in horror: the monster and grotesque bodily transformations. Walking on two legs and still wearing clothes, Larry Talbot's werewolf was both man and monster. His transformation into the eponymous creature, though perhaps now low-quality in its cheesy dissolves, slowly strips away his identity to replace familiar human flesh with the fur, claws, and teeth of a creature that defies all norms and violates the rules of what makes a good person. Rather than appearing as simply an animal, Larry embodies the Other. The film emphasizes the ability of a monster to lurk inside a seemingly good man in the poem repeated throughout it: "Even a man who is pure of heart and says his prayers by night may become a wolf when the wolfbane blooms and the autumn moon is bright." The real horror in the film isn't really Larry's attacks on townspeople but his own monstrosity.

BY THE END of first grade, I was already a Weird Kid, the kind that horror often attracts. Painfully introverted, bookish, constantly afraid I was the butt of some larger joke everyone else was in on—but also drawn to dark things. I scared my cousins with my own made-up horror stories and got into trouble for it. With the Satanic Panic still fresh in their memories, the grownups seemed to pride themselves on warning me about the dangers that lurked around every corner, waiting to prey on little girls. I didn't tell them I'd already learned that lesson. I kept quiet partly from humiliation, but also partly because I wanted to protect *their* innocence. For their own safety, I let them think the monsters on my tapes were the only monsters I knew about.

That year, I also received my first lesson on being too close to other girls. A friend and I sat together before class every morning, bonding over TV shows that scared us. At recess, we started planning the house we wanted to have together when we grew up. The house would be in Wyoming, not because either of us had any connection to the state, not because of any mournful queer significance people found in it a few years later when Matthew Shepard was murdered there, but because of a picture we'd found in a calendar. The house would be brick, which seemed luxurious to us then, would have real working shutters, and would be decorated with all the fanciest things from the mail-order catalogs our parents received. It had only one bedroom. I made the mistake of telling an adult about our plan. We were forbidden to sit together anymore.

THERE'S A GREATLY mistaken belief that there are no queer people in Appalachia. Let me assure you: there are plenty. Their existence has historically been a quiet one: obscure bars and gathering places, gender nonconforming relatives, men who are "funny but mean well," stony, unmarried women with lifelong "friends." Appalachia is simultaneously a terrifying and beautiful place to be queer, and it is also contradictory. There's a deep sense of danger that being outed could mean the end of one's livelihood or life altogether, yet amid that danger there's a solace in the cultural value of being left to one's own business. The bonds of queer community are hard-won there, but they're strong, or at least stronger than those I've experienced elsewhere, including New York. Outside the hypercompetitive metropolitan world I now live in, where financial, social, and cultural capital often dictate even casual friendships, Appalachian queers seem to recognize each other as partners in the same fight despite our individual differences.

With increased attention to queer issues on the news in the '90s, our churches and families had to actually talk about queerness, and many did so with disgust they learned from conservative media. Ironically, although it would be a few more years before I linked werewolves to lesbianism, I learned the word *lesbian* from a news report about a fatal dog attack. The woman's death was, I was told, justice for her crime against God. She was in hell now, but her surviving girlfriend might yet be saved if she repented. God was merciful, after all.

One Halloween night, my cousins and I ran ahead of our parents as we trick or treated. We'd been going door-to-door, but The Dads shouted for us to stop as we crossed onto one home's lawn. The porch and interior lights were on, the universal signal that trick or treaters are welcome. But catching up with stern, worried faces, The Dads explained to us that *lesbians* lived in that house. By this point, I had a much more detailed image of what a lesbian was. In the religious tracts that our parents kept in their Bibles, lesbians were ugly, unlovable women, God-haters, predators, child abusers, every bit as perverse as gay men were thought to be. Who knew what they'd done to the candy they handed out to innocent children that night?

As The Dads led us away from the house, I felt as if I'd been the one to do something wrong. But I also hoped those women hadn't seen us kids coming through their lawn, hadn't noticed that we never rang their doorbell.

MY FATHER WAS still my connection to horror even after I'd memorized every image and line of every film in the VHS cabinet. He spent many days away from home hauling freight across the country, then he'd come in off the road, shower, and sleep. Like his own father, he was a disciplinarian with a soft side except where sin was concerned. But Friday nights brought out the best in him as we'd sit in the bedroom, where my parents kept a smaller TV, and watch *The X-Files*.

Stories of filial piety compromised by the son's shameful otherness have always resonated with me. The figure of the *son* is key to that resonance somehow. My relationship to this figure clearly owes something to Biblical roles of sons, as well as to pop culture's typical recognition of shameful Otherness in queer men's narratives while not-always-but-often presenting only a watered-down acknowledgement of those feelings in queer women. It may also owe something to the fact that most of my friends in the teen years of queer realization were queer boys, who treated me as if there were no difference between us. Yet, even those explanations are inadequate. There's some kind of *truth* to that role, and any attempt I could make to codify it is certain to become a complicated mess with disclaimers, footnotes, a song lyric, a collection of images sans context. But there would be no comfortable answers, and certainly no easy ones.

Maybe it would have been different if I'd seen *Dracula's Daughter* first. But I didn't find this gem until college, and so, when I think of my father, I think not of the Count's sapphic daughter but of the Talbot son.

THE CONFLICT OF *The Wolf Man* isn't just between Larry and himself as he becomes a werewolf, knowing that he can't resist the monster lurking in his own body, but rather between Larry and his father. Portrayed by Claude Rains, Sir John Talbot represents the elitist traditions from which Larry has fled. He speaks with a crisp British accent and comports himself with poise. Larry, meanwhile, is an American whose speech and movement convey a sense of leisure. He is a large man. Compared to his father's physical slightness, he almost appears as a naive, graceless giant. Yet they do love each other. As the townspeople realize that Larry is the werewolf that haunts the woods at night, Sir John insists that his son suffers from delusions. To him, Larry is sick, under a pagan influence, but curable and certainly not a monster.

At a family barbecue when I was thirteen, the adults sat on the porch and shared their disgust over two women, clearly a couple, who had been in a doctor's waiting room with me and my parents earlier that day. I'd recently had the surgery that would leave me permanently hard of hearing, but I was still close enough to hear every word the adults said about the couple. They were sinners, monsters, surely a sign that the End Times were upon us. But I'd felt something for those women—not longing or admiration but a fascinated comfort. One woman's hair was dyed in a black-and-blond pattern I'd never seen before, and the other was called "Daddy" by their son. In the waiting room, I wanted to sit closer to them.

As host of the barbecue, my father put an end to the talk. "I'm disgusted by it," he said—*it* now going beyond the lesbian couple to include all queer people. "And I know everyone here is too."

I wasn't sure if the kids counted in that "everyone here," but my heart fell into my stomach when he said it. I wasn't like those women. I *couldn't* be. I'd already had boyfriends. I hated kissing them, hated the way their tongues poked into my mouth, hated the way their hands felt on my skin, but I was a Christian, a model student, a Good Girl. I couldn't be a monster. But something in me *was* disgusting, and I begged God to take it from me.

Within a year, that feeling in my stomach developed into a chronic pain like a fist squeezing my guts every time I felt anxious.

I also met a girl. *The* girl.

THERE IS SOMETHING especially visceral about the werewolf's violence. The vampire's bite, at least, looks erotic. The werewolf, though—it doesn't just want a taste or to remake you as its immortal companion. It wants to tear you apart. Lacking any semblance of human morals or even social codes, the transformed werewolf has no compunctions about killing its victims. And unlike the vampire, the werewolf doesn't *need* to kill to survive. But it does. And so the werewolf is irredeemable.

The first werewolf of *The Wolf Man* isn't Larry Talbot but the fortune-teller Bela (portrayed, no less, by Bela Lugosi). Bela looks into Jenny's palm and sees the pentagram, the in-film sign of the werewolf and a symbol deeply feared within my family. He knows the wolf inside him will want her. Rather than act on the wolf's desire by allowing her to linger, thus ensuring she is nearby when he transforms, Bela begs her to flee. As she obeys, the camera lingers on Bela, who looks horrified at his own existence—and still attacks her moments later.

His horror is repeated in Larry. The aloof irreverence that so separates Larry from the stuffy old townspeople disappears as he realizes that not only is he a monster but that his condition can't be reversed no matter what he does. For the rest of the film, his brash American cheer is replaced by depression.

Bela's mother, Maleva, is the only person who offers Larry real help. Larry watches her deliver a benediction over Bela's coffin that absolves the werewolf of blame for his own condition. She alone understands that the werewolf isn't evil. She alone recognizes her son's and Larry's suffering under the weight of their own monstrosity. When Larry is caught in a trap, she repeats her benediction and temporarily restores him to his human form. But she can't offer him any more help. His face is a picture of wild terror as he hears hunting dogs drawing closer. If he is caught, he and Maleva both know, his condition means his death.

UNLIKE THE VAMPIRE, who retains enough human consciousness to enjoy the sensations of their new existence, the werewolf has no control over their own body once transformed. Just as they are bitten without consent, werewolves change and succumb to violent animal instincts without any autonomy at all. Despite his masculine posturing and American bravado, Larry is clearly traumatized by being bitten, and his transformations continue to use his own body against him.

I'm old enough and, as an academic, steeped enough in theory to recognize a link between my love for horror, my sexuality, and my trauma. All of it combines in the werewolf and, in my first favorite movie, in Larry Talbot's growing awareness of his nature and betrayal by his own body. Without knowing what I was angry at, my church taught me that my anger was a sin. But horror gave me a power to reckon with what happened and with my increasing difference. In those monsters, even those who weren't as sympathetic as Larry Talbot, I found people and creatures like me. A product of Appalachia himself, Pumpkinhead seemed more like a faithful companion than a demon. Chucky gave me nightmares, but these were somehow more comfortable than many other social interactions. Every year at Halloween, a family near Main Street dressed up as famous horror characters to scare trick or treaters. My cousins screamed when the man dressed as Freddy Krueger moved his knife-fingered glove toward them, but I loved him. I'd stand on the dark wooden porch while candy was being dispensed and stare at him, daring him to move, waiting for that thrill. The irony of liking a child predator isn't lost on me, but back then, Freddy seemed to be just another one of those dark things to which I felt a kinship. Monsters, not heroes, were my friends.

After those old VHS tapes, I burned through any horror movie I could find. When The Dads took us kids to Video Connection, I went immediately to the horror section and smuggled the goriest covers to the counter in hopes that The Dads wouldn't see how bad they were before the clerk exchanged them for the blank rental boxes. My increasing tolerance for horror violence became a badge of honor. My family joked about my ability to eat spaghetti while watching the "Freddy Krueger movies" that made my cousins feel sick. Even the much older, much larger boys couldn't stand the amounts of screaming and blood and gore that I relished. I knew early on how easily they could hurt me, but I also realized they couldn't stand the sight of evil and pain that I could look at without flinching.

What *did* terrify me was myself. In my teens it was the slow sense of separation from God and my parents, the mounting interest in girls who were soft and pretty, girls who looked more like boys, girls who were new and looked lost in the hallways at school, girls who made sure their underwear showed through their gym clothes, girls from homes surrounded by junkyards, girls from the backwoods who cursed and wore dirty boots. If I looked at one too long, I could feel the last threads connecting my soul, God, and my family coming unstitched.

We had that satellite box for most of my childhood. To me, it was normal to listen to movies I couldn't actually see on the channels our mysterious and possibly illegal connection couldn't fully pick up. One night I was listening to *Species* on Showtime. All I knew about the 1995 sci-fi movie was that it had a female alien in it, and female villains have always fascinated me. I *didn't* know that the film's central conflict involved that alien's quest to breed with human men. I pretended not to realize the sounds coming from the TV were sexual. The sounds of sex and horror-movie violence are, after all, embarrassingly similar. Suddenly, the picture cleared to reveal Natasha Henstridge's naked breasts. My heart stopped. I knew it was wrong to look but I did, still feeling something beneath my shock and fear that I wasn't ready to understand. Then I heard my father walking through the next room and shut the TV off.

I was afraid to gamble with newer movies on the distorted channels after that. But those old black-and-white monsters could still keep a secret.

AT THE END of *The Wolf Man*, Larry is killed by his own father. Sir John doesn't know the werewolf he beats to death is Larry until it is too late and he sees the monstrous body transform back into that of his son. He looks at the dead Larry and then the murder weapon—Larry's own cane—with horror. Though Larry is much larger than his father, his death makes him appear smaller and vulnerable. Sir John sees that his son was indeed the monster terrorizing the countryside, but, rather than recoiling from him, kneels beside his son's body and strokes his face.

MY FATHER AND I don't talk much anymore. I've moved several hundred miles away and he's in poor health. He only rarely mentions old horror movies and *The X-Files* when I visit, but we haven't watched either together in over a decade. Instead of classic horror, his choice of entertainment now is right-wing religious conspiracy theories, pro-Trump videos narrated by uncanny automated voices, and evangelical sermons on YouTube. He speaks constantly of the End Times. He waits for the Rapture, for Jesus to come take His children away from the evils of this sinful world. Whenever we do speak, he reminds me of the need to get right with the Lord so I won't be left behind. It would be easy to ascribe this to political antagonism, but he means it. He genuinely wants his family to be with him in eternity in a celestial land where there are no monsters.

Ever fearing that I'd turn out to be a lesbian, my mother warned me once that if I was one, to "never to tell Daddy because it would break his heart." So, I never told him the truth about the girl who stepped out into the hallway while I was skipping world history. Her face still had smears of pale makeup from a scene she'd been doing in drama class. She wore red eyeliner. She told me she'd played Dracula.

My father knows her, but doesn't know who she was to me then or who she still is now. To this day, my sexuality remains unspoken between us. I pretend most of my daily life doesn't even exist. Sometimes I think he must know and that he simply doesn't acknowledge it because doing so would mean admitting that his only child is bound for hell. Sometimes I think he knows there's *something* different about me, the same way other members of our community always seemed to, but can't identify it because surely a girl who elected baptism at only five years old couldn't be so sinful.

Recently, the woman who used to be the girl who played Dracula asked me what my favorite part of *The Wolf Man* is. I told her it's Larry's first transformation and night as a wolf, but my second choice is that last moment between Larry and Sir John, when Larry is revealed as both man and monster—and, still, a son. It's not a happy ending, but it's a damn good one.

Just Come a Little Closer

KIRSTY LOGAN

Raze

"*Women fighting to the death is a different thing to men fighting. Men fight to kill and be victorious—but for women… it's far more emotional, coming from somewhere maternal and instinctive and sad.*"

—Zoë Bell, in an interview about *Raze*

THE FIRST TIME I watched *Raze* was near the start of a month-long writing residency in Iceland, working on a collection of feminist horror stories, *Things We Say in the Dark*. The second, third, fourth, fifth and sixth times I watched it was also on that residency. I kept the film with me like a security blanket, like a talisman, the file always open on my laptop.

I don't know what to call the state of mind I was in during that residency. 'Breakdown' is too strong a word. Let's say I was having a strange mental health time. I didn't look after myself very well. The place was isolated and I isolated myself within it. Every day I walked for about an hour down the one straight road that ran through town, then turned around and walked the hour back. I passed fields and fences and a couple of horses. I never reached the next town. Every other day I went to the outdoor pool and swam laps until I went into a daze, barely conscious, my body moving without me telling it to.

Iceland, geographically at least, isn't too far from my home, which is in Scotland, with my wife. We'd been married for three years and were about to start trying for a baby. Much of the book I was there to write was about that: my fears of committing so permanently to someone, of becoming a mother. How could I know if I'd be any good at it? What if the secret awful things in me were in the marrow of my bones, in the very words I spoke and thought, and I passed them on to the baby? How could something good ever come from someone like me?

But still, I knew it was a good life. It was the life I wanted, the one I'd been working towards for a long time. There was so much love in my life, and tenderness and grace and support and solidarity and community and positivity. All our family and friends were excited for us to have a baby. Our village was ready to help and love this new person.

But I was not with my village. Not at home. Not making a baby. Not even writing.

I was here, alone in the snow, watching a horror film over and over.

Here's what I don't understand. Why, when in my real life it was all about women together, women being tender, women listening to one another, women loving one another, women using their bodies not to take life but to make it—why, right then, was I obsessively watching women beat each other to death?

RAZE IS A 2013 exploitation film starring stunt performer Zoë Bell about an all-female fight club. But not in a hot way. But kind of in a hot way? It's confusing.

We open on a woman's face. She's in a small room lit by red lights. She's wearing a white vest, black bra and grey tracksuit bottoms, rolled down at the top to show her toned belly and up at the bottom to show her bare calves and feet. We follow her down a long red corridor and into a circular pit. The ground is sand, the walls are stone. The red eye of a camera watches her. And so do we.

In flashback we learn she's been kidnapped – and so has, presumably, the woman she's trapped in the pit with: Sabrina (Zoë Bell), who says: "Same thing happened to me. We're the same." And they do seem the same: trapped in this pit together, dressed identically, watched by the silent red eye. But something is wrong. They're not quite the same. Because Sabrina knows what's happening: the women have to fight, and one of them has to die.

So they fight. This isn't a fists-up, fast-feet performative fight. The punches are loose and rough, the injuries brutal and bloody. It's harsh. It's sad. The music is the haunting strings of a tragedy; the gasping, desperate breaths of both women; the turning fan like the steady thrum of a heartbeat.

Sabrina straddles the woman and breaks her arm, then punches her in the face over and over. The woman looks up at her, eyes begging, not even fighting back. Sabrina pauses, then keeps hitting. Sabrina's hands are red. Sabrina's face is red. The woman chokes on her own blood. Sabrina is crying. She's begging the woman: "Stop, stop."

Sabrina wins. Or rather, "wins". She stands up, distraught and weeping. She sobs at the sky, at the camera's eye, at us: "How many more do I have to kill?"

THE FIRST QUESTION, when hearing the setup of *Raze*, is obviously: Why don't they just refuse to fight? Well, because then a mysterious cabal of powerful people—mostly men, though not all—will kill someone they love. For Sabrina, that person is her teenage daughter, given up for adoption as a baby. For the others it's mothers, husbands, fiancés.

The women don't fight for glory. They don't fight to win a prize, defeat a bad guy or save the world. They fight for one thing. Love.

Well, all except for one woman: Phoebe.

When I say I watched *Raze* over and over, that's not technically true. I didn't want to—or couldn't—watch it all. I didn't like the extreme violence of the fights or the plot-dumping scenes of the overarching mythology. I watched two small sections multiple times a day, more times than I can count. The first is when Sabrina, blood-spattered and sobbing, rocks back on her heels over the body of a woman she's just beaten and wails: "How many more do I have to kill?" The second is later, leading into the third act.

Phoebe is the only one of the women who seems to enjoy killing. Like all the others, she's survived trauma (childhood sexual assault in her case; the others mention domestic violence and military combat). Now Phoebe is about to fight and kill the closest person Sabrina has to a friend—or, maybe more accurately, a child substitute.

Phoebe marches down the corridor. All the cells are empty except for the locked one containing Sabrina. "You're dead, you're dead," Phoebe chants, pointing to the empty cells one by one. She approaches Sabrina's cell, where she'll be forced to watch Phoebe's fight on a TV screen. For Phoebe, all of this—the taunting, the killing—is a performance for Sabrina.

"Please, just come a bit closer," Sabrina mutters from behind her locked door. "Just come a little bit closer, please, just come a little…" Phoebe pulls closer, then snaps just out of reach as Sabrina's hand snatches out for her. "Fuck!" shouts Sabrina, smacking her empty hand on the door. All we see of Sabrina in this moment is her hand. Knuckles red. Nails short. Forearms wiry.

The intimacy of it. The closeness.

The women in *Raze* only touch when they're killing each other. Sabrina wraps her legs around a woman to suffocate her with dirt. Sabrina straddles a woman to punch her. Sabrina holds a woman along the length of her own body to strangle her.

Raze is a film of intimacy. It's the opposite of the distant, bloodless, baddies-fall-down gun deaths of many action films. To kill, you have to get close. You have to use your hands. You have to grab a throat, and hold a face close to your own, and squeeze.

I WANT TO TALK also about strength. About (sigh) the Strong Female Character.

On that Iceland residency, I walked or swam (or walked and swam) every day. As I felt my mind looping in circles, obsessing, disconnecting, weakening its hold on everything I'd left at home, my body got stronger. Every night I went to bed with my muscles aching, and every morning I got up and did it again. I thought that if I could exhaust my body, then it would allow my mind to work. And my mind did work, very efficiently, not at writing the book I was meant to be writing, but at getting obsessed with *Raze*.

Josh Waller, the film's director and co-writer (the other two writers are also men) said he wanted to treat the film "as seriously as if it were men that were abducted and forced to fight each other." I've spent a lot of time thinking about that phrase, as it makes such little sense to me. Surely women being forced to fight is *more* serious? Men fight all the time. I live in Glasgow; I could go to any pub on any weekend night and see them, flinging their fists and yelling shit. But perhaps Waller's point is that *Raze* is, as he sees it, part of the "largely exploitative subgenre of women-in-prison." There's no nudity in *Raze*. No one attempts to seduce a male guard for extra leniency or as an escape attempt. The most intimate interaction with a guard, in fact, is when Sabrina flicks some of her own shit in his face.

It feels strange to talk about *Raze* as a feminist film because I don't know that it is. I think it wants to be, but it doesn't quite hang together. I want it to explore concepts of femininity and intimacy, sexuality as performance, violence as performance. Perhaps what I most like about this film is the version of it that exists in my head.

But I do like how it treats the Strong Female Character, which is a term I have always hated. Buffy Summers, Lara Croft, Xena: Warrior Princess, the stars of superhero films. I never felt empowered by these characters, as it seemed to me that they were only strong in ways that a certain type of cishet man understands (i.e. physically strong and violent), and also that they were heavily sexualized, always wearing tight, skimpy clothes and—of course—with perfect hair and makeup, even when that makeup was bloodied.

Raze is not exempt from the male gaze. These women are all beautiful in a specific sort of way: slim and muscular, styled hair, clear skin, straight white teeth, hairless legs and armpits. During the fights they're pulled around by their long, blow-dried hair but they never cut or shave it off. They get hit in the mouth, but never lose teeth. They're artfully bruised—a little cut to the lip, a small gash on the temple—but never get ugly injuries like a broken nose or jaw.

But the fights are undeniably brutal. They beat each other's faces into meat. This feels like the typical male-gaze Strong Female Character taken to an extreme. You want a woman who can fight? Here's a goddamn fight.

And most interestingly to me, Sabrina doesn't like violence. She doesn't think it's desirable or empowering, or even justified or necessary. She knows that in these fights she's not killing a black-hat baddie or a destroying a monster: she's killing other women. "We're the same," she says. She cries as she kills.

This is what makes the fights so hard to watch. Not just because of their gore or violence. The women cry as they're killed, and they cry as they kill. None of them want to be there, in this place together.

LET'S COME BACK to the "largely exploitative subgenre of women-in-prison." Every time I'm on a residency I get obsessed with depictions of confined women. It's relevant to my writing, in an oblique way; but I'm not going to pretend I have noble intentions. My interest isn't academic. It isn't analytical. I don't quite know what it is.

While in Finland writing a novel about a teen girl experiencing first love and grief on a small mythical island, I obsessively watched British 1990s women-in-prison drama *Bad Girls*. While in Sweden writing short stories about women being kidnapped or abandoning their children, I obsessively watched Australian 2000s women-in-prison drama *Wentworth* (a remake of a 1970s women-in-prison drama *Prisoner*). I rationed the episodes out, watching two every evening, only allowing myself to start after I'd had dinner and it was dark. In the daytime, between writing sessions, I read episode recaps and scrolled through screen grabs of the episode I'd watched the previous night.

I didn't know at the time why I was doing this. I don't know now. I wish I did know.

What I loved about these stories was the forbidden love aspect. In *Bad Girls*, it's a romance between a prisoner governor and an intellectual, rabble-rousing prisoner. In *Wentworth*, it's a romance between the outwardly brutal but secretly tender 'top dog' and the one woman who sees the truth of her. It's dangerous to fall in love—with this woman, in this place—but they do it anyway. These love stories are a kind of building, and I tell myself that's what I love about it: finding queer love, making a space for tenderness among violence and brutality.

But the violence is an integral part of it. And in *Raze*, I can't even argue that it's about queer love. There's love of a sort, the type of love you'd kill for; but it ends horribly. There's no hope. No happy ending.

HERE'S HOW *RAZE* ends. Sabrina escapes and kills her way up— the guards, the man and woman who run the place—and just when it appears she will escape, she's shot dead.

But that's not the ending that matters. To me, the real ending is just before, when Phoebe and Sabrina finally fight.

Phoebe and Sabrina work their way through all the other women, fighting them all to the death. But Phoebe killing Sabrina's friend is the final straw. "I want to fight!" Sabrina yells. She's never wanted to fight before—but for Phoebe, she will. She's a caged animal, bouncing around her cell, full of red mist. Phoebe is already in the pit, waiting. Sabrina is released. She rockets out of her cell, down the long red hallway, and into the pit.

Sabrina, finally, is alone with Phoebe. This is the strongest display of emotion in the film. This is the central relationship.

This is a story I watched, over and over, while being in love, while hoping for a child. Every time I'm away from home, I choose to inhabit worlds where women are confined, women are controlled, women beat one another and plot to kill one another. I could choose instead to watch stories about queer hope or queer tenderness; about women building things together, making things grow, just like I want for my real life. I could. But I don't.

THE SEVENTH (and, I think, last) time I watched *Raze* was to write this essay, five years later. Now I'm not gently losing my mind alone in the snow in Iceland. I'm at home, with my wife, in our bed, the volume turned low so as not to wake our one-year-old, asleep between us.

I was nervous about watching it with her. I'd never mentioned it to her before: my obsession, the way I'd used the film as a talisman, the way it had accompanied me during that strange time. I worried she'd think the film said something about me; something I didn't want her to know about me, or even admit to myself.

All these years, I have been slightly ashamed about my obsession with *Raze*, in a way that I'm not ashamed about my love for other horror. Was it because I didn't want to admit to the intensity of this obsession? Because I knew that this film did not justify this sort of obsession? But rewatching it, I changed my mind about it. I started off by calling it an exploitation film, but now I'm not so sure. It's a sad film. It's a horrible film. It's a film that—if I choose to interpret the ending, which disappointed me, in a generous spirit—is about how when women try to play a man's game, they will always lose, because the game is rigged. It seems to have the same intent as *Showgirls*, which I watched for the first time recently, and which I'd been led to believe was a camp classic, a fun so-bad-it's-sort-of-good popcorn film, but which I found profoundly depressing.

I don't know if I wanted my wife to like *Raze*. I don't know if I wanted to still like *Raze*. Maybe it doesn't matter. All that matters is that it haunted me. The long red hallway. The dirt-floored pit. The women in their low-slung, rolled-leg tracksuits. The way Sabrina holds the other women tight and squeezes. In the end, it doesn't matter what I wanted my wife to think about the film, because she fell asleep fifteen minutes in.

I lie beside sleeping wife and sleeping baby. Watch credits roll. Think about putting it back to start and watching it again—or maybe just those scenes, the two I know by heart. I could watch them again. And again and again and again.

I close the laptop and switch off the light.

Twin/Skin

ADDIE TSAI

Dead Ringers

TEN YEARS OLD. Matching black leotards. Matching pink tights. Matching black shiny patent leather tap shoes with matching red ribbons tied in big matching bows. Our mother is chatting up Miss Michelle, our teacher at Dance Tree, while in the background a stranger is fawning, not at the outfits—every other girl here is dressed identically to us—but at our faces. This reaction to us, the novelty of our twin skin, will teach me just how much the world reads into faces. The fawner approaches my mother, coos over our doubled face and our doubled ponytail.

"Oh, you *must* show them the movie *Twins!*" she insists.

Our mother enthusiastically engages in the conversation, as she always does.

Our discomfort doubles, too.

TO LIVE IN the world as a twin—a doubled body, a mirrored self—is to also live with others' misperception that you're somehow interchangeable. It's fitting that the first two film-twins I was exposed to (aside from Arnold Schwarzenegger and Danny DeVito, whose dizygoticity was both the joke and the punchline) were radically different sides of the same twin-trope coin. The first was *The Parent Trap*, which embodies the fantasy of suddenly learning you have a separated-at-birth twin who immediately becomes your best friend, who looks and talks and acts and thinks just like you, and, of course, is game to trick people by pretending to be you, because does anyone really know you well enough separately to even notice if you switched places? The second was *The Shining*, its infamous hand-holding ghost sisters reduced to metaphor and murder victims.

THE MORE PROVOCATIVE fetishization of twins—both in the cishet world and the queer (male, more frequently) community—often relies on the fantasy of twins desiring one another, but the twin relationship itself is not inherently sexual; it is, however, inherently, and instantly, queer. After all, my twin was the first body with which I interacted, in the intimate space of body and fluid and womb. She was my first connection, before birth, before language, before mother. It is my twin whose body pressed against my own, as it tried to grow and understand itself. It is through this queer relationship that I understand all other bodies I encounter throughout my life.

I CAN'T REMEMBER when I first recognized that the intense feelings I had for another girl wasn't friendship but infatuation. I didn't come out until my late twenties because, for many years, I found it especially hard, as a twin, to make sense of same-sex attraction. Were these primal feelings I had for my "friends" evidence of queer desire, or simply residual complications from the relationship I already had with my twin, this other same-sex body I could never create distance from since she was always with me? I had no tools or theories to make sense of how queerness related to my twinhood, because, unlike the Electra or Oedipal complexes, no one knew how (or perhaps cared) to theorize the twin bond. This was not, as Freud deduced, about mother or father but about a self which is not *the* self, an *other* body I knew as well as my own because it *was* my own.

It Came From the Closet

I CAN CONCEDE the very likely possibility that not all twins are born into an endless, excruciating system of comparison the way that she and I were. We were at once "the same" and yet, at the same time, nitpicked meticulously for the tiniest differences between us. It was hard for me not to give in to the desire to satisfy others' needs for us to fulfill their twin fantasy. It is also true that for most of my childhood, I *did* want her to be my best friend. I oozed affection for and onto my twin from an early age, pathologically hovering within her orbit. For many years, that fantasy was true: we spooned each other cookie dough in our bedroom, cuddled with easy intimacy, recorded ourselves enacting our favorite Disney sequences on an old boombox. We hid underneath blankets in our father's living room, pretending to speak his birth language, Mandarin, pointing and laughing at each other's messy mimicry until out of breath.

AS WE GREW, so too did the eyes of others, asking, always asking *which one is shier which one is louder which one is prettier which one is uglier which one's eyes are too far apart which one has the uneven cheekbones who is curvier who is skinnier who is more popular who is smarter who is more talented who is sexier who is who*

EVENTUALLY, my twin wanted nothing to do with me. I tried to get closer to her, but she couldn't get far enough away from me. I learned to accept, in time, that the person I loved most was filled with disdain for me. Her attitude and treatment toward me turned, like any horror-movie character revealed to be the villain, from the sticky-sweetness of honey to a piece of fruit that was rancid and rotting.

TWENTY-FIVE. A boyfriend's sister, upon learning that I am an identical twin, excitedly insists we rent *Dead Ringers*. I have long grown tired of all the twin film suggestions thrown at me, but I'm a pleaser, so.

Dead Ringers, written and directed by David Cronenberg, is loosely based on the lives of real-life twin doctors Stewart and Cyril Marcus, who died together under mysterious circumstances. The twins, played with eerie nimbleness by Jeremy Irons, were found dead in their apartment on the Upper East Side, most likely by cause of barbiturate addiction. Cyril was found lying facedown on a bed, wearing only undershorts. His brother was found lying faceup on the floor, nude. A macabre mirror image. Twins in birth and in death.

The title, *Dead Ringers*, plays with a colloquial notion of likeness that is experienced by those who aren't twins. The twins are the surprise. Once you watch the film, however, you get it. The "dead ringer" is part of the act. As in most films featuring twins, there is a dominant twin and a submissive twin. It is through the parallel between sibling relationship and sexual relationship that a horror film can play with the erotic connections that are often made of twin relationships. In this case, Bev is the passive twin, and Elliot is his dominant brother. *Dead Ringers*, then, like all twin stories, eventually becomes about replacement. In Cronenberg's telling, Elliot routinely diminishes Bev, even impersonating him and having nonconsensual sex with Bev's lover, Claire.

"You haven't had any experience until I've had it, too," Elliot reminds Bev. "You haven't fucked Claire . . . until you tell *me* about it."

"Then I haven't fucked Claire," Bev concedes, allowing this autonomous act of intimacy to be disappeared by Elliot.

When Claire discovers the disturbing truth of this violation that's been committed against her, she confronts the brothers. "Can't get it up unless your brother's watching?" she snarls at Elliot, whom she correctly identifies as the dom while undermining his perceived power over Bev. Still, she throws a drink in Bev's face and storms off, leaving him sobbing pathetically. Bev may be subordinate to Elliot, but he's no less culpable. Two become one, the terrible merging achieved.

ONE OUT OF every four pairs of twins are actually mirror twins, a nick of time separation before things go too far and conjoinment takes place, causing the twins to be born with mirroring features. The easiest way to identify mirror twins is that one is left-hand dominant, while the other is right. My twin and I have a freckle above our lip, but on opposite sides. When we walk, we swing the opposite arm. But in more medically dangerous cases, mirror twins can be born with organs on the opposite sides of their bodies. Even fingerprints and hair patterns whorl in the opposite directions.

To look at my mirror twin, then, is to see not a reflection but a refraction.

MY TWIN (once) loved me as no other person on this earth has, or ever will.

My twin (once, possibly still) has hated me as no other person on this earth has, or ever will.

SHORTLY AFTER I experienced *Dead Ringers* for the first time, my own twin had suddenly begun to encroach upon my life in destabilizing, cinematically preposterous ways. I had developed a career, community, and life around my writing and teaching, the only spaces in my life that felt entirely mine. How foolish of me, I think now, to believe anything was ever only mine. My twin began to frequent the coffee shops I wrote in, take workshops with friends of mine, and warn writers she'd only just met that I was a pathological liar. At the same time, she would chat me up, ask to see my latest poetry, and put on a persona as amiable as we always pretended for the rest of the world, even as our connection became fractured.

It wasn't until I published an excerpt from a memoir-in-progress that my twin committed her most calculated act of thievery: my name and all that came along with it. She acquired (stole) three domain names: my first name, my full name, and the title of the memoir; she'd later insist she only bought the domains so she could someday "publish cute stuff about *us*." Years later, she would admit, matter-of-factly, that she used me as currency, as a way to legitimize and ingratiate herself into the writing community. But what she really meant to say is that she used our twinning, our likeness, our apparent interchangeability, to her benefit because, after all, had I actually had any creative experiences unless she had them, too?

"YOU HAVE TO kill her, or you'll never be free," my therapist said once, early in our work, as I tried to untether myself from my phantom twin. She meant psychologically, of course.

DEAD RINGERS HAS become a staple for me, something I revisit often—not out of entertainment but out of necessity. It is uniquely and specifically horrifying, and it allows me a space to understand the type of twin relationship that feeds on itself, that treats the boundaries between twinned bodies as porous. Sunken into deep depression following Claire's dramatic exit from his life, Bev begins to spiral from a heroin addiction. He reminds Elliot that whatever one twin does, so must the other; Elliot, adhering to his own dark logic, shares in the experience, which subsequently kills them both.

THIRTY-THREE YEARS OLD. The day that I learned my twin had stolen my domain names, I could feel the pull toward a fate similar to Bev and Elliot. I began to crumble beneath the weight of what it signified for my identical twin to take from me the few territories that grounded me in the world, gave me a sense of the line where I ended and she began. It had been half my life since I had felt any urge for self-annihilation, any impulse to self-harm. If my twin was already intent on eradicating me from the world, why not take it all the way? I wept into my hands as I sat in front of my laptop on my mattress, her name next to my domain names on the screen, blinking back at me.

And yet, the urge to fight for a singular selfhood was stronger than my twin's attempt to snuff it out. Instead of relinquishing all control to a cipher whose existence meant a doubling of not only my face but also my pain, I turned to art. I propped a mirror in the center of the room, and began to create self-portraits. I painted my face white and my lips a scarlet red, lined my eyes black. I faced the mirror with a video camera and smeared the other face I had painted on top of my own, documenting the transformation, the ways it both obscured and exposed.

The shared womb is a metaphor, not a mandate.

Loving Annie Hayworth

LAURA MAW

The Birds

THERE'S A SINGLE moment in Alfred Hitchcock's *The Birds* that I find undeniably sexy, even now: Annie Hayworth, dressed in deep red, lights Melanie Daniels's cigarette for her. Fourteen minutes into the film, it's the first time they meet, and their chemistry is palpable, if tentative. The fact that Melanie (Tippi Hedren) has arrived in Bodega Bay to seduce someone else, Mitch—by delivering his younger sister two lovebirds for her birthday—seems almost irrelevant at the moment she meets Annie (Suzanne Pleshette). Standing on Annie's porch, they are charmed despite themselves—despite, or perhaps because of, the other's mysterious motives, their inability to read one another fully. It's a conversation coded with desire.

Annie removes her gardening gloves. "You know," she tells Melanie, "I've been wanting a cigarette for the last twenty minutes. I just couldn't convince myself to stop. This tilling of the soil can become compulsive, you know."

On the way to her car, Melanie is playful, accusing Annie of seeming covert. Annie leans on her car door, grinning, flirtatious.

"Do I? I don't mean to. Actually, I'm an open book I'm afraid." She glances down at the car seat. "Lovebirds?"

The camera is fixed on Annie, resting her elbow on the red mailbox, as Melanie drives away. Her expression is one I know well: the beginnings of longing, and beneath it, a feverish anxiety. Despite myself, I was obsessed with Annie Hayworth. *I just couldn't convince myself to stop.*

LOVING ANNIE HAYWORTH was a distraction from another, more anxious, love. Laura would light my cigarettes in that same, intimate way when we were eighteen: speaking with her own cigarette bobbing between her lips, angling herself toward me, folding one hand into the pocket of her red coat. Lingering at the fringes of two connected friendship groups, we barely spoke for a year—our interaction back then was a furtive glance across the room at best—but I knew her. She cut her dark hair to her jawline and countered never remembering her homework with offers to recite the essay she would have written. She was difficult, unpopular, and far more intelligent than anybody I knew. I was obsessed. I kept my distance for as long as I could—not smiling when she told our teacher that his use of the word *disenfranchised* was, actually, wrong; not reacting when she hissed *I've been sleeping with your wife for the past sixteen weeks* while singing Pulp's "I Spy" unprompted—but we had almost every class together. I couldn't avoid her, and I didn't want to. That spring, we were inseparable, but wary of each other, our easy intimacy charged with threat. Beneath our affection was an overwhelming anxiety: I was afraid of how much I loved her; I was afraid, too, that in loving me back she would give form to that fear as well as that love. Sometimes, midconversation with someone else, I would look up to find her gaze fixed on me, her hazel eyes filled with disarming flecks of gold—soft, jealous—as if she were deeply involved in some private calculation. When I met her gaze, she looked away, and it was this way for a long time: one of us would tentatively move toward the other, and she would move back. It was addictive, circling around a question neither of us wanted to be the first to ask.

We were together, sitting side by side on the floor of her living room, when I first saw Annie Hayworth on screen. Laura had recorded *The Birds* the night before, and we had skipped our classes that afternoon to buy cheap wine. I brought my knees to my chest on the carpet, both afraid of and giddily anticipating touching her. We watched Annie lean toward Melanie, shielding the flame of the lighter with her cupped hands. I was instantly enchanted by Annie's seductive, husky voice, her easy confidence.

Laura saw it first: "She looks like me, kind of. Maybe this is us in the 1960s."

It was a throwaway remark, but I saw the parallels: that effortless charm, that dark hair, that affinity for red. A little later, Laura reached past me for the wine bottle, and her hand brushed my knee. I turned to her. Her face was lit up by the emerald glaze of the television. She stayed still and glanced at my lips. My heartbeat was sticky, heavy. But she didn't touch me; she tipped the rest of the bottle into our glasses, suddenly energized, her voice louder, compensating for the previous quiet. "Let's get drunk."

A hot, shameful ache in my throat. That afternoon was the first time I tasted rosé: the tangy fizz on my tongue; my dizziness inseparable from nerves when I stood up to drink water in the kitchen. I would remember that single moment—that fierce jolt of lust and panic—for years afterward. On screen, when I returned, Melanie was back at Annie's doorstep, explaining that she hadn't planned on staying very long, but she needed somewhere to stay for the night. Annie looks at her, curious.

"Did something unexpected come up?"

Melanie seems embarrassed, caught off guard by the directness of the question. She bristles. "Yes."

Melanie returns that night after her dinner with Mitch and finds Annie sitting in a white dressing gown on her sofa, reading a newspaper.

"Would you like some brandy?" she asks.

It's the film's most intimate scene. Annie talks openly about her previous relationship with Mitch, assures Melanie it's over. She is witty, flirtatious, charming. Like their earlier conversation on the porch, it's full of subtext: Annie offers Melanie her sweater; she tells her, coyly, that it's extremely cold in her house at night—and they both pause here, uncertain. There's a palpable friction in this scene between desire and the anxiety of its expression; both women are wary of vocalizing it too directly and opt instead for coded phrasing, double meanings, invitations that are both sexual and platonic. But certain emotions slip through—at times, it sounds like a conversation between two lovers in the aftermath of infidelity: "Annie, there's nothing between Mr. Brenner and me," Melanie insists. Annie asks, "Isn't there?"

It was a conversational rhythm I knew well: the punctuating sparks of jealousy, the careful negotiation between vocalizing and disguising desire—when to move toward it, when to move back. On screen, they are interrupted by the telephone. It's Mitch. As Melanie talks, we see both women in the same frame: Annie smoking in the chair; Melanie in the background, cautiously glancing at Annie. Annie lifts her cigarette to her mouth, looking intently at the ceiling, as if determined not to return Melanie's gaze, as if absorbed in some private push-and-pull of emotion.

I NEEDED TO GO; I knew that. My anxiety had reached a fever pitch. When the film finished, I sat on the stairs, lacing up my shoes with trembling fingers. Laura stood silently with her back against the front door, her arms folded behind her, watching me intently. I felt sick. I knew something had changed, and wondered if she knew, but I wasn't prepared to ask her. We always said goodbye like this: her unthinkingly blocking the door while I lingered, not really wanting to leave. That afternoon, she said, "Wait, it's cold outside. Take this with you." She wrapped her red scarf around my neck. I didn't tell her that I only needed to walk to the car outside; I was afraid she'd take it back.

THAT SPRING, I rewatched *The Birds* obsessively. The anxieties the film presents looked a lot like my own. Some of *The Birds*'s most disturbing scenes don't stem from the horror itself but in the arousal of suspense: Eerie silences; gradually tightening shots; frames shifting away from the source of tension. The film's most iconic moment—in which Melanie waits outside the Bodega Bay school for Annie and Mitch's sister, Cathy—lingers in this impending threat: The camera toggles, back and forth, between a closeup of Melanie and the jungle gym behind her. Each time we look at the playground, another crow has settled. To me, it's hard not to read this scene as a visual expression of queer anxiety; equally, it doesn't seem implausible to say that Melanie is thinking—pleasurably, anxiously—about Annie here, repeatedly glancing back to the school. The camera then follows a single bird through the sky as it settles on the jungle gym, and we see the structure is swarming with crows: a horrific mass of twitching wings, slick, shiny bodies juddering against one another. The horror here is not about action. It's about anxiety—anticipating what will happen without quite knowing. This was, too, what my relationship with Laura felt like: orchestrated by the thrilling agony of suspense. After that day at her house, I fixated on the next time we would be alone. What would happen? Would she kiss me? I felt feral with anticipation, turning the various scenarios over in my head. Anxiety had knotted itself with desire—its intensity visceral, nauseating—and I waited, foolishly, for it to pass. I fantasized about this mythical end point: the point at which I would be unafraid, would slip out of coded phrases and coy invitations. I would tell her, I decided, in the summer.

June that year was unusually hot—fans were wheeled into all of the classrooms, and one of our friends had started buying packs of ice from the shop in town. Laura and I walked to the sea whenever we could, giddily sucking cheap beer from cans, smoothing her red coat out on the sand to lie down. We'd developed a habit of hissing "the birds!" at each other whenever we saw a flock of them perched ominously somewhere, and she leaned over me one afternoon to gesture at the seagulls lining the pier. Her lips brushed my hair and she whispered, "Look." The joke was worn out immediately, but we kept repeating it, desperate to acknowledge that afternoon without discussing the specifics of what had changed between us. We were preparing for exams that summer and spent hours sitting at the edge of our now-merged friendship group in the sixth form conservatory; our spot was at the end of the table, facing each other. I wasn't studying that day but reading a collection of Virginia Woolf's letters—a book she had bought me, writing *all my love, forever and always* on the inside cover. Laura wasn't studying, either: she was designing invitations for my birthday party later in the year, sketching the cover of Bowie's *Aladdin Sane* with a biro. Our friend, B, looked up from her biology textbook to tell us that a person's pupils dilated when they looked at somebody they loved. B turned to J.

"What do my eyes look like?"

J looked at her, uninterested. "I don't know, they look like they always do."

Laura and I met each other's gaze involuntarily. B looked at us from the end of the table and rolled her eyes. "Obviously Laura's pupils will be huge when she looks at Laura."

Neither of us knew which Laura she was referring to. We looked away from one another quickly, our gaze split by sudden exposure. Nobody said anything. Laura's expression was blank, and with a red pen she began coloring the lightning bolt on Bowie's face. Her hand was steady; she gave nothing away. The ambiguity was agonizing: Which of us was looking, and which of us was being looked at? Did everybody know how I felt by the simple fact of the way I looked at her? I stared at B, desperate to know how she—how, maybe, everybody else—saw it: Was Laura the initiator of this love, or was it the other way around? I had thought that our relationship was private, but in that moment, I knew with awful clarity that it wasn't, and it chilled me: the thought that perhaps B had seen something I couldn't, something I didn't realize was visible. In my bedroom that night, I sobbed: I couldn't stand to have anybody else acknowledge what we hadn't yet named.

ANY ANXIETIES Annie and Melanie feel about their own sexualities in *The Birds* don't only affect them but other people, too, as the residents of Bodega Bay start to suspect the source of the disruption. It didn't, to me, seem like a coincidence that the birds begin attacking the Bay from the moment Annie and Melanie meet—and it doesn't seem that way to the characters in *The Birds* either. After the attack on the harbor restaurant and parking lot, Melanie stumbles, exhausted, into the corridor. A woman walks toward her, furious.

"They said when you got here the whole thing started," the woman shrieks. "Who are you? What are you? Where did you come from? I think you're the cause of all this. I think you're *evil*."

This, perhaps, is the epitome of the film's queer anxiety: We dwell not only on Melanie's own anxious desires but in the reception of those desires too. We reckon with the idea that those desires might unravel the social fabric of the small town; that they might—that *she* might— be the source of horror. This sentiment is echoed, too, by the customers at the restaurant, buoyed and enraged by the mayhem: One resident declares, "It's the end of the world!"; a mother pleads with a waitress, "Could you ask them to lower their voices please? They're frightening the children." I can't help but read this dialogue as a metaphor for the subversive power of queer desire: its disruption to heterosexual norms, to the nuclear family, to the social status quo—its perceived impending horror. At the restaurant, in the face of accusation, Melanie is silent; instead of speaking, she retaliates by hitting the woman accusing her. Perhaps she, too, couldn't stand to have anybody acknowledge something she could not name, couldn't stand the idea that her disruptive desires were apparent to people other than herself. That shame of being seen wanting without the certainty of being wanted back. That acute mortification.

ANXIETY, more often than not, reaches resolution in horror cinema. Unlike fear—which is a response to immediate threat—anxiety is, according to critic Mathias Clasen in *Why Horror Seduces*, "a future-oriented emotion, an emotion that occurs in response to anticipations of danger or threat."[1] Anxiety, then, looks toward the frightening possibilities of a future event, and it is resolved once that event takes place—either in the sense that the threat has passed, or its extent has been misjudged. In horror, this rhythm of anxiety lowering and heightening is a familiar one: it's a cycle that repeats itself until the third act, in which—usually—the threat is escaped and the possibility of future threat is eradicated. In queer narratives, this type of anxiety—one that has an end point—is a familiar convention too: this anxiety exists in order to be overcome, eventually, by the sheer force of the protagonists' desire; as if desire and anxiety were separate entities, as if one merely blocks the other, like an eclipse. But anxiety is not resolved—either by the eradication of threat, or by the antidote of desire—in *The Birds*.

Ambiguity—rather than resolution—is the final note of the film: Melanie, Mitch, Lydia, and Cathy walk from the Brenners' house to the car. They move slowly, tentative and uncertain, surrounded by birds. Climbing into the car, they drive away from the house. But the camera doesn't follow the car very far: we don't see it leave Bodega Bay. We're left not with an image of resolution but the presence of potential threat: hundreds of birds gather ominously on screen, just as they have before prior attacks. There's no indication that the characters will manage to escape Bodega Bay. It's fitting that the film's last image is one of uncertainty, that it explicitly lacks resolution. Watching that afternoon with Laura, I wondered how Melanie felt, driving away in the car. We can't see her in the final moments of the film, but I imagined her expression: that she might be thinking not about her life beyond this point but about what life she has left behind—what love she has lost.

1. Mathias Clasen, *Why Horror Seduces* (New York: Oxford University Press, 2017), 27.

Shortly after the woman in the restaurant accuses Melanie of causing the Bodega Bay attacks, she and Mitch travel to Annie's house to find Cathy. They find Annie lying on the pathway outside, covered in blood. When Melanie realizes what has happened, she screams and begins to cry. Beyond the symbolism of Annie's death—necessary in that her existence was an obstacle to the film's heterosexual coupling, and her death makes room for their union—it also functions to reveal unresolved feeling. When Mitch rescues Cathy, Melanie is still sobbing about Annie, begging, "Don't leave her there." He carries Annie into her house.

I knew that I wasn't supposed to feel a connection had been cut short when Annie died, but I did. Their last conversation at Annie's school, where Melanie instructs her to evacuate the children for their safety, carries, by necessity, none of the intimacy or depth of their conversation at Annie's house. If they had known it was the last time they would talk, would they speak differently? Would they say something more urgent? When Annie dies, Melanie is left with unresolved desire, a relationship that never began, love left unspoken: her emotion left hidden by code, insinuation, double meaning. She is sobbing, maybe, for what could have happened between them but now no longer can; she is not only mourning the loss of a woman she might have loved but also their potential future. Melanie's desire for Annie reaches an end point only insofar as its future expression is made impossible in the face of Annie's death—as if the only path out of her anxiety is for its source to be cut from the narrative. Her anxiety about her own sexuality, in other words, is not resolved—its direct cause is merely removed.

DESIRE WAS NOT an antidote to my own feverish anxiety, either. I still remember the sensation of standing in my bedroom, my heartbeat thickening—pleasurably, anxiously—as Laura closed the door behind us. I knew I had to tell her. The words came clumsily. "I think I like you—like that."

We were both drunk, and my tongue was sour with wine. She looked at me for a long time with an expression I couldn't decipher. Very gently, she said, "I know. I don't know if I feel like that. I don't know."

I nodded, humiliated despite, or because of, her softness.

She said, "There are moments—like, the other day with B, when I felt sure I felt the same. But other times . . . I guess I don't know, Lau."

She held my hand. I kept nodding, repeating useless affirmations, as if the facade of acceptance could cancel out the white-hot feeling of shame. B, and everybody else—including Laura—had known, and I hadn't realized. I had thought my anxiety would dissipate once I had told her, that the source of my anxiety was in keeping this secret from her, that once I had spoken the words I would be freed of the problem, but it didn't happen like that. I had expected a yes or no; I hadn't anticipated her uncertainty. I didn't know how to respond.

It was this way for a long time: we lingered in the erotic ambiguity, as we always had, reliant on it like an energy source. In our French class one afternoon, our teacher, bored at the end of term, handed out temporary tattoos to us: images with their translations underneath. A shooting star—*étoile filante*—or a tube of red lipstick—*rouge à lèvres*. Amused, I peeled a sticky heart from the plastic. *Cœur éclaté*: broken heart. I was about to turn to Laura, grinning, but her hand found mine under the table. Her eyes were huge and glassy. It was a look I knew well. Before, I had interpreted it as proof of her love, but that day—months after her confessed uncertainty—I didn't know how to translate it. It was there, still: that same wary affection, almost involuntary. After that day, it happened gradually: She began holding my hand, discreetly, whenever we sat together; she found excuses to drape her leather jacket over my shoulders between classes; I sat on the girls' bathroom sinks and she stood between my legs, our thighs touching, carefully blending my eyeshadow with her finger while my skin turned hot. We didn't vocalize the shift in dynamic, and I was anxious that acknowledging what I hoped was true—that she felt the same way—would disrupt the energy we relied on. I tried to cultivate neutrality, as if the expression of my emotion alone could mute her affection.

I already had a blueprint for our ongoing uncertainty, the risks of pressing Laura about it. *The Birds*, too, is orchestrated by Melanie's uncertainty, her indecision, the push-and-pull of her emotion. She is uncomfortable with fixed commitment to plans, opinions, and other people; she is uncomfortable with direct questions that expose these uncertainties ("Don't you like Bodega Bay?" Cathy asks. Melanie replies, "I'm not sure yet."). At Annie's house, she's unsure whether or not to join Mitch for dinner.

"Do you think I should go?" she asks.

"It's up to you," Annie tells her.

Melanie seems overwhelmed by the weight of the decision, unable to work out what she should and should not do, unable to translate her own emotion into action. She solicits advice because she can't untangle obligation from desire: Is she going to dinner with Mitch because she wants to, or because she feels she should? Does she rely on coded phrasing to flirt with Annie because she is unsure of Annie's feelings— or is it to mask her own uncertainty, to give her desire some elasticity, to move back from it if necessary? Arriving at the Brenners' house later, she presents Cathy with the lovebirds she brought from San Francisco—the ones Annie spotted in the seat of her car. Cathy is delighted, examining the cage.

"Are they a man and a woman? I can't tell which is which."

"Well," Melanie hesitates. "I suppose so."

Uncertainty is Melanie's protection: If she never commits to the vocalization of her desires, she is free to dismiss them as joke, whimsy, boredom. She cannot be rejected by the recipient of those desires, or punished for their expression. Safe in ambiguity, she cannot, in other words, be hurt.

I DIDN'T REALIZE that there was no antidote to anxiety, no balm, no end point—not even the moment I'd routinely fantasized about. The nature of the conversation is hazy now; I remember it in fragments, discussing the universities we were going to after the summer was over. We were sitting in Laura's bedroom, books spread over the floor between us.

"You'll forget me," she said.

I laughed. "If I'm lucky."

She said nothing for a moment, scratching her red nail polish off with her index finger. It was only when she smiled—slowly, resigned— that I realized the playfulness had worn off.

"I wouldn't blame you," she said. "But . . . you know that I really love you, right?"

I looked at her, not sure if she was really asking the question. Her palm lay flat on the carpet between us; studying my expression, she moved closer to kiss me. I kissed her back. I had anticipated this moment; I had imagined my anxiety being eclipsed, finally, by something else. But on the way home that evening, I felt uneasy: not because of the kiss itself but because my anxiety had not dissipated like I imagined it would. I knew how capable we were of hurting each other so deeply, and I found other uncertainties to anticipate—moving to different cities at the end of the summer, meeting new people. Anxiety was, as Clasen writes, a future-oriented emotion: it wasn't fixed to that moment of kissing her but somewhere beyond it, anticipating new difficulty at being apart. We didn't speak about the kiss the next day; instead, we spoke about the coursework grades we received, which cemented our university offers. Our dynamic shifted back to a tense, thrilling ambiguity. Later, I wondered if she had planned to kiss me to say goodbye, if it was meant not to signal a beginning but an ending. In the end, it signified neither.

Loving Annie Hayworth

THE SPRING I rewatched *The Birds*, I fantasized about what Melanie and Annie's relationship might have been like. Maybe Annie might have driven to meet Melanie in San Francisco. They might have bought a ridiculously elaborate array of tropical fish at Davidson's Pet Shop. They might have sipped whiskey on cubes of ice in Melanie's apartment. Annie might have watched Melanie slide her pistachio-green jacket off her shoulders. They might have kissed, might have slept together, might have loved each other. I allowed myself to fantasize. But maybe it would look a lot like the relationship I had with Laura in the years that followed, driven by an ongoing—and unresolved—ambiguity, that space between anxiety and desire. We saw each other sporadically in our different cities, our meetings always mitigated by the arrival of other people, the flow of other conversations and—by then—the presence of other partners. I visited Laura and her boyfriend, D, at their flat once. The evening was uncomfortable: D rarely left the room so Laura and I could be alone together, rarely let more than a few minutes pass without speaking to tell a story only he and Laura would find amusing. I felt sulky, jealous, competitive—and relieved when he stood up to get another bottle of beer from the kitchen. Laura and I sat in silence on the sofa. Her hand was ice-cold when she touched mine, her fingers white from gripping her drink. She looked apologetic.

"Glad he likes me," I said.

She was silent for a moment, then lowered her voice. "He said when we're together we make him feel like he's invisible." We heard the clinking of glass bottles in the kitchen. "I don't know how I can change it." She gestured back and forth between us. "I can't change this."

The three of us walked to the train station in strained silence. D walked ahead of us, and we lingered back. I held Laura's hand, stroking her thumb through her gloves. She looked at me with an expression I could only read as *I know, but stop it*, and dropped my hand. As if knowing I would move toward her, she pushed me back and ran to catch up with D. I watched her take his hand.

At the station, she wrapped her red scarf around my neck.

"I don't know when I can give this back," I said.

She looked hurt, as if acknowledging the fact that we rarely saw each other was something I had deliberately engineered.

"Keep it," she said. "We'll see each other soon."

I studied her expression. She wouldn't meet my gaze for longer than a few seconds, but I knew she was going to cry. I dug my fingers into the spongy wool around my neck, the red fibers sticking under my nails. A streetlight buzzed above us. I watched the orange digits on the clock; the train was about to leave. I wanted to say something, but could only think one thing, like it was all I knew: I didn't know how to love anybody else while I still loved her. I thought about telling her this. But the look on her face told me she knew it already: because she didn't know how to love anybody else, either.

MAYBE, leaving Bodega Bay that evening, Melanie is thinking about how her relationship with Annie might have unfolded: the whiskey sipped in apartments, the feverish kisses. Maybe she's ruminating on the pain of that lost, unknown love. But, maybe, she's thinking of a different kind of pain: the possibility that, even if Annie had lived, their love might still have been unknown. That years might have passed and things might have remained unsaid. Maybe, on that journey, Melanie is reckoning with the possibility that their love's greatest driving force might have been ambiguity. The possibility that, even if Annie had lived, Melanie might still one day be making this same journey: traveling away from Bodega Bay, lamenting a lost love, alone.

The first time they meet, Annie is gardening. She confesses to Melanie, "I just couldn't convince myself to stop." Their conversation is open-ended, ambiguous in its intent, orchestrated as much by silence as it is by dialogue. *I just couldn't convince myself to stop*. It's a phrase that comes to stand in for their relationship: compulsive, addictive, ongoing—brought only to a resolution by Annie's death.

For as long as we knew each other, I knew there could be no resolution to my relationship with Laura. There was only the same ambiguity, the same flirtation circled with no end point. After that night, the months between our meetings developed into a year, and then longer still. We both let it happen. When she asked me to meet one summer, I agonized over a reply, and, not knowing how to tell her what we both already knew, never sent it. I wondered, in the weeks that followed, whether she might have been relieved: to have avoided the responsibility of making that decision neither of us wanted to be the first to make; to have had the outcome she wanted without needing to bear its burden. I began to see our relationship's lack of resolution as an answer in and of itself: Our chemistry depended on the thrill of uncertainty, desire simmering alongside anxious hesitation. It's the same uncertainty that orchestrates the plot of *The Birds*: anxiety doesn't reach an end point because no resolution is offered; Annie and Melanie's relationship reaches no conclusion, nor does their desire for each other. My relationship with Laura never seemed to be over because it never began; I couldn't turn away from it to look at anything else. It was an ongoing question: an enduring, compulsive, complicated love. For years, I would carry that love with me. *I just couldn't convince myself to stop.*

The Same Kind of Monster

JONATHAN ROBBINS LEON

The Leech Woman

THE SMOKE CLEARS, the Nando tribesmen carry away Paul's lifeless body, and June is young again. Gone are her dark circles and puckered forehead. Her hair tumbles in creamy, Hollywood curls. And her face! It's as though Kevyn Aucoin has been hiding in the smoke with his arsenal of makeup brushes.

Five minutes before, we may have questioned her coldhearted willingness to have Paul sacrificed for the sake of regaining her youth. Now, however, it all seems worth it. She's not just young. She's young and gorgeous. What's one dead husband when you can look like Coleen Gray?

At nine years old, I get it. Without a doubt, I would slit Paul's throat myself to look that good in safari gear. I move to the edge of the bed, clinging to the footboard in anticipation. The volume is low so that the television won't wake my mother, who's asleep beside me. As a rule, I'm not allowed to stay awake past ten o'clock on weeknights, but when my stepfather goes away for work, we buy a giant bag of peanut M&M's and laze around like chubby raccoons watching TV in her bed.

Tonight's fare is *The Leech Woman*, an early '60s B horror flick presented via an episode of *Mystery Science Theater 3000* and advertised with the tagline, "For her there could be no love . . . only horror!" The portrayal of African culture is cringeworthy, the performances at times laughable, and what the film has to say about women and aging isn't so hot either, but I'm too young and too absorbed in the plot to see any of the movie's obvious flaws. I look back to make sure my mother's still sleeping and turn the volume up a little.

It's nice to be ourselves, to enjoy each other's company without my stepfather's scrutiny. Ordinarily we creep around the house, giving the living room, and him, a wide berth. His presence is a weak acid, slow-acting, but given enough time, it could reduce you to bone, or liquefy you completely. I try to stay quiet and out of the way, but arguments develop around him like hurricanes in warm waters. Arguments I never win.

Until he came into our lives, I thought I was a good boy, but I have since learned that I am too sensitive, too feminine, and interested in all the wrong things. Yet there are worse faults, once dormant, but slowly waking within me. Brimming beneath my obsession with sketching all of the dresses worn at the Oscars and my fervor for all things Lisa Frank lurks something more sinister. It's the reason I sometimes look over at other boys at the urinal. It's the reason I've committed the page number of Michelangelo's David in my mother's art history textbook to memory.

Even at this premature age, I've already moved beyond theory and fantasy. There's a boy I see at parties and church picnics, his family close with ours. When we can sneak away to a back bedroom or a barn, he likes to forcibly cover my mouth and go down on me. Where he got the idea, I can only imagine. I'm supposed to scream and try to wiggle away, he says, but I only fight so hard. I'm horrified to find that I like it, and that I like even better when he says it's my turn to put my mouth on him.

We've been caught, this boy and I, but everyone has dismissed what happened as childish curiosity. For me though, I cannot shake what we have done. Rubbing myself against my sheets at night, I think of the moist warmth of this boy's hand over my mouth. My homosexuality looms over my family like a specter in the sky, but for now, we are still pretending it is just a cloudy day.

I don't know anything about camp aesthetic yet, but I'm drawn to this film by instinct from the first scene. June slugs back two fingers of whiskey while her bedraggled stole slips from her shoulders, and I'm hooked. She's been lured to Africa by her husband, Dr. Paul Talbot. Having witnessed how Nipe, pollen collected from a rare species of orchid, can prolong life, Dr. Talbot tracks Malla, a 152-year-old Nando tribeswoman, back to her village to watch her regain her youth in a secret ceremony involving human sacrifice. After downing a concoction of Nipe and pineal secretions, courtesy of a slaughtered tribesman, the skeletal Malla is transformed into a bombshell played by Kim Hamilton (whose exquisite face makes it unfathomable that she wasn't a bigger star). Talbot is thrilled by the commercial possibilities of what he's learned, but he gets more than he's bargained for when Malla offers to share this last flowering of youth with his wife.

Brought along for the expedition only as a human guinea pig, June is ten years older than her husband. Paul doesn't bother to hide his revulsion for older women, and her in particular. He's dragged her along in the hopes of making her young again, to use her as living proof of his discovery. But of course, a man must be sacrificed in order for the potion to work. "Any man I wish?" June asks Malla.

"Any man."

The dejected June wastes no time picking Paul for the job, and he's hauled away by two men in loincloths. The ceremony is repeated, a tribal priest stabbing Paul's spine with a hooked ring, smoke flooding the screen, and June is made young again.

I don't make the connection then, but the film's promise of transformation is similar to my prayers as a child. When I first began to understand that I was different from other little boys, I prayed to god for a miracle. At six years old, I promised to dedicate my life to him, to be a kind and devoted Christian, if he would only let me wake up as a girl. Then I could wear dresses, play with dolls, and think about kissing boys without worrying that I'd fall, crack my head open, and come to in the fiery bowels of hell (my family was largely Baptist, and hell had been so vividly described for me that I had regular nightmares about ending up there). June's willingness to sacrifice her husband is understandable to me in the same way that I knew exactly why Ariel signed Ursula's scroll, or why Madeline Ashton swallowed that dubious, glowing potion: they each wanted a miracle.

Looking back, I don't think I ever wanted to be a girl, but my parents had kept me so sheltered, closely monitoring everything I watched or read, that I lacked other references. In my narrow mind, boys had to be boys, and girls had to be girls. If you didn't fit the mold, you'd better get down on your knees and start begging Jesus to erase your family's memories and rechristen you in the middle of the night. When I grew up and learned that it was possible to transition, I reflected on whether this was something I truly wanted and came to the conclusion that no, I'd just been a little boy desperate to play with dolls and suck dick, but in my heart, I was not a girl. Yet, while I eventually came to terms with my identity, I was forever marked by the shame of feeling that I was a deviant: wrong, broken, and so very dirty.

Knowing they'll be executed if they remain with the Nando, June and her jungle guide escape, thinking nothing of throwing dynamite at the Nando village and stealing the Nipe and murder ring for themselves. She and the guide end up tangled in each other's arms, June impossible to resist now. When she wakes, however, the Nipe has worn off, and June is even more hideous than before. Her guide staggers back from her aged face and clutching, gnarled hands, running and falling into swamp water. He tries to crawl out, only to become June's second victim, a startled cry escaping his lips as the ring is plunged into the back of his neck.

June returns to the United States, passing herself off as her own fictitious niece. She's set her sights on Neal, her hunky lawyer. The question of why June would chase a dud like Neil is moot. I understand that Neil isn't just Neil; he's all men. He's all the people who can only love me and June if we keep them ignorant about the worst parts of ourselves.

It only takes about three minutes for June to wrest Neil from Sally, his simpering fiancée. If we're supposed to feel bad for Sally, I don't get the memo. She reminds me of every pretty girl I know, taking for granted the enormous coincidence of being plopped into a body and environment that affords them the luxury of living the kind of life suited to them without fear of persecution. Because no one has yet educated me about the many pitfalls to being a woman, I only see the majesty of it and am enormously jealous that girls are never asked to toughen up or ordered to the garage to help their stepfather work on a car.

June intends to take full advantage of her regained youth and spends the movie murdering people left and right to keep it. The only trouble is, every time the potion wears off, she is left a decade or so older than before. How could Neil love her if he sees her true form? I know that fear. My friends and my family have not quite puzzled out who I really am. Neither have I, but I know that the self I am hiding is far more repulsive than Coleen Gray covered in wrinkled latex.

Even decades later, out and proud, married and a father, the urge to hide, to disguise myself remains with me. As a little boy, I made myself palatable by pretending I liked playing outside, that I had an Ultimate Hair Queen Amidala doll because I loved *Star Wars* and not because it was the closest thing to a Barbie my parents would let me buy. As an adult, I make myself palatable by pretending that my husband and I are like Mitch and Cam from *Modern Family*: just like the straights, but with more paisley. I allow my parents to think we're monogamous and that we're raising our son with religion.

I even hide parts of myself from my husband. While he brags about bagging some toned twentysomething on his lunch break, my exploits are impossible to share. I know the look of disgust he would give me if he knew, for example, that sometimes I like to be obliterated, to submit myself to the most unkind and revolting men I can find. In some ways, those men see me more clearly than my husband, knowing how willing I am to deprave myself, to offer up my body even as another part of myself recoils from their touch. Afterward, I feel defiled and fulfilled, a complex combination that I know my husband would never understand.

Shame is a part of my identity. Having spent so long in its embrace, I sometimes need to feel it wash over me again to know that I am myself. Even with the surprising amount of love and acceptance in my life, I will likely never shake the feeling that I am Selina Kyle, too wicked to ever accept Bruce's offer to live with him in Wayne manor. I'm Melisandre, desirable only out of context, but don't remove my necklace.

I'm June Talbot, too, and Sally is right to try and run me out of town at gunpoint. It's a testament to how much I identify with the monster of the movie that, as a little boy, I actually clap my hands when June kills Sally, the ring gutting her spine of the precious fluid June needs to remain young. I want June to get away with it, or to at least have a hot weekend with Neil that would justify the trouble she's gone through to get him.

Yet just as June gets Neil to herself, the police burst in, having figured out that the unsolved murders of late can be traced to the widow recently returned from Africa. At nine, I'm crossing my fingers that they don't open the hall closet where June has stashed Sally's body. I recognize that there is something personal at work here, that this is no longer just a movie for me. My own loathsome desires mean that the forces of good will always find a way to burst in on me too, thwarting any chance of satisfaction. It is me crawling up the stairs in shame as Neil watches, the Nipe wearing off, my true hideousness exposed.

I'm right in thinking that there will one day come a climax, a reveal when my parents will see me as the detectives and Neil now see June. They will find a diary where I have detailed each of my transgressions, and they will know that the little boy they once loved is dead, and in his place is this degenerate, a person who has made himself filthy and unworthy of love. It will take so many years of healing, of forgetting, for us to be family again. Yet still I know better than to reveal too much of myself to them, and they know better than to go hunting for any diaries.

In the movie, the closet has spilled its secrets now, and June is trying to explain that she can become young again, hurrying up the stairs to show them. Poor girl. Doesn't she see their faces? Doesn't she know that it wouldn't matter if she became young again now? They know her for what she is. They have seen behind the curtain, and now loving her would be impossible.

June learns too late that the Nipe only works when the sacrificial victim is a man. Reduced to a withered hag, she throws herself from the balcony. Neil and the detectives burst into the room and spot her body on the patio below. The camera zooms in on her shriveled apple face, her hair now shock-white. The detectives stare not at her but at Neil, their faces pinched with repulsion. How could he have loved this? The final scene feels personal and correct. I turn off the television and crawl into bed next to my mother.

For now, I still belong, though it will only be a handful of years before I fully crack the lid on my sexuality. I'll encounter a man at the flea market, decades older than me. He'll take me to his van, and I'll do everything he asks because I'm afraid, but also because I recognize him as the same kind of monster. I will learn from him and others what kind of creatures we are and how splendid it feels to reveal ourselves to one another, to cast off our clothes and dance before the bonfires we've erected to summon our strange gods.

They, too, will hide themselves, cruising for sex in public bathrooms, despite this no longer being necessary, there being hotels and bars where our kind can meet. For some of them, these anonymous encounters are the only way they can get hard, the knowing of names taking the bloom from the rose. The shame clings to us. It is a facet of what it means to have been queer in a time before *Glee*. It is a portion of our specific inheritance, part of why we cherish figures like Lady

Macbeth, the Wicked Witch of the West, and Baby Jane. We understand what it means to be the monster lurking in the dark, our desires twisted against us until we disgust even ourselves.

I don't yet know if we will pass this toxic treasure down to future generations, but it's my hope that they have no use for it. Today's baby queers seem better at understanding themselves, better at brushing off the world's attempts to control, define, and limit them. What use have they for June's stolen Nipe powder and ceremonial ring? What use have they for a miraculous transformation when they can look in the mirror and fully accept what they see?

But all of this, the man at the flea market, the men after who will punish and shame me in the way that I crave, all of this is still some years away. I am only nine. I curl against my mother's back and make myself small. I fall asleep hoping that tomorrow isn't the morning when the Nipe wears off and I'm left withered and exposed. *For just a little while more*, I think, *let me hide here.*

Centered and Seen

SUMIKO SAULSON

Candyman

ONE BY ONE they appeared, sporting brightly colored hair in shades of hot pink and royal purple, lime green and fishbowl aqua. Manic Panic and Directions dye-streaked undercuts, mullets, and fringes atop their queer, gender nonconforming heads. Some wore gothic black lace, others draped themselves in the unmistakable rainbow hues of the pride flag. Every single one of them connected to the San Francisco Bay Area LGBTQ and Leather Community—queer and kinky folks I am proud to call my friends. We'd spent the pandemic separated from one another, interacting behind Zoom and Discord screens, but when Nia DaCosta's *Candyman* arrived, so did we, renting out the entire theater for a private, vaxxed screening of the long-awaited sequel to Bernard Rose's 1992 classic of the same name.

My girlfriend, Staci—in a short, powder blue frock over serpentine tights, square and sensible heels with a peek-a-boo toe, long flowing locks of hair, and a wizard-like beard—stood beside me outside the cineplex as the family reunion descended upon us. Despite the joy of the moment, when we entered the theater I couldn't help but notice that I was the only Black person in the room about to take in this Black film. I didn't let this fact pull me away from how wonderful of an outing it was, and we all had plenty to share and say about the film, particularly how queerness was unexpectedly and deftly included in the narrative. But there was no one there to identify with on the subject of Black centering, no one else for whom the movie spoke to in the ways it spoke to me.

Although I am polyamorous, neither of my other two, nonwhite partners could attend that night. Wednesday, a genderfluid, non-Black

POC, had to work. Empress, who is African American and lives across the country, went to another theater in another city at the same time as us so we could talk about it later. But when they got to the theater, they decided they wanted to see the Aretha Franklin biopic *Respect* instead. Ms. Franklin coincidentally died around the same time my mother entered the final phase of her life. Multiple myeloma, the cancer my mother eventually died from, is a bone cancer in the same family as leukemia and lymphoma. It affects people of African heritage at a rate twice that of the general population. In an alternate universe, I would have seen *Candyman* with my mother, who was a tremendous horror buff. In this universe, my mother was gone and I saw *Candyman* with a bunch of queer white people instead.

Candyman, in all of its iterations, relies heavily on Black pain and trauma to instill a sense of horror in its audience: overcrowding, gang violence, and drug use in the housing projects; violence enacted upon Black bodies by lynch mobs and law enforcement; and the vilification of Daniel Robitaille, a victimized Black man who returns as the titular Big Bad. Much of what is depicted in the *Candyman* films, sometimes on the periphery, has affected me and my family in real life; I've seen it up close. Perhaps this is why the original *Candyman* remains one of my all-time favorite horror movies. It depicts, in a manner both realistic and sympathetic, the struggle of African Americans living in poverty in America, hunted both by the police and their neighbors. It was groundbreaking for its time and remains achingly relevant today. *Candyman* also turned on its ear the white savior narrative that would become popular in the near future with feel-good films like *Dangerous Minds*.

The heroine and white savior of *Candyman* is Helen Lyle. An affluent graduate student researching urban legends, Helen becomes involved in the lives of the residents of the Cabrini-Green projects in Chicago to both their and her detriments. Everything Helen does to try to "save" those around her is tainted by her personal involvement in the systems of oppression. Her presence at Cabrini-Green causes tension with gang members who have been using the legend of Candyman to instill fear in the projects' residents and maintain their authority. The angry ghost of Daniel Robitaille, the Candyman himself, has leeched onto Helen because she is ostensibly the reincarnation of the woman he loved—and who inevitably caused his lynching. Even Helen's ultimate act of self-sacrifice at the end of the movie, a grisly immolation inside of a huge bonfire as she saves a Black infant from Candyman's grip, is dimmed by the inconvenient fact of her being the one to awaken Candyman to begin with.

When *Candyman* came out in 1992, I immediately developed a celebrity crush on Tony Todd, the man who brought Robitaille to iconic life. Todd's undeniable charisma aside, *Candyman* was one of the few horror films (or any film for that matter) with an African American star. It reminded me of when I saw the original 1978 *Dawn of the Dead* as a child, awed by the impressive screen presence of its Black protagonist, played by Ken Foree. Like *Dawn of the Dead* and 1968's *Night of the Living Dead* before it, *Candyman* centered a Black character in a white-made film. Like both of those early films, it integrated America's issues with race into a horror story. And like *Night of the Living Dead*, it maintained a gritty, somber tone, forcing us to take its subject matter seriously. But unlike *Night of the Living Dead*, the Black character did not stay dead. Candyman was no martyr in Uncle Tom's Cabin mode. Candyman rose up to enact revenge upon others for his horrific lynching.

Staci, a pink-haired and pink-bearded nonbinary transfemme, shares my lust for Tony Todd as Candyman. And, as we are both nonbinary femmes, pansexual and polyamorous, shared celebrity character crushes is essentially one of our love languages. We're both kinky people, and Staci, my life partner of nearly three years and collared submissive of more than two, has a hypnofetish. Fey fantasizes about being Helen Lyle, played to perfection by Virginia Madsen. Staci is utterly fascinated by the fact that actual hypnosis was used to get the actress more deeply into character.[1] Director Bernard Rose brought in a professional hypnotist to work with Madsen and learned to use hypnosis himself in order to help her more convincingly achieve a trance-like state when under the influence of Candyman.

As members of the LGBTQ community, kinky folks, and writers, Staci and I also feel a kinship with openly gay horror author Clive Barker, the craftsman behind the 1985 short story "The Forbidden," which birthed the entire *Candyman* franchise. Anyone who has seen *Nightbreed* or the *Hellraiser* franchise, or read the stories they are based on, knows that Barker has a deep penchant for unapologetically kinky horror. "The Forbidden" takes place in England and digs into topics of class inequality as well as the strength and persistence of urban legends. It was director Bernard Rose who insisted that the topic of race be introduced and decided to set the film adaptation in 1990s Chicago. He even went so far as to have the script vetted by the NAACP[2] to minimize perpetuating stereotypical or dangerous tropes about Black men, though it's debatable how much their notes shaped the final film.

I, of course, have a relationship to the Blackness of *Candyman* and the melanated denizens of Cabrini-Green cast as background in the original film that Staci does not—cannot—share. The deep, bloody pain related to certain plot points of Candyman resonate with me on a cellular level. I am a biracial Black and Ashkenazi Jewish person. Anti-miscegenation, the hatred of race mixing, is the foundation of *Candyman*. Daniel Robitaille was murdered by a white lynch mob for becoming romantically and sexually involved with a white woman. The only way to validate his life and avenge his death was to become a

1. Eammon Jacobs, "Real Hypnosis Was Used in the Making of This Classic Horror Film." *Looper*, June 9, 2021, https://www.looper.com/432415/real-hypnosis-was-used-in-the-making-of-this-classic-horror-film/.

2. Phil Hoad, "How We Made Candyman: 'I Got a $1,000 Bonus for Every Bee Sting,'" *The Guardian*, June 25, 2019, https://www.theguardian.com/film/2019/jun/25/how-we-made-candyman-virginia-madsen-tony-todd-bee-sting.

monster who instilled both curiosity and fear among the masses. They wouldn't likely remember Daniel Robitaille, just another lynched Black man, but Candyman—that was a name they'd keep in their mouths.

My love for the film notwithstanding, I cannot ignore the white-centering in a film that revolves around Black pain. The film offers many suggestions as to why Robitaille obsesses over Helen, in addition to her being the apparent reincarnation of his forbidden love; most urgently, Helen's college thesis on urban legends threatens to disprove his very existence and, in turn, suppress his power. Like a monstrous Tinker Bell, Candyman relies on people believing in him. However, by heavily implying that Helen is a reincarnation of his lover Caroline Sullivan, whose father drummed up the very lynch mob that killed him, Robitaille's murder becomes reduced to a backdrop for his revenge spree and, more pointedly, his victimization of Helen. The decision to emphasize Candyman as a terrifying movie monster ultimately minimizes Robitaille's own victimization, and in effect centers whiteness. This dimming of Black experience happens, as it often does, subtly and corrosively, right in front of our eyes until we, the audience, are complicit.

I also feel some kind of way about how in the second and third film, two poorly received sequels that are best left forgotten, the "one drop rule"[3] was used to establish that Robitaille's forebears were cursed due to being distant progeny of a Black man. In a misguided retcon of the original film, Candyman's origin story was expanded to include the existence of a daughter named Isabel, born to him and Caroline. Caroline and her murderous father decide to raise Isabel as white. Somewhere in this new, convoluted mythology, Robitaille

3. ". . . the 'one drop rule' has meant that anyone with a visually discernible trace of African, or what used to be called 'Negro,' ancestry is, simply, Black." David A. Hollinger, "One drop & one hate," *Daedalus* 134, no. 1 (Winter 2005).

must murder off his own bloodline to be "free." It also manages to eke out the flimsy revelation that Helen Lyle's resemblance to Caroline Sullivan is a result of being a descendant of the Sullivan-Robitaille bloodline, thereby attempting to replace Helen's white savior narrative with a new story regarding white passingness.

From the moment I heard about Nia DaCosta's 2021 *Candyman*, it felt like a vindication. Not a remake but, as its marketing touted, a "spiritual sequel," the film returns to Rose's original landscape and deletes the problematic, lesser sequels from the canon. My excitement soared the moment I saw the first trailer and recognized Vanessa Williams reprising the role of Anne-Marie McCoy, the resident of Cabrini-Green whose infant son was kidnapped by Candyman and saved from a fiery death by Helen Lyle, and pieced together that this story would focus on her now-adult son, Anthony. In under two minutes, I was overcome with the realization that this would be the first *Candyman* to properly center Blackness, to reckon with Black pain rather than simply use it for narrative purposes.

When I say that the original film was built on Black pain, I mean it quite literally. In 1985, a fifty-two-year-old Black woman named Ruthie Mae McCoy was murdered by two men who climbed into her apartment through the medicine cabinet behind her bathroom mirror that adjoined an empty neighboring unit. Because she had a history of mental illness, Ruthie was not believed when she called the police. The Grace Abbott Homes were a Chicago housing project very near Cabrini-Green. Ruthie Mae's story was gently folded into Rose's film—a woman tells Helen the story while she's interviewing residents for her thesis—and it's surely not a coincidence that the surname McCoy is assigned to Anne-Marie and her son Anthony. There are key scenes in *Candyman* where a hole behind a medicine cabinet leads into a labyrinth of walls and abandoned units. The reality of Ruthie Mae McCoy's murder and all of the systems that failed her are expanded on—and exploited—in Rose's film. After all, it is Helen who goes on to explore and document these graffitied tunnels that double as shrines to Candyman. Helen is often alone in these scenarios, a white blond woman glowing in the darkness of the haunted bowels of Cabrini-Green.

Like the original film, and in a contemporizing of the Gothic horror tradition, DaCosta's film casts the Cabrini-Green projects as a central character in the story. Set in the present, the Cabrini-Green towers have been torn down and replaced by expensive condominiums where Anthony McCoy (Yahya Abdul-Mateen II) lives with his girlfriend, Brianna Cartwright (Teyonah Parris). Brianna's name, of course, invokes Breonna Taylor; it will not be the last such evocative moment in the film. In an early scene, Brianna's out gay brother Troy and his white boyfriend, Grady, pay a visit to the apartment and, over wine, it is Troy who recounts the legend of Candyman, reminding them of where they stand. In a white-centered film, Troy would be a victim of the magical Negro trope, inorganically summarizing all the deets of the original film for those in the audience who don't know or don't remember. In DaCosta's hands, since most of the characters are Black, Troy is instead a magical *queer* character, perhaps a winking reminder that Clive Barker, the progenitor of Candyman, was queer (and lest we forget about Barker, there's a comically pompous art dealer named Clive who gets his at the end of the first act). Like an omniscient narrative voice, Troy knows all, and his retelling of the legend of Helen Lyle (albeit, a somewhat inaccurate retelling broken down over time) is presented to the audience in an eerily effective paper puppetry sequence.

What Troy doesn't know, though, is that in this *Candyman*, Daniel Robitaille isn't the only one—just the first. Candyman isn't a person but rather a whole hive of monsters made manifest from the pain of wronged Black men. This revelation is delivered by William Burke (Colman Domingo), a longtime resident of Cabrini-Green, who now lives among the sad remnants of the past, in ground-level projects that survived the tearing down of the concrete towers. It is Burke, left behind to witness and withstand gentrification and the erasure of Candyman's legacy, who will ultimately be responsible for resurrecting Candyman by orchestrating events that allow Anthony to step into the destiny Daniel Robitaille had instigated thirty years earlier, the one Helen set herself aflame to prevent.

In the final act, we'll learn that Anthony's mother, Anne-Marie, has spent the last thirty years trying to inoculate her son from any knowledge of Candyman or Helen Lyle, as she had previously seen firsthand that spreading his story only strengthens him. In the end, her efforts have failed, for Anthony's body has begun the process of transformation, skin charring as though he himself has been burned, his spiritual and physical reunion with Daniel Robitaille, his initiation into the hive nearing completion.

Though I should have anticipated it, the onscreen destruction of Cabrini-Green and its aftermath came as an emotional gut-punch for me. I remember back in the 1990s when all of the concrete housing projects in San Francisco, where I lived at the time, were condemned and pulled down. They were replaced with new, condominium-style projects that housed one-tenth as many residents. Given only a $2,000 voucher for first and last month's rent in the middle of the dot-com boom, Black folks were forced to leave San Francisco in droves. Tenant crime was cited as the predominant reason that concrete projects like the Geneva Towers in San Francisco were torn down, the reasoning that overcrowding, lack of sunshine, and a dismal quality were creating dissatisfaction which led to illegal activity. But many of the tenants, local public access[4] television producers,[5] and independent filmmakers[6] asserted that it had been in retaliation for the election of San Francisco's first Black mayor, Willie Brown.

My mother, brother, and I personally canvassed for Willie Brown, distributing door hangers in the concrete projects in the Western Addition. We were told that it was the first (and last) year a polling place would be set up in the building. Black folks came out in droves to vote for Willie Brown—and were later chased out of their homes by the San Francisco Redevelopment Agency.

The Geneva Towers came down in 1998. Cabrini-Green in Chicago was torn down in 2011. What remains of Cabrini-Green—the low houses that surround the tower, the ones from which Burke watches the world pass by—closely resembles housing projects near City College of San Francisco, and ones my aunt Gloria used to rent in Watts, in Southern California. Gloria was once robbed by some people who spray-painted YOU BEEN ROBED across her wall. I was about seven years old when it happened, but I remember well standing in Gloria's apartment looking at the writing on the wall, hearing the story, my parents explaining to me how Gloria had made a mistake in calling the police, that she'd then been harassed and punished for reporting the crime.

As a queer African American, as a nonbinary, gender-fluid Black femme, there are many things I share with the Black community, and many I share with the queer community. Sometimes the two intersect. In DaCosta's *Candyman*, queerness and Blackness converge as well. Burke, the left-behind Cabrini-Green resident who longs for Candyman's reawakening to set things right in a gentrified police state, and Troy, the queer, too-smart-for-this-shit Greek chorus who refuses to say Candyman's name the requisite five times, are the film's central storytellers. As a result, their otherwise marginalized voices are made important, given weight they otherwise wouldn't in white-centered, white-made narratives.

4. Will Roscoe, "Brief History of Bayview-Hunters Point," *FOUNDSF*. https://www.foundsf.org/index.php?title=Brief_History_of_Bayview-Hunters_Point.

5. Public Broadcasting Service, "The Fillmore: The Story," PBS. https://www.pbs.org/kqed/fillmore/learning/story.html.

6. Rachel Brahinsky, "Fillmore Revisited—How Redevelopment Tore through the Western Addition," *San Francisco Public Press*, May 5, 2021, https://www.sfpublicpress.org/fillmore-revisited-how-redevelopment-tore-through-the-western-addition/.

Centered and Seen

Because Troy exists predominantly as an envelope character—telling the story and connecting the dots—he lives, both literally and figuratively, in the safest place in the movie. The film does fall back onto some African American horror comedy film tropes in order to make Troy both palatable to straight audiences and relatable to Black filmgoers (Troy familiarly represents the Black man who says "hell no" to going into the basement in a white horror film), but DaCosta subtly deepens and complicates his character by placing him in a relationship with a white man. After all, Troy and his partner, Grady, do not live in shiny new condominiums in a dangerous neighborhood on land that used to be a part of Cabrini-Green. They live elsewhere, likely in a part of town where they can safely be an openly gay interracial couple. Proximity to whiteness keeps Troy safe.

After the screening of *Candyman*, Staci and I offered some friends a ride to the BART subway station. Naturally, on the way down we excitedly discussed the movie. Staci quickly registered themes of class, particularly involving Anthony and Brianna's detachment from their roots. Fey noted class issues similar to those of Jordan Peele's 2019 film *Us*, but fey did not pick up on *Candyman*'s emphasis on the impostor syndrome[7] that African Americans experience. I had to explain to Staci and my friends that the narrative isn't just about class and how it hits African Americans. Sure, that's part of it. But another part of it is how people like Anthony and Brianna have feelings of community betrayal related to impostor syndrome, how they've been forced to neglect the communities they came from in order to advance and progress. They are living on hallowed Cabrini-Green land, but as well-to-do, artistic Black millennials who must finely thread the needle between the past and the present. But a larger, more gaping

7. Pauline Rose Clance and Suzanne Imes, "The Imposter Phenomenon in High Achieving Women: Dynamics and Therapeutic Intervention," *Psychotherapy Theory, Research and Practice* 15, no. 3 (Fall 1978).

part of the narrative is how Black pain gets mined and milked repeatedly to humanize Black folks in non-Black eyes.

Burke, our other storyteller, who does not have a safe existence outside of what's left of Cabrini-Green, brings that message home in literally every scene he is in, reminding us all of how the now-villainous Candymen all started out as innocents. Innocents who were routinely made responsible for their own victimization by the oppressor. The ghost town version of Cabrini-Green Burke occupies is a symbol of the erasure of Black communities in the name of government assistance. And so, the stories about what happened to the Candymen are no longer just revenge porn; they are a reminder that portrayals of Black pain are necessary to humanize the subject. Still, DaCosta's film laments the cost of Candyman's continuance—the inevitable loss of more Black life—and acknowledges that it is one too great to make it an even trade.

IT'S NOVEMBER, three months after the *Candyman* screening, and Staci and I are attending another reunion: the memorial service for my aunt Gloria, who passed away quietly in her home in Castaic, California. The event, held in a ballroom at the Grand Hotel in Long Beach, takes place on Gloria's birthday, the day before Thanksgiving.

Staci and I hold hands as we walk in together, each of us clad in an ankle-length black dress. Fey wears practical square-heeled black leather boots, but I've chosen my glittery purple knee-high platforms. My hair, in two perfect Afro-puffs, is currently half-purple, half-red. As we enter, it quickly dawns on me that I have not seen most of the people in the room since my own mother's memorial in 2019, since before the pandemic that indiscriminately separated our communities from one another, created distance among people who had fought so hard to maintain connection. I immediately greet and console my cousin Damon, who has organized the event. There is an open bar, a banquet, and an elaborate birthday cake. As I take it all in, the lengths to which Damon and the rest of the family have gone to make this day a celebration of life rather than a dwelling on death, I'm reminded how so often Black pain can be alleviated by the presence of Black joy.

Later, my cousin Coco starts a line dance, so of course a whole lot of us jump up and join in. Before we know it, we are all bumping our hips and doing the slide. My aunt Gloria loved to dance, and so do her children, and her grandchildren, and her great-grandchildren. When I get up to dance, Staci, one of only two white people in the entire room, leaps out of eir seat and joins me and my family without hesitation. Once we center ourselves on the dance floor, my thirteen-year-old cousin and their friend approach me and Staci, and shyly ask us what our pronouns are.

"Mine are fey/fem/fear, or e/em/eir, or be/bim/bos," Staci explains with a little curtsy.

"Mine are ze/hir, and they/them," I add with a smile.

"Mine are they/them and she/her," my cousin replies gently, returning Staci's curtsy. Clearly elated at having shared this information, they excitedly grab their friend's hand and run back onto the dance floor.

Through the night, Staci and I line dance, couple dance. We are a natural part of the fam-bam and, like *Candyman*'s Troy and his love Grady, we glitter, and we belong.

Blood, Actually

GRANT SUTTON

Friday the 13th, Part II

HIS FAVORITE SWIMMING spot is a small beach on Black Creek in Mississippi's DeSoto National Forest. It's the kind of day a wise-cracking, gum-smacking movie character would cheerfully compare to the start of a horror movie, irony thick as Karo syrup. The county is named for Nathaniel Bedford Forrest, the founder of the Ku Klux Klan. We do not discuss this trivia.

When we arrive, we find an unoccupied pickup truck on the side of the road. Probably just someone out canoeing. Gunshots fire in the distance. The sound cuts between us. It could be fifty feet away, maybe a mile. Is it hunting season? The remainder of a dead squirrel flanks the sandy path, tufted fur and teeth but missing a tail.

It looks so much like where I grew up on the Cape Fear River in North Carolina. It's so stereotypically Southern that it almost feels like a movie set. The relative comfort and tolerance of New Orleans, where we both live, does not extend here, and authorities in places like this would be just as likely to bash our brains in as the imaginary Super Predator Redneck I fear is following us. Even at forty, kissing a man outside the privacy of my home or a gay bar is still transgressive, perhaps worthy of punishment.

His name is Alex, and he is an archaeologist. He travels constantly, and when he comes back he brings me gifts: a piece of petrified wood from Big Bend; coffee from Puerto Rico; a rusted betel nut knife and blanket from India, where he unearthed a crashed plane from World War II in the Himalayas. He is not afraid of dying. He can't wait for his body to break down, to be reduced to ejaculations of spores.

Blood, Actually

He is passionate about historic preservation, breaking and entering, and my cock.

His most recent assignment is to exhume a mass grave of children discovered in a rural part of Puerto Rico. There's been some conflict, both inner and overt, about whether the Puerto Rican team should be handling it alone without the aid of interlopers from the continental United States. When he finds an arrowhead or piece of pottery or a skull fragment, he never slips it into his pocket the way that I would. It belongs to the land, to the dead.

On our first date we met in City Park under the hulking live oak trees, their branches covered in outrageous amounts of Spanish moss, like girthy arms with tacky bracelets. We met just before midnight, in the peristyle, and split a six-pack before he grinned at me. A tiny jewel glued to his bicuspid flashed like a warning light. He overwhelmed me like a fever, and in my haze I agreed to break into a nearby cemetery with him. We leaned against a mausoleum and made out like goth teenagers.

Alex tells me he discovered Black Creek with a former lover who is also a former lover of mine. I do not ask follow-up questions.

"The rot clings to you if you swim too long," he warns as we survey the water.

In my youth, I swam in creepy lakes and rivers just like this one. My eyes were always trained on the shoreline. Every fish flopping or tree branch falling into the water frightened me then, as it does now. I am always wondering—who could be watching us from the trees? With a lover, I am even more aware of every sound, every movement bringing me just enough discomfort that I cannot relax: *if someone is watching and something happens, people will say I had it coming.* I know I will wake up at 4 a.m. in a sweat, taking inventory of all the reasons my eventual murder will be my fault: I should have worn a more modest bathing suit; I should have "butched" it up more; I should not have lain so close to him on the worn painter's tarp I brought for our picnic. Did

I arrange the pink lady apples and the perfect muffuletta too artfully? Even my apple choice feels preposterously gay. This lead blanket of worry, crushing me. Self-censure familiar as sunburn.

Now he's reading Foucault's *History of Sexuality, Part 1*, the bright pink edition, a spot of contrast to our earthy surroundings. I want to impress him. I tell him about the course I took in college dedicated to Foucault, and how my final term paper had discussed our university grounds as a panopticon. As I drone on about Bentham's structure—an inward-facing circular prison with a central watchtower that made every prisoner feel on display whether a guard occupied the tower or not—he pulls off my shorts. Goosebumps from excitement and shoulders hiked as I feel eyes on us, staring out of the woods.

WHEN MY MOTHER and father were still in love, we lived on the marshlands of the Intracoastal Waterway, and you could smell the sea and watch the buoys that marked our crab pots bob like severed heads in inky water. I was working up the nerve to check the pots on my own one day, even though I was scared of the crabs they imprisoned, when I heard my mother scream "Cottonmouth!" from the deck. Terrified, I sprinted back toward the house. Our handsome collegiate gardener, my first crush, was trimming the azalea bushes in the front yard, but he grabbed a shovel and made his way to the back, where danger lay coiled, head shaped like an arrow, ready to strike. The sliding glass door framed him, and I enjoyed the long, uninterrupted view of him wearing not much more than work boots, a pair of tight jeans, and a thin layer of sweat. He looked just like Mark, the counselor from *Friday the 13th, Part II*. In one decisive motion, like Zeus hurling a thunderbolt, my hero severed the snake in two. Wiping the sweat from his brow with one gloved hand, he scooped the pieces into a garbage bag, and peace was restored. I wanted to thank him, to give him a kiss for his gallantry, but I resisted.

Blood, Actually

When my parents divorced, we moved to my mother's home: a twist in the road, a clearing between tobacco and cotton fields. There were more snakes, no father, and no Mark to save us. Instead of counting out daffodil bulbs for her garden, she now counted her fears about all the ways she was afraid to ruin us. I collected her fears like she collected our baby teeth in her jewelry box: LSD-laced Cracker Jack tattoos, suffocating to death in a refrigerator, kidnapping, home invasion, the constant threat of poverty. I learned to write the perfect thank-you note, to carry a pocket knife, a clean white handkerchief in case I encountered a crying woman, and ChapStick (always plain, never cherry).

When I was seven, I came out to our neighbor, who told my mom, who confronted me. I denied it, pretending I didn't know what she meant. I planned to hang myself from the banister with my white karate belt.

Whatever happened next is chained to the bottom of my memory, struggling to breathe, waiting to resurface. Everything fades to black.

EXT. CAMP CRYSTAL LAKE — EVENING

The screen door slams shut just as the rain begins to pummel the camp. Tiny ricochets turn to a constant roar as Mark, the beautiful brunette counselor in a wheelchair, glides down the ramp to search for Vickie, who wanted to change before they went off together to make love in an empty cabin. As she runs around in the rain in her brown satin sex panties, Mark starts to worry: What is taking her so long? Menacing music scores the moment that the machete appears from nowhere, slicing into his gorgeous face, the force of the blow so powerful that it sends him flying backward down not one but two flights of stairs, the latter impossibly long, descending into nothing. The screen freezes on the back of his head with the machete lodged in the front. Flash to white. Smash cut to the next teen sacrifice.

THE MURDER OF Mark, played by Tom McBride in *Friday the 13th, Part II*, an out gay actor and self-described "A-List Gay" who went on to die of an AIDS-related illness in New York City, was not the first time I learned that Sex = Death. On the way to school one day, my mother handed me and each of my brothers our own copies of *People* with Kimberly Bergalis on the cover. The photo of the thin sorority girl who'd allegedly contracted HIV from her homosexual dentist, David Acer, bore the title "The Dentist and the Patient: AN AIDS MYSTERY." My mother wanted each of us to read it so we could talk about it as a family. The article discussed how Kimberly's mother worked with patients living with HIV and AIDS in a Florida clinic and recognized the hollow cheeks as a telltale sign that something was wrong with her daughter. No one knew how she could have contracted it because she claimed to be a virgin waiting for marriage, and she didn't use intravenous drugs. The only possibility: her homosexual dentist must have intentionally infected his patients as an act of violence and rage motivated by his own impending death. This was never proven.

At this point, my sweet fantasy of marrying a Mark of my own and living together forever in a snake-free castle decayed into the tobacco fields we were passing on the way home. Whether the Bergalis family meant to ignite this gay panic or not, gay men were ripped from the shadows and elevated to public enemy. The word *AIDS* slashed across all the headlines, the bold red letters made every trip to the grocery store a test of endurance, avoidance. News programs showed Lady Diana visiting patients living with AIDS and all I could see was myself, my skeleton protruding through my thin skin, eyes sunken in, reaching for her hand. People applauded her for touching the patients and treating them like human beings as if she'd performed a feat of strength. President Reagan didn't even acknowledge HIV/AIDS for six years, and only because Elizabeth Taylor manipulated him into it. The "personal responsibility" doctrine of the Reagan era taught Americans that fault lay with gay men and their enablers, and AIDS was a just cure for their existence. Nancy Reagan stood by in her bloodred dresses, red as an AIDS ribbon, red as gore. Often the evening news featured our United States senator Jesse Helms, my mother's favorite politician, suggesting that people with HIV should be quarantined, or William F. Buckley calling for gay men to be identified and tattooed on the buttocks, and it taught me to hide my feelings. Shame and fear gripped my shoulders, pulling me into a solitary hell. I would escape to my room, where I created elaborate versions of ways I would eventually die when it was my turn. Gay blood must be toxic, and I visualized it clogging my veins like black Jell-O.

At bedtime, every single night, I petitioned Jesus not to let me die of AIDS. Sleep felt like a trapdoor for death, a time for all of my worst fears to creep in. Sometimes, in the darkness, I counted my heartbeats and wondered how many I had left. I lay awake thinking about my abdominal cavity, a butcher shop case of throbbing organs writhing together. I categorized each spasm, waiting for my insides to turn on one another, and then on me. I obsessively counted the number of times I might see my family members again in my lifetime, feeling guilty for wanting to run away from them all, dreading the day my mother would acknowledge my homosexuality and condemn me, or when my pediatrician would out me by diagnosing me with HIV. I would brainstorm escape plans to New York, tracing the route I'd walk in an imaginary atlas. I wrote down lies in my diary with the flimsy lock to throw my mom off my path (I don't think she ever read it). The only way to keep the trapdoor sealed was by staying up late reading V. C. Andrews novels about incest, madness, and damask with titles like *If There Be Thorns, Dark Angel, Fallen Hearts*. And when I was older, I watched horror movies.

I started with *Nightmare on Elm Street, Halloween, Texas Chainsaw Massacre*. I'd convince my mom or dad to let me rent whatever I wanted. They were too guilty or too tired to object to my selections. Entering the horror movie section at Videomax, decorated with fiberglass and papier-mâché Dracula and Frankenstein's monster and the

Mummy, felt like the first exercise in bravery. Next came looking at the scary art on the box covers, then reading the descriptions. Every tiny step felt like training for the fear that I was learning to live with, incremental poisoning to gain immunity.

Each villain was deformed, disfigured by scars, and masked. Often these figures were the objects of early shame for some disability outside their control. Pushed to the fringes, they became experts in the behavior of their victims. There was something about the simplicity of *Friday the 13th* that especially appealed to me. In the original film, Jason's mother is the killer. It opens by putting the audience into Ms. Voorhees's point of view as she kills trysting counselors in the boathouse. Grief-stricken and unhinged, she attempted to assuage her grief about the accidental drowning of her son by murdering any new counselors who wanted to reopen Camp Crystal Lake. In her mind, all of the teens deserve their grisly fate—they should know better. After his mother is murdered by Alice at the end of the first film, Jason Voorhees takes over the blood feud, avenging her death. Armed with his relentless silence and tenacity and a white hockey mask, broad and pocked like the surface of the moon, he dispatches his victims, one or two at a time.

As I got braver, I watched all of the *Friday the 13th* films. Rather, I studied them. I memorized the names of the actors, the characters, and all of the creative ways that Jason would kill people. If I focused on the trivia long enough, I could escape the true horror that kept me awake at night. He has the most kills of any slasher series, and he lives in a dirty shed in the woods near "Camp Blood" (except when he went to Manhattan on a shitty cruise ship and when he went to space and when he went to hell) so creativity is necessary. Among Jason's improvisational weapon choices: a pitchfork, an RV wall, a space anchor, an electrical box, a tent stake, a noisemaker, a trimmer with saw blade attachment, a flaming machete, a screwdriver, a tree pruner, a heroin needle, a fire poker, a wrench, a harpoon, a radio antenna, a scythe, a liquor bottle, a claw hammer, a fence post, a spaceship hull breach, a camper-filled sleeping bag, an oil drum filled with trash water, hot stones from a sauna, a deep fryer, a bone saw, a signpost.

Slasher films gave me a way to order the violence and death that occupied most of my attention. My toxic blood seemed less terrifying when I saw fake blood spilled on screen, knowing that it was probably chocolate sauce, corn syrup, or pixelated gore. If the blood was fake, then maybe, just maybe, all of reality was fabricated, and knives and ice picks always retract, bullets are always blanks, and no one is ever murdered by a machete-wielding killer. No one is ever really harmed. Anxiety is temporarily relieved as the credits roll, a vulgar catharsis. When real fear creeps back in, just rewind the film and start again.

But my research, like my mind, eventually turned in on itself. Even on film sets, I learned, people were vulnerable. Inescapable reality comes for everyone. Brandon Lee died in Wilmington, my hometown, on the set of *The Crow* when someone mistakenly loaded a broken blank in the gun's chamber. He was brought to the hospital on the same day my grandmother was there recovering from a fall, the same hospital where I was born. A teacher from our local high school was attacked in a Winn-Dixie parking lot by a man who'd hidden along the banks of the Cape Fear, carrying a rusty dull machete. The teacher survived the attack, only to die from a blood infection. Danger was just out of sight, but it always left a bloody trail.

Rewind the film. Start again. Go to Crystal Lake in your mind.

THE SUN DESCENDS, and the breeze cools. I can see the candlestick tattoo on Alex's abdomen tighten from the shift in temperature, and I hold him closer to warm him. When we are apart, his tattoos shrink and grow and rotate and rearrange in my memory. I want to keep a field guide, so I don't forget them, but that seems a little stalkerish.

A low roar begins miles away and creeps toward us. Our eyes widen and we wait for what the noise will bring. A monster? An apocalypse? It surges forward then dissipates as it reaches us, shaking the trees and sending a swirl of dead leaves to encircle us like something out of a fairy tale. They drift into the sand and the river to continue their cycle of decay. Bare limbs scratch the sky as we embrace, the familiar comfort of him pressed into me cut with the feeling of being watched. That fear still slices through me when a man tries to hold my hand on the street. Despite my lurking anxiety, we spend a half hour on our knees, kissing on Black Creek Beach. We toy with the idea of doing more, and we move into the woods for more privacy, entering the area where I sense invisible watchers hunting us. He lays me down, the pine needles pricking my skin, the layers of dead forest cut his hands as he climbs on top of me.

THERE'S A SCENE IN *Friday the 13th, Part II*, when a couple of counselors are boning in a bunk bed and just as the man is about to climax, the woman beneath him sees Jason in the doorway but fails to roll her lover off in time to prevent being speared together, forever locked in a bloody embrace. Instead of losing myself in the moment, kissing this man, I am looking over his shoulder, waiting for a rod to penetrate us both.

Jason: the ultimate Power Top.

This will be how it ends.

YOU MIGHT THINK that once you've seen one *Friday the 13th*, you've seen them all. But you would be incorrect. The finer points distinguishing each film may seem negligible to a layperson. The story is told repeatedly, repetitively, almost obsessively, every time. A group of attractive teenagers arrives at a reopened summer camp, no trace of the murders from the previous summer. Repainted cabins flank the lake, which seems to be impossibly high in naturally occurring lithium, given the chipper attitudes of each fresh set of victims. The endlessly refreshed archetypes are all guilty of something outside of their control. There's always the funny one, the hot one, the stoner, the jock, the nerd, the biker, the clown—and they all want to get laid. Except for the Final Girl.

Everyone recognizes the Final Girl. The term is so commonly used that if you use it around even a moderate horror fan, you might see their eyes roll back in their heads. The Final Girl is beautiful—not too beautiful—smart, funny, charming, wholesome. But she's often aloof or possesses some skill or ability or insight that ends up saving her in the end. Something she may or may not value about herself. She is the ideal victim. Does anyone want to be the Final Girl more than the young closeted queer? Brimming with unseen inner power, waiting to demonstrate her strength.

During the last act of each film, the Final Girl and Jason lock into a grisly pas de deux. Each makes their move, struggling for primacy. Each fulfills their function. The coda is almost always his unmasking, revealing the true, repulsive, unlovable face beneath the mask. But by enduring this horrific spectacle, her previous sense of safety is permanently annihilated. Once a part of the crowd, now permanently apart from the crowd, she will always be isolated by this experience, and now she must wear the mask. Her friends are all gone, and she must learn to live knowing that they are gone forever, victims of an unconscionable act of violence for which no one could prepare.

AS AN ADULT, I live in a great city. When I started taking PrEP, I had to mourn my past as I realized how much the fear of contracting HIV had affected all of my intimate partnerships, my sex life, and my self-perception. HIV and AIDS permanently shaped me. Now, I am one of the oldest participants enrolled in a groundbreaking medical study, developing an injectable prophylactic medication to prevent the spread. Now, HIV and AIDS are manageable conditions for those with access to care. Here in the Gulf, seroconversion rates are still alarmingly high, seeking care still stigmatized. I struggle to locate and connect with the few elders from the generation most decimated. How can the younger queers I love understand what it was like? Is it better that they do not? I am grateful they are spared the horror.

As it turns out, being raised in a homophobic, misogynistic, racist culture forces you to behave in sociopathic ways. Nobody wants to be the poor, disfigured boy who grows up to be a serial killer. Even though I want to be a Final Girl, I'm more of a Jason Voorhees. They are both survivalists in their own ways, but I've used my improvised skills to hurt people deeply, to hide from my pain. My tongue is my machete. I can be just as nimble and industrious, constantly scanning the room for threats or potential lovers, sometimes treating both as opponents as they surface. I used to hunt in gay bars or gay.com, the library stacks in college, and now I hunt in Scruff profiles that showcase floating torsos and feet and round (and not so round) asses, trapped in orderly, grid-like graveyard plots. I built a persona out of pain. But the world has changed. Now that I live somewhere more tolerant and I have more sexual freedom, what do I do with my arsenal and killer instinct? Does Jason retire when he gets sick of the murder business? Does he just want privacy at Crystal Lake? Does he murder so he can finally take his mask off and be alone in his murder shed with his mother's severed, screaming head?

Maybe he's just like me, bad at ending things, more comfortable being alone and pretending to be impenetrable.

ON THE WALK back to the car, Alex holds my hand and occasionally stops to kiss me. I am ashamed of the control my fear still wields over me. I wish I was braver. That night, I confess that I was scared for much of the day. He reciprocates, telling me that even though he loves that spot, it isn't always safe. A group of his queerdo femme friends had asked him where they should go for a long weekend in the woods. He drew them a map, marking all the relevant signposts and giving them the coordinates, even going so far as to lend them his canoe and describing when to take the path to the left, to go past the place where the willows bend. They hiked in, following all of his instructions to the letter, leaving the pistol in the VW Vanagon. One of them argued that the gun made them feel safer, the other said it made them feel less safe. As night fell, and they lit a fire and began to get stoned and drunk and laugh, the noises began, coming from all around them. It was way too loud to believe that it was just the hissing of sap boiling out of the wet pieces of firewood they'd collected. When the whispers turned to jeers and taunts, they hid inside their tent. No one slept at all that night. The voices stopped around dawn, and his friends fled back to New Orleans, leaving their gear behind. He apologized for not mentioning it before. He didn't want to scare me.

Part IV

WHATEVER YOU DO

DON'T FALL ASLEEP

The Trail of His Flames

TUCKER LIEBERMAN

A Nightmare on Elm Street

IN THE 1980s sitcom *Just the Ten of Us*, Heather Langenkamp played a pious Catholic teenager, the eldest of eight children. An avid watcher of the show, I didn't know she was already more famous for her role in *A Nightmare on Elm Street*, which had come out in 1984, when I was just a preschooler. I wouldn't see *Elm Street* until the midnineties, when I was closer in age to the iconic horror hero Langenkamp portrayed: Nancy Thompson.

Back then, I had the same first name as Langenkamp, and so I identified with her in that small, surface way. Unlike her character on *Just the Ten of Us*, my family was Jewish, my father was a corporate lawyer rather than a sports coach, and, at the time, I had only one sibling. The world of her Nancy character on *Elm Street* made more sense to me. Nancy inhabited a surreal, dystopian version of quiet, majority-white suburbs with '80s telephones, decor, clothes, and cars. Nancy and I lived in terror of our own imaginations, forces we couldn't control. She was taking a crash course in managing nightmares because she was in a horror movie, and I watched horror movies because they mirrored and interrogated the emotional infrastructure in my dreams. She was more willowy, more brave. She would show me how to wage spiritual warfare against my nightmares of pod people and zombies.

The glitch in looking up to Nancy—which you know if you've seen the film—is that she doesn't win. She does everything right and fights off the monster. Yet, in the final scene, when it seems she's resurrected the murder victims by waking up from her nightmare, the monster reappears and seizes them all again. There wasn't ever a way for her to win. The message, perhaps, is that we might not be able to fight the monster after all, which is what makes the original *Elm Street* so scary.

Hit fast-forward a few frames: I did not entirely identify with Nancy insofar as I did not feel like a girl. In 1998, my senior year of high school, I started testosterone injections and had surgery to reshape my chest. That story is fairly "by the book," the book in question being the fourth version of the American Psychiatric Association's *Diagnostic and Statistical Manual of Mental Disorders*, according to which I was diagnosed with "gender identity disorder." In 2007, I married a gay cisgender man; this marriage lasted only a few months, for highly unpleasant reasons outside my control.

In 2015, I had another surgery to reshape my crotch. Soon after, at thirty-five years old, I fell out with a good friend who I'd known all those intervening years. He was one of the few people who knew about my surgery in 2015, and moreover, he comprehended how it worked physically and what it meant to me. Suddenly he was gone from my life. I couldn't sleep, I couldn't swallow food. I began to exercise compulsively and drink huge amounts of water. I lost weight unintentionally, and my thinking was disordered. It is hard to lose a friendship. Friendships that travel along the axis of a certain queerness might be especially hard to lose because it is through each other that we come to know ourselves.

After several months of emergency-level anxiety—tied to my internal narrative about the loss of the friendship—I asked my doctor for a pill. I received Klonopin, which is a benzo tranquilizer. For three weeks, the nightly pill put me to sleep, but I awoke each morning to even worse anxiety. Most alarmingly, while on Klonopin, I began to hallucinate setting myself on fire. *Hallucinate* may not even be quite the right word, as other people surely have hallucinations more potent and persuasive than mine, but what then should I call it? How to label things seen-but-not-seen? How to distinguish the sense of watching a movie from watching something in the real world?

When I stopped taking the pill, the fire hallucinations, too, immediately vanished. They had occurred every fifteen minutes during waking hours, so about a thousand times in all. Since I still had anxiety, I tried a different pill: Trazodone, an antidepressant. That pill was a dream. A *good* dream. It got me to sleep at night, and it also helped smooth out my distress during the day. I took that for six months. Once my feelings became a little more manageable, I stopped that medication too.

I want to talk about what precipitated the friendship loss that so deeply impacted my mental health, yet I am loath to offer identifying details or discuss things not mine to discuss. This friend and I never hashed out "what happened," so my information and perspective remain limited. Fortunately, there are other stories we can step into in order to "tell" our own. So, instead, I am going to tell you the story—well, a version of the story—of how Nancy faced Freddy.

AS NANCY, DAY 1

It's the opening scene of the movie and I am Nancy, walking to school with my boyfriend, Glen, who lives across the street from me. My friend Tina joins us, while her aggressive suitor, Rod, trails behind. Glen and I agree to stay at Tina's house overnight while her mother is away because she's been having nightmares. Later, at Tina's house, she and I realize we've been having the same dream: a man with fingernails "more like fingerknives." Rod surprises us all and drags Tina to the bedroom like the jerk he is.

That night, the man with the fingerknives murders Tina in her dream. Rod wakes up just as her invisible attacker drags her across her bedroom ceiling against gravity and slashes her torso with four invisible razors. When Glen and I rush to the bedroom, we find Rod standing over Tina's body. When Tina dies in her dream, she dies in reality.

REFLECTIONS

In some obscure way that has yet to be revealed, Nancy, Glen, Tina, and Rod were *all* at fault: the monster came out of their collective nightmare. And yet there is nothing obvious they could have done differently.

It reminds me of the day something popped out of the shadows and changed everything for me. During the summer of 2015, this friend I'd known for nearly two decades was staying in my house and behaving oddly. I decided to give him some space for the weekend and take a much-needed retreat for myself, so I left Boston on a Thursday and drove three hours alone to pitch my tent in the Vermont woods, planning to enjoy my retreat until Sunday night. There was little cell-tower reception where I was going, and I'd forgotten a charger. Nonetheless, the phone let me retrieve an important voicemail. My friend's alarmed brother was turning to me as someone he hoped could possibly do a welfare check on him and help him out. This was not normal. I didn't know his family, and they had never contacted me before. My phone couldn't return the communication from the woods. Since I couldn't advise my friend's brother that I was unavailable, I left the woods a bit earlier than planned and drove back three hours to make sure my friend was all right.

He was still there in my house. My concern was illegible to him, at least in his mental state. He assumed that I, along with his family, was against him somehow. He remained in my house but would not speak to me. Within two days, without his collaboration and without even warning him, I arranged for him to go to a psychiatric hospital, where I told the truth to the doctors about what was going on. They agreed that he needed to be held for a while. This marked the end of our friendship.

It was also the end of the world for me as far as my emotional hydraulics were concerned. For the next year, for me, our disagreeable confrontation was always-happening-again in an "eternal now," and I struggled to understand why I could not unbuckle from the nightmare. My brain melted and took years to reshape itself into something useful again. Yet, as morally filthy as it felt to put a friend in the hospital and as painful as the consequences felt, I still lack the creativity to imagine an alternate solution for this exact scenario. Here is part of the problem: When we are in a sticky spot, we can tell the whole truth, lie, or elegantly obscure certain details, but, whatever route we choose, it does not change the baseline situation. *Something bad is happening,* and we may be traumatized no matter what response we choose. Sometimes monsters jump out of the closet and all we can do is barge through escape routes we will later regret. I often think about how I drove home from work during lunch hour, put my friend in the hospital, and drove back to work. It was a private apocalypse, and yet it was unmentionable, and I was expected back at the office. The way the world isn't ready to hear the terrible weirdness of our catastrophes is part of the trauma.

In *A Nightmare on Elm Street,* some parts of Nancy's life seem normal. She lives in a large, well-kept house with her mother; her father has moved out, but she still sees him frequently. Her boyfriend, Glen, can easily climb up the rose trellis to her bedroom to visit her, which is an arrangement they both like. Yet we start to get the sense that Nancy's idyllic, suburban life is itself a nightmare. Despite the overnight murder of Tina, school has not been canceled.

AS NANCY, DAY 2

Mom tries to persuade me against going to school—not so much because I saw Tina with her belly slashed open but because I'm tired. (Glen, who didn't come to the police station with me, will later claim he slept "like a rock.")

Dad, a Sergeant at that precinct, however, lets me walk to school so he can use me as a decoy to attract Rod, who's now the murder suspect. Indeed, Rod—in his usual sociopathic way of initiating conversation— jumps me and drags me into the woods, pleading with me to believe in his innocence. The cops arrest Rod, and Dad lets me continue on my way to school.

I nod off during a Shakespeare lecture as the teacher drones on about gravediggers and nightmares. Next thing I know, I'm dreaming about Tina. The fingerknives murderer corners me in my dream, and I burn myself deliberately on some hot pipes to jolt myself out of the nightmare. I wake up screaming in the middle of Shakespeare. The teacher dismisses me on compassionate grounds, but warns me, "You'll need a hall pass," before ordering the other students: "Back to work."

I notice the burn on my skin is real. I've brought it back from my nightmare.

At the police station, I'm allowed to speak to Rod privately through the bars of his cell. Rod mentions having had the nightmare, and I'm now sure that Fingerknives killed Tina and is coming for Rod too.

Later, at home, I fall asleep in the bathtub, and the monster appears and nearly drowns me. I find Stay Awake pills in the medicine cabinet. I also wish to fall asleep to explore my dream, which is contradictory, and I don't know what I'd do if I found the monster.

With Glen agreeing to stand guard, I fall asleep easily. In my dream, Fingerknives walks *through* the bars into Rod's jail cell, taunting me. He chases me home, and we wrestle in my bedroom until my alarm goes off, saving my life (a useful backup, as Glen had fallen asleep).

Was my dream prescient? Glen and I run to the police station. Dad disapproves and delays. When we reach Rod, he's dead in his cell of apparent suicide.

REFLECTIONS

Rod's death is the exact midpoint of the film. By now, we know something is wrong not just with Nancy's nightmares but with her waking life. Her parents are ethically and psychologically dysfunctional. Her public school administration is on another planet. Her boyfriend is more oblivious than most teenagers. There is something wrong with the whole town. We might start to wonder if her "waking life" might be another layer of the same nightmare.

There was a time in my life, right after the incident with my friend, when I would have done anything to hit rewind and record a different outcome. I mentally replayed the events of that day on infinite repeat. I wanted the chance to undo, to edit, to undo edit. I didn't know exactly *what* I ought to have done, but I wanted to try again. I emphasize that I "would have done anything" in my present—that is, I would have sacrificed a lot—to be granted the opportunity to change the past.

I went to work as if everything felt normal when it definitely did not. I took pills to keep myself regulated even though I wasn't sure exactly what the pills should or could do. The first type of pill, Klonopin, caused me to hallucinate, and I persisted in habits that weren't helping. (The chief unhelpful habit was taking that pill. Others were: continuing at a stressful job, scribbling invective against imaginary demons in my work notebook, and spending evenings and weekends sprinting in circles around the neighborhood.)

I couldn't really talk to anyone about this. Our world sets itself up so that we do not understand each other, and the suburbs throw their own veil over the "midlife crisis" or "nervous breakdown." A waking nightmare: The system is misbehaving and will never own its shit. If I am not understood, how can I understand myself? If I don't understand others, what do I give and receive? I couldn't pierce the membrane of ignorance and isolation. Even if I had, where would I have been? Where are we when we "come out"?

It can always get weirder. The first half of *Nightmare on Elm Street* just establishes the premise. It could have gone in a number of directions. The second half of the film, unrolling across Days 3 through 6, detaches itself from comprehensibility.

AS NANCY, DAY 3

The next morning, we put Rod in the ground. The funeral is a small affair. My parents and a dozen people unknown to me attend; Glen and I are his only classmates present. The priest implies that Rod deserved to die by suicide for killing Tina.

After the service, I tell Dad, "The killer's still loose, you know." He seems curious for the first time, so I describe the killer's burned face, his clothing, the murder weapon. But Dad treats me like a rambling toddler.

Mom, more helpfully, drives me to a sleep disorder clinic. The young doctor admits that dreams are poorly understood. He tapes electrodes to my forehead to quantify my sleep activity.

The EEG shows my dream starting off as a 3. A nightmare, in the doctor's words, might be "5 or 6." As I thrash, the EEG readout jumps to 30.

I find Fingerknives in this dream, of course, and this time I grab his hat. I am still holding it when I wake up.

3. "5 or 6." 30.

The last number validates my problem, but I receive no diagnosis and no further treatment, just a bandage on my arm—and the nightmare monster's hat that I get to take home like an arcade prize.

REFLECTIONS

No funeral for Tina? No autopsy for Rod?

How hard it is to talk about the loss: to acknowledge *that* it happened and to find out what *really* happened. I kept my friend's hand-me-downs, as if by wearing them he were still with me. But he was not. He left my house without an autopsy. A doctor gave me a pill to put me to sleep, and, if I'd been hooked up to a nightmare EEG detector, I would have burst 30.

AS NANCY: THE CELLAR MONOLOGUE

His name is written in the hatband: Fred Krueger.

Mom tells me to trust her. She swears I'm crazy. She admits recognizing Fred Krueger's name but assures me he's dead.

I go for a walk with Glen, who admits he no longer sleeps, yet he offers a strategy to combat fear: turn my back on the dream monster. "Take away its energy and it disappears," he tells me. I don't tell him I've learned the monster's name.

Returning home, I'm furious to see that my mother has installed security bars on every window. She and I go down into the unfinished cellar for a chat. You know, where normal families have normal talks. Here's where things get *really* weird.

Fred Krueger, Mom begins, "was a filthy child murderer who killed at least 20 kids in the neighborhood." He was arrested but was freed on a technicality. When he returned to the murder site, the parents took matters into their own hands. "We took gasoline, poured it all around the place and made a trail of it out the door, then lit the whole thing up and watched it burn . . . He's dead, honey, because Mommy killed him." She shows me gloves with long blades attached like claws: "I even took his knives." They're exactly what I've seen in my dreams. She's stored them in the cellar all my life.

REFLECTIONS

Nothing about this makes sense.

Nancy's mother recently assured her that Fred Krueger couldn't hurt her because he was *dead*, yet then she installed window bars to protect against him. More significantly, the backstory doesn't make sense. A serial killer eliminated two dozen kids in the same neighborhood, and families continued to live there? The suspect was freed on a technicality and was allowed to return to and hang out at the same abandoned site where he'd committed the murders? He, in turn, was executed extrajudicially and no one was penalized for that? Nancy's mother can't remember exactly how many children were murdered? Nancy never heard this story from her mother or anyone else in the neighborhood, despite her neighborhood missing two dozen kids who would have been about her own age? Her parents would have been young when this happened (the actors who play them are only nineteen and twenty-eight years older, respectively, than Langenkamp), but they would remember. At least now we understand better why her school administrators are unfazed by losing Tina and Rod on consecutive days—this amount of child death is normal for this town. But why wasn't Nancy's father, the cop, interested in the familiar, distinctive wounds on Tina's body: Four knives like claws? And the murder weapon that her mother keeps—not only is this a bizarre souvenir but how did she retrieve it while incinerating Krueger's living quarters?

We still don't know what Krueger wants. How old were the two dozen "kids" he murdered? This is not just a point of curiosity. We need to know why Krueger has waited so long to pursue Nancy and her friends. Was he waiting for them to reach his preferred age for victims?

MY CELLAR STORY

Queerness is a narrative sitting askew, moving uncannily, resisting taxonomy. It's not a fixed point in space-time. Concretely and in the narrowest sense, "queer" is a sexual label meaning gay or bi, and sometimes it's also about gender. More expansively, it means socially marginalized or conceptually slippery, sometimes in ways apart from sexuality and gender. The queerest stories are the ones that are hardest to tell.

When a story is queer, it is often queer in multiple ways. The storyteller or the characters may be queer, of course. In a memoir, the storyteller is also a character. Look at me in 2015: Someone once socialized as a girl. Conflict-averse. Previously escaped a brief marriage to a man with a severe mental illness. Recently exhausted by a new genital reconstruction while not missing a beat of overwork in an office that only knew me as "a man" who had been out for "a surgery." It is one thing to do the gender transition. It is another thing to invisibly maintain this historical-and-ongoing process. They assume I am a cisgender man when in fact I am a transgender man. They assume this, not because I deceive them but because I live with some privacy and some assimilation—two things everyone needs to some degree or at times. There are reasons why houses, rooms, and closets have doors and why it is sometimes good to close them. (Probably no one cares what kind of penis I have, and neither do I need to talk about my penis with people who don't care about it.) That I am "out as transgender to anyone who asks" is a hypothetical, as this outness requires someone to ask. I have left a door half-open in a neighborhood where no one notices my house.

A story can be queer based on how it keeps secrets. See how I navigate my friend's presence in this story. I nearly idolized him, was taken by surprise by his apparent mental instability, and handled it in a way that pleased neither of us. I am afraid that, if I reach into the dreamworld and confront my horror story, I'll grab a hat off someone's head and you'll all read, inside the hatband, the name of the friend I lost. And I don't want to hurt him again by outing him.

If the hat came out of the bag, I might just end up crouching in the cellar telling you the whole backstory, knives-out. That could hurt me too: Reliving details that don't matter but that I have somehow spun into a trauma story. Besides, I might tell it wrong. Then I'd be reliving a fictional trauma. I might sit in that cellar outright making stuff up and, tragically for me, never realize my error.

AS NANCY, DAY 6

Because of the damn window bars and the broken rose trellis, Glen can't sneak up to my bedroom anymore. We speak by telephone. With purple bags under my eyes, I tell him I haven't slept all week. I reveal to him the satanic name: Fred Krueger.

I ask: Will he try again to stand guard over me while I sleep? This time I elaborate my plan better. Twice have I returned from my dreams with physical evidence of Freddy. Can't I pull Freddy himself out of my dream? I assume Freddy is mortal, so Glen can kill him.

I swallow Stay Awake pills although I'm planning to sleep.

Almost midnight, and I try to call Glen but his parents take the phone off the hook. Freddy calls me back. I pull the phone from the wall, breaking the cord.

I want to run across the street to Glen, but my mother has locked the front door so I cannot escape. The police arrive with flashing lights. My father tells me over the telephone, casually, that my boyfriend is dead. I can imagine the blood volcano. He's this week's third teenage victim murdered in close proximity to me.

I booby trap the house: A heavy hammer outside my bedroom door and an exploding lamp in the living room. One of these should kill Freddy, I hope.

I tuck Mom into bed and reassure her that everyone will be okay. She tells me she hid information to protect me. Sometimes it's good to "face things," she says, while other times "you have to turn away." Which approach will help me now?

Just in case Dad doesn't arrive in time, I set my alarm.

Now I'm dreaming. In my dream, I poke around my cellar and look for my mother's trophy: Freddy's fingerknives. But they're gone. Freddy must have them. I call out to him in my dream. We pounce on each other, and my alarm goes off.

I am awake. And I have brought him back. My booby traps only lightly injure him, buying me a few moments. Freddy and I make it down to the cellar, where *I set him on fire* and run back upstairs. He somehow manages to pursue me. I push him back down the stairs. He ascends again, igniting the staircase carpet. Footprint-sized bonfires. I can follow the trail of his flames.

He takes his fourth victim: my mother in her bedroom. My father arrives. I tell him gently to give me some time alone.

Now I am talking to Freddy. I turn my back on him, as Glen told me to.

"I know the secret now," I tell him, with my back to him. "This whole thing is just a dream." I order him to bring my mother and friends back to life. "I take back every bit of energy I gave you. You're nothing. You're shit."

This seems to do it. He dissolves, collapses, falls into me, vanishes. He has returned to where he came from, and he cannot hurt me.

REFLECTIONS

That was supposed to be the end.

Turning one's back on Freddy was extraordinarily interesting advice to me as a teenager. I don't think I interpreted it as applying to power, systems, concepts, or bullies; I understood it as applying literally to the nightmares I saw when I closed my eyes.

But it was not the end of the film. The filmmakers revived Freddy in the last several seconds of the movie to create the possibility of a sequel. It's a bright, beautiful day, and Nancy has voluntarily seated herself in a car, but then the car is haunted, somehow *is* Freddy—the convertible top red and green like his sweater—and the vehicle she can't escape takes her away.

I think about how I came home from work to talk to my friend but he wasn't having it. How I thought there was a psychiatric emergency, as it resembled a situation I had seen years earlier during my brief marriage, one I regretted not acting to stop. How I placed the 911 call, according to instructions provided to me by one of his colleagues, who I believed knew the appropriate procedure and the right time to use it. How I waited the small eternity. How my friend guessed what was happening (perhaps it was not the first time someone had done this to him) and ran past me downstairs to the garage, turning his key in his car's ignition. The garage door lifted slowly, delaying his exit, more and more light streaming in. The cops, almost too late, parked in the driveway and blocked his escape. They spoke to us, locked him in their vehicle, and drove him away. And that was the end of the movie we'd made together.

FOUR LETTERS CHANGE EVERYTHING

There's a four-letter typo in the script. A deliberate one that made all the difference. Freddy's character was originally supposed to be a child *molester*, according to Wes Craven's original script, but the film's creators supposed it might come off as crass or insensitive, so Freddy was changed to a rarer bird: a child *murderer*.

Swap out four letters in *m[ol]e[st]er* and you get *m[urd]e[r]er*.

That is: The movie was made less offensive by causing it to *make less sense*. If you understand Freddy as a molester, the mother's speech in the cellar is crystal clear. Play it again: Krueger "was a filthy child [*molester*] who [*abused*] at least 20 kids in the neighborhood." After he was freed on a technicality, "a bunch of us parents tracked him down ... We found him in an old abandoned boiler room where he used to take his kids ... I even took his knives." Now we understand why the parents continued to live in that neighborhood: most of them didn't know, or weren't willing to see, that someone was hurting their kids. Their kids did not outright *disappear*. They weren't literally *murdered*. They were, rather, *invisibly hurt*.

Now, too, we understand what Nancy's mother is telling her: *Your classmates carry these memories, possibly repressed. You might have these memories, too, and that's what's been coming back slowly in your dreams, now that you're a young woman who has a boyfriend. You remember Fred Krueger's name, clothes, fingers, knives. Somewhere, you heard he was burned to death.* The teenagers aren't experiencing an assault that comes out of nowhere; they are reliving memories of an old assault. And it doesn't matter if there was never a knife. Freddy didn't *carry* a knife. His fingers felt like knives.

Nancy's mother is also indirectly supplying a coping strategy. *In your dreams, take charge, and don't give into fear. Pull him into the "real world" where you can confront him consciously. You can't permanently kill him because he's already dead, but you can remember that we torched him and you can relive our victory, and alternatively you can sap his energy for a while if you just forget about him.*

If they had made the movie this way, it would have been a more serious exploration of trauma. Instead, by making Freddy a *murderer*, the kids who supposedly *weren't* attacked are the ones having the dreams. That's a little weird. The movie never describes, names, or pictures Freddy's murder victims (unless you count the ghostly girls skipping rope for a few seconds at the beginning and end). This may be one reason why the film is scary. Not only is it about a young woman who reports being stalked and isn't believed, the film script isn't ever honest with viewers about the nature of the original crime. We're fed a piece of false information in the cellar scene and it's never debunked for us.

HOW SHOULD WE TELL THE STORY?

The monologue by Nancy's mother in the cellar is chilling in how little sense it makes and how earnestly her mother tells it as if she believes it. Here, I am reflecting not on sexual abuse or murder but on secrets more generally, and then about secrets I hold. Unburying a secret is always a fraught endeavor. Discussing transgender identity is fraught in specific ways. First of all, for those of us who had to pursue a "gender identity disorder" diagnosis to be allowed to transition, we were encouraged to stick to that narrative mold. There is also the general problem of queer visibility: when you are invisible, you are inadvertently excluded, but when you are visible, you encounter more direct prejudice. And because gender is inherently public information, people often make related assumptions about your physical sex, who you date, what you do in bed, and what your gender means to you. How should you disclose having previously lived in a different gender role, for example? It's easy to let people assume wrong information. Often there doesn't seem to be an appropriate time or a reasonably easy path to disclose that you are transgender, or that you are transgender *and it doesn't mean what someone else thinks it means.*

I learn to hide the real information. I could put in a typo, change the script, feed people false information disguised as truth. This is what they ask for. Don't divulge; hide. If I am illegible to others, they can ignore or dismiss me. Hiding is considered *polite.* I start with a seven-letter first name, delete four letters and add three new letters, and now I'm a different person. I don't talk about the first name I had prior to 1998. (This is the first time I've alluded to it in print.) I don't talk about surgery on my genitals nor about the friend with whom I had a special connection that can never be replicated and who is still not talking to me, nor about how I despaired over him until I needed a tranquilizer, nor about how the tranquilizer made me hallucinate setting myself on fire.

My nervous breakdown was likely mimetic: I empathized with my friend's distress, replicated his disorder, paid him crude homage through what felt like peak religious experience, and attempted penance and absolution by performing a descent into anxiety. The mind can be melodramatic and embarrassingly shitty in its appropriation of other people's pain. It can persuade itself to suicide, whether I do or don't call the cops to have a chat with it. Just because I might be imitating someone or acting out a scripted drama doesn't mean I can stop it. Imitation is, counterintuitively, one kind of realness.

Gender and sexuality are mimetic. It's the nature of social categories and interpersonal relationships: we copy each other. Gender and sexuality are also individually authentic. My nervous breakdown was shaped by ideas that "came from somewhere," but its exact manifestation was uniquely mine, and it had something to do with being a single gay transgender man.

The particulars of this mental illness remain a mystery. When I hallucinated a thousand times over three weeks, I am not sure why I saw fire rather than, say, bunnies. I don't know why I fixated on setting myself on fire, why I kept seeing it over and over, as if in a movie, as if in a waking dream, to no apparent purpose or resolution.

I do wonder if it came from *Nightmare on Elm Street*. Nancy thought fire would kill Freddy, and Freddy also seemed to fear it would kill him, but it didn't destroy him after all. He could run upstairs while he was burning. He could show off by leaving the carpet in flames.

If I hide "what really happened" in my life—the gender transition in 1998, a brief first gay marriage in 2007 to a man who endangered me, the loss of a long-term friendship with a different man in 2015, the nervous breakdown that resulted—other people may still dislike me. They would dislike me without understanding why. It would be because my stories won't quite make sense.

There was a little girl jumping rope. We pretend she never existed. If you keep dreaming about her, I might tell you she died, but the lie would grow more elaborate and eventually I wouldn't be able to spin a coherent version. She wasn't murdered. She was transformed. That's why I'm still here to tell you this story today.

I turned 35 and a close friend stopped speaking to me. To hide those details for *his* privacy is what transgender people learn to do for ourselves and others: to withhold, to gloss over. But if I said there never was a friend, or if I made up a story about what happened to him, I'd be lying, right? Just as if I said there never was a little girl, or that the little girl was "murdered," I'd be lying about my own past. To what end? Secrets and lies can make queer life more scary.

I am 41 now, and that's the truth.

"A nightmare now would be plus or minus 5 or 6," said the doctor at Nancy's sleep clinic, observing her stats. For six years now, my friend hasn't been talking to me. All this time, I have been watching my nightmare EEG for a novelty in the pattern. It might be time to stop watching. His absence may not be a nightmare. It's starting to look like real life. If there is one good thing about discovering that a terrifying loss is real and not merely imagined, it is that I can navigate my fear, sadness, and regret within a comprehensible reality system.

We maintain some privacy without hiding, accept some labels without lying, let go of profound pain without erasing, and learn to "turn away" and yet "face things." That means we deflate imaginary monsters of our own making while accurately recalling what has been done to us and what we have done to others. If we forget the real story, we dream ourselves back into our cellars, setting our own misremembered trauma aflame.

The Me in the Screen

STEFFAN TRIPLETT

Us

MY SEMESTER ABROAD was the first time I had sex with someone who wasn't already my boyfriend. I'd planned for this to happen,
even though it was something that, before, I'd told myself I *wasn't*
planning on. I'd convinced myself it was something that I wouldn't
do or that I was uninterested in. It was 2013, and I was twenty years
old, still shaking off the rhetorical and emotional baggage that came
with a southwestern Missouri upbringing, tinged with morality and
religion, the abstinence-only sex education carved into my memory
of middle school. I was still fearful of sexuality, even by association:
when my father brought me to the airport, I panicked that the small
box of condoms I'd put in my carry-on would sound off an alarm,
alerting everyone that I was *sexually active*. So I took my bag in the
bathroom and switched the box into the suitcase that I was checking. When I brought it back out, my father, unhappy with how we'd
packed things earlier, insisted on rearranging them. He unzipped the
suitcase and saw the box.

"What's this?" he said as he was opening it.

I froze. A moment passed as he glanced at its contents. He closed
it and we never spoke anymore about it. I was horrified. These were
all free condoms I'd amassed that year as a college student at various
on-campus events, though I told myself I wasn't actually planning on
ever using them anyway.

And yet, I spent many nights in Madrid kissing men in clubs
and following them back to their apartments. It was easier than I
expected, both to do away with my previous inhibitions, and also to

catalog what then felt to me like pleasurable transgressions. I kept a list of names of men I'd hooked up with. It quickly grew larger than the list I'd kept in my non-abroad life, and with each addition to that list, I left the old me in the US, giving myself permission to deny my current reality. This type of sexual freedom didn't fit with the more respectable self-image I'd crafted in my head. This version of myself did not, and would not, exist back home. *None of this counts,* I told myself. *None of this is real.*

THE FIRST SCENE in Jordan Peele's *Us* is a scene about misinterpretation. The camera slowly zooms toward a television set as commercials roll on an ordinary evening. We're not just watching a local broadcast near Santa Cruz in 1986, we're actually watching someone else watch it; she's a little girl—you can make her out in the TV reflection, wearing a blue top with ruffles and white piping, rapt, alone in the living room. You can see her in the black of the blank air space between commercials.

The focus here seems to be on the commercial, but it's really on the screen, on the girl watching it. We notice her after the fact; notice her noticing the Hands Across America event happening that summer—a human chain connecting American citizens from one coast to another. It was a strange (real-world) fundraising attempt to fight homelessness and hunger, touting a narrative about connection, how we're all the same and might band together to fix the world's problems. The girl is taken with this idea. It will drive her later on, becoming the visual basis for the statement she will make years later after being stuck underground in a life she never asked for.

The little girl is one of the film's protagonists, but not the one the audience expects. *Us* is really a film about two versions of her. There's the young Adelaide we watch watching the television. On a family trip to the carnival on the Santa Cruz Beach Boardwalk, that

The Me in the Screen

Adelaide encounters another version of herself in a hall of mirrors.

Unknown to the audience, Adelaide's double switches places with her and takes over her life. The adult Adelaide we follow across the film, now married to her husband Gabe Wilson and mother to two kids, is not the same Adelaide as before—that one is now going by "Red" (both are portrayed by Lupita Nyong'o). Thus, much of one's initial viewing of *Us* is a misperception too. We spend the whole first viewing of the film thinking we're watching one life when it's really been someone else's. At the film's end, "Adelaide" kills her double, yes, but in "reality," Adelaide destroys herself.

IF THERE'S A double in literature or film, there's always the threat that they'll take the other's place. I've watched enough seasons of *The Vampire Diaries* and plenty of late-night horror and science-fiction films to know as much. More unsettlingly, during my semester abroad in Spain, we'd read short stories about men from Barcelona and Madrid trying to take one another's place; the professor told us it was the product of anxieties about masculinity and class-jumping due to a national history and economy I was new to learning about. It all read as vaguely homoerotic to me, something I was too embarrassed to offer up in the classroom discussion at the time.

At night in my homestay, I'd go to bed dreaming of someone trying to disappear me, of secret passageways in apartments behind bookcases and mirrors that led someone from one big city to the next, littered with images and storylines I'd only half understood. I found the idea titillating, a rivalry and intimacy only complete after self-annihilation—or sex. So, in a film where two characters look the same and are played by the same person, it's always in the back of my mind as a viewer: At what point will one try to be the other?

I'LL ADMIT I was disappointed by *Us* when I first saw it in theaters in 2019. Jordan Peele's *Get Out* is about as cleanly executed as any genre film can be—everything in the right place, the reveals exciting, yet inevitable as day. By the end, however, *Us* is less clear-cut and more opaque, and it's executed with a heavy emphasis on its reveal in the film's final moments. But the ending brings more questions than answers. What I didn't like about the disproportionate focus on the reveal—that the two young Adelaides switched places in the hall of mirrors—is that, if you're only watching for plot, it's too inevitable, too easy. As a queer viewer, I was much more interested in the other themes and ideas of the film's unnervingly familiar undergrounds, its subconscious imaginations running through those tunnels.

I now understand the film to be more lyrical and complicated than the focus on the twist would otherwise suggest. The self is a slippery thing. The "us" can be the many selves inside one's own being. I spent hours wracking my brain thinking of where either Adelaide's knowledge might end and begin, thinking of how one might possibly erase something they once did from their memory. What if she doesn't remember she took the original Adelaide's place? What if she can no longer tell which one she is?

I once had a dream that I was best friends with myself. We were identical and got along famously and had sleepovers in my apartment. During one of these sleepovers, I woke to myself lying on top of me, staring into my eyes. It wasn't friendly or romantic, it was sinister. Suddenly, my viewpoint changed: I was the one on top of me, looking down at my other self. Then, I woke up.

What if I'm not the one I thought I was?

I couldn't shake the feeling.

NEITHER "DOPPELGÄNGERS" nor "clones" is ever uttered in *Us*, because it's not that these are different people that just look like the others, or that they're independent beings concocted in a lab. They're closer than that.

So, what are they, exactly? The Wilson family can't seem to agree. "It's *us*," Adelaide's son Jason says, when the four Wilsons finally see their doubles all lined up together, Red and the doubles of Adelaide's husband and kids having broken into their summer home. At first they think they are simply intruders, a different family standing menacingly in their driveway; but, of course, they look just like *them*. It's something they can't wrap their eyes or minds around. The scene quickly erupts into chaos. It's clear that the doubles are out for blood, and only one family, only one version of them, can survive.

And so, one by one, the Wilsons are forced to kill their doubles. Red, the only surviving double, takes Jason underground, beneath the house of mirrors that leads to the tunnel world from which the doubles emerged, forcing Adelaide to follow. In the film's big moment of exposition, Red gives us more insight, if still somewhat impenetrable, into how they're connected: "We're human too, you know. Eyes, teeth, hands, blood. Exactly like you . . . I believe [humans] figured out how to make a copy of the body but not the soul. The soul remains one, shared by two."

Red goes on to explain that the actions of those above control the Tethered below, the opposite of what was originally intended when they were formed. It's a lot of information at once. I sensed my own resistance in this moment because I thought, *none of this really matters*, it's all window dressing to explain why these two selves exist. It all seems to inhibit the more interesting ideas that put people in the theater seats: What if there's another one of you, standing in your driveway? What are they like? What do they want? What would you trade from your own life and give to them to preserve the rest?

THE YEAR BEFORE graduate school, I lived in an apartment across the street from a strip of gay bars in San Antonio, the music and bass drifting up from its interiors calling me toward it each weekend night. It was hot in Texas and the summer heat gave me an excuse to show off the legs and youth I knew were fleeting. I'd dance the night away hoping to meet someone. I wasn't as precious about my purity as I'd been in Spain, more consciously embracing this new look toward pleasure. Yet, I couldn't escape this sense of the other me, tentative and fearful, lurking nearby, ready to remerge what had been divided.

A queer person is used to keeping secrets, telling lies, sectioning off parts of themselves. I spent many years wishing that parts of me weren't real, and, eventually, they became that way. I had forged two selves. I could assign all the bad stuff to the "pretend" me. All the things I didn't like about myself, that I was ashamed of, that I didn't want anyone— myself included—to know, were kept away and pushed onto the flimsy sketch of myself that lived somewhere in my head, but whom I never had to acknowledge.

That other self, his first sexual experience was not one he signed up for.

So sex became something I was always running from, hiding away, burying down deep in a mental basement, just like the one that it happened in. It was too much to think about, something that wouldn't be pulled out from me until therapy over a decade later, so, accordingly, I just pretended none of it was me. I was not that person. *None of it counted*. It became easier than I thought it would be to simply not think about the actions I didn't want to associate with myself, to not think of the more complicated version of myself I'd pushed down below. The version of myself that, try as I might, I remain tethered to.

The Me in the Screen

WHEN I REVISIT *Us*, I see myself in the reflection of the television screen, watching young Adelaide, who will become Red, watch herself watching something that will drive her to her end. I watch her in those early scenes, drawn to mirrors and different reflections and refractions of herself. Sometimes fearful of them, sometimes succumbing to the horrors the world will soon throw at her. My own reflection makes me, ever so briefly, consider the person in the screen, the person I've become since the last time I watched. How I've gone on each year to find myself a little more, and resolved to take myself with me.

Sight Unseen

SPENCER WILLIAMS

The Blair Witch Project

EVEN IN THE present, a ghost story always turns toward the past. It has to. A ghost is a matter of memory. A haunting is unfinished business. A reminder.

I want to tell you a ghost story, but I don't know where to begin. We could start in the woods near San Bernardino, where I learned to pray by folding in half. Or in the boxed room I grew up in, four walls dressed in third-grade folk art. Or maybe we could start in a different wood, the ones near Julian, where I went camping with my dad and his friends each summer. Their boys, my age. The stream we swam naked in, unconscious and brave in the face of snakes and bears. Or we could start in Tatiana's pool, getting scolded by her mother for yammering too loudly about our ideas of what sex would be like. Or, we could begin in Winston-Salem, in the backyard of my cousin Andrew's house. My small body flying down the street on a bike I wasn't taught how to brake. Andrew chucking stones at me, yelling, "Go faster! Faster! Faggot."

Leading up to the summer release of *The Blair Witch Project* in 1999, IMDb listed the three actors featured in the film as deceased, presumed missing. To drum up interest, the marketing team baited audiences with the mystique of death, the prospect of witnessing the final moments of a life abruptly snuffed out. Fade to black.

At screenings, they handed out proof of disappearance, posters featuring the actors' faces like those on the side of a milk carton. No Q&A with the cast. Just the bleak air of their absence and a piece of paper. The public wanted to see, with their own eyes, how a person goes missing. But in the distribution of materials, their want gave way to a collective unease. People left the theater, poster in hand, feeling haunted, like they'd just watched something they shouldn't have. Perhaps some wondered why they'd wanted to watch these people trudge their backpacks and cameras into the mouth of the woods in the first place. The trailer for the film told audiences they wouldn't come out. Upfront, the film said there'd be no happy ending. So why endure the inevitable? Why not look elsewhere? What compels one to voluntarily sit inside their fear?

Flash forward to 2008 and I am sitting on my childhood friend's vast living room sofa, watching *The Blair Witch Project* for the first time. Already living in the age of Internet forums and Google, I know the film playing out in front of me is a work of fiction. But knowing this doesn't make the watch any easier. My friend is playing with a gaming console on the sofa next to me, unbothered. Her fingers tap away at some animated creature while, onscreen, the grain and wobble of a camera pans to the scattered dead of leaves on the forest floor. "This part is freaky," she says, not looking up from her screen. And so I watch alone as a woman—Heather, the director of a film within a film—unfurls a bundle of sticks wrapped with twine that looks like dental floss. A pause. The two of us, Heather and I, stare at its contents, the jam-red of pulled teeth. A litter of tiny bones. Then, Heather screams and her breathing reaches a crescendo. She chokes on the air, then begins to weep. Her friend had gone missing in the woods the day before, but it's not the sound of mourning that I hear. In place of grief, there is fear. Heather is still lost in the woods, and in the brutal equation of present circumstance, Heather and her friend's teeth have been made equal. Neither of them will be found again.

IN THE EDITING booth, I flip through the stills, run back the footage. There's me, or someone who looks like me as a child, standing among other children in a circle. A college-aged guitarist strums a rock hymn, his arms covered in cut-out socks to hide tattoos still peeking out from holes in the fabric. My childish doppelgänger holds up his hands to the stage, trying to give them away. It's an unnerving spectacle to watch. I am so far away from a childhood in service to a presence unseen. But my boyish self is anything but weary. His hands clasp together now. His eyes shut. He is praying and singing at the same time, proof of his unwavering belief. The song ends. Is that a tear I see? God must be somewhere in the room, I think. I squint at the footage, zooming in and out. After a while, I have to admit I can't see shit.

MY FAVORITE KIND of horror film includes found footage as its central gimmick. Something about the awkward posturing with a camera in hand appeals to me, the want to document, to record a truth on tape no matter how dark or ridiculous it sounds in the mouths of strangers. I love the camera-holding protagonist and the doubling of self: there's always the performative-self conducting interviews squaring off against the actual-self reviewing footage once the sun goes down and the equipment is slipped back into its case.

And like any good hook, there's always a piece of the puzzle missing in a found-footage horror. No matter the story, the cameraperson wants to unearth the hidden darkness of the subject at hand, be it a commune of religious folk who seem dodgy when asked about their customs or curious decorum, or working-class townsfolk who live beneath the shadow of an old legend. Usually, unearthing the secret comes at a cost. Rarely does the found-footage protagonist survive. And when they do, they usually return to the world possessed by some unseen entity or irreparably damaged by what they have witnessed. But mostly, it's the footage that survives. The demons of the world seem to ignore handhelds or SD cards. Where a body once was, an apparatus remains. The footage thus becomes a stand-in for the voice that is no longer there. The camera is like a ghost you can hold in your hands.

I BEGRUDGINGLY identify with the Blair Witch. Described by locals as a gangly woman covered head-to-witch-toe in hair, the obvious parallels to the experience of trans womanhood—the constant plucking and tweezing and fussing for the purposes of achieving that impossibly twisted feminine-coded hairlessness—arise like a fly-laden stench from some swampy creek. In the face of crushing cis beauty standards, my desire to retreat into the woods and live out the rest of my days like Sasquatch becomes more and more of a pressing want. In this sense, the Blair Witch offers a radical template. Rather than pass in public as human, she opts to simply disappear. Indeed, what I latch onto most with regards to the Blair Witch, more than anything physical, is her anonymity, her refusal to be seen or captured in frame.

The Blair Witch gives a master class in nonpresence. While subsequent sequels attempt to glimpse her in all of her hunched-over, cryptozoological glory, I prefer the original film's commitment to the titular character's erasure. She is at once omnipresent and undetectable. She's there in the ornamental twig-art she leaves dangling from the branches of naked, looming trees. She's present in the ectoplasmic slime she casts upon film equipment and in the stone monuments erected outside of our unlucky trio's tents during the night. But thankfully, you never see *her* standing aside the products of her terrifying labor. In the gap she exits from, you're forced to imagine her there, arranging her nature in such a way as to appear foreboding. You're made to make your own portrait of her. What might she look like? How did locals describe her? What color hair? In your imagining, you have no choice but to abandon your need for closure. Whatever you come up with surely won't be accurate.

There's a moment in the film when, awakened at night by the uncanny sounds of childish laughter, Heather and Mike exit their tents into pure darkness, running panicked around the woods, but not in any particular direction. Just running, as if somehow the act of moving might keep them safe. Heather turns her head to the side, alarmed at something running beside her. The screen wobbles through the throat of the night, but doesn't once shift to get a clean view. Still, we don't need to see what Heather does to know her blood has run cold: her throat-shredding screams of "WHAT THE FUCK IS THAT?!" are enough for any bodily hair to rise in rapture.

But it's her. She's right there. You can feel it.

IN THE FILM classes I took as an undergraduate at the University of Iowa, my subject was always the self. I never made narrative work, too afraid of failing my lofty ambitions. The self as a documentary subject felt more intimate somehow—truer, safer. For who better to know the intricacies of the human spirit than the human herself, pointing the camera at her own flesh? The logic was obviously flawed. For one, in order for the self to remain true on camera, another body needed to present so as to guide and redirect moments that felt emotionally false or overwritten. Without a crew, the directorial-self mistakes aloofness for candidness. Alone with only myself and a Canon 7D, there was no harsh truth I could offer about myself or the world as I saw it, only curation.

It is painful to glance back at the footage from back then. For one, I am a woman now, not an egg running from the prospect of trans embodiment. My face looks different, stranger-esque. My eyes shift awkwardly in every direction but straight. My hair is a buzzed-off blast-zone of DIY patchiness. My clothes drape over my wide shoulders like a sheet pulled up to cover someone's massacre. Stubble intrudes upon my chin, an army of black spots that won't wash out.

I am also not a good filmmaker. My shots are always too close, too tight, too obvious, and out-of-focus. An argument could of course be made for transness as a perpetual state of out-of-focusness. To do so here, though, would be to give my younger self too much credit. My cuts are harsh, with no regard for temporal or spatial continuity. My audio buzzes with background static and conversations. My film-making is an aesthetic nightmare, caught between a desire for Giallo sensibilities and an underwhelming budget. It's hard to look, to see the limits of one's talent clash with the mind's attempts at grand flourishing. I could never get the tripod to angle the camera exactly where I wanted it. I could never stare into the lens in the private dark of my room and feel anything but mortification. How does the self as a subject build their own narrative, when they are simultaneously embarrassed by it? How could I give you the truth without first claiming it for myself?

Heather has at least one thing going for her: a crew. Mike and Josh are her cameramen, her confidantes, her buffers. While Heather is obviously keen on making a documentary on the legend of the Blair Witch, she is equally interested in herself as a historian. We see her directing Mike and Josh from in front of the camera, reading off-scripted sections about witch trials and scared publics. These curated centerpieces for the film she wants to make come off as hokey, too practiced. In this, we are alike. It is only when the performance fails—when control ceases—that the work becomes interesting. Once lost in the woods, Heather chooses to document everything, from arguments with her crew to her own mental breaks. In the film's most compelling moment, Heather—defeated, tired, and hungry—places the camera directly beneath her nostrils and offers an apology. She is sorry for dragging her friends into the woods with her, for acting like she was prepared even though she wasn't, for being selfish. By the end, her face is distorted in liquid—a deluge of snot runs down her mouth like a river splitting into two pathways. Her eyes are dewy, glistening emptily in the faint light of the camera. It is a moment of realness that can't be faked, a desperation that functions both as elegy and what Heather wanted all along: the truth, plain and ugly.

WHILE AT SCHOOL in another state, my mom calls me and asks if I still have the short videos I made of her, my dad, and me, from the family road trips we used to take together in the summer months of July and August. I had forgotten about these videos, filmed with an old MacBook using the iMovie app. In each montage I sit in the backseat of my parents' car, wondering aloud when we will pull into the next hotel, when I might be allowed to eat something other than the rice cakes in the bag upfront with mom, or when I might have access to Wi-Fi again. These moments of bratty teenage narcissism are interspersed with shots from the window—the plains of America speeding past us, old towns with populations smaller than my high school, gas stations without patrons, rolling hills, sand dunes—all disappearing behind us. The natural elements I captured juxtapose starkly with the familial drama of being trapped together for five hours per day. But in capturing my surroundings and my childish wants, I also captured my younger self in the throes of great change. My wrist flicks and twirls with theatrical flair, emphasizing my disdain for parental company. My eyes roll so far back in my head as to become not eyes but hollows of white. My voice, a product of California, stretches gravelly and fried across the footage, as though the Grudge decided to have a beach day. And my boy-coded version in all his budding queerness, the one who believed his room was haunted by demons, the one who desperately wanted to believe in a God that was on his side, who couldn't ride a bike but wanted to impress a cousin who performed boyishness more believably than he did, hit record and outed himself on video. I, in the present, watch as my younger self discovers her sense of body, her freedom, her entrapment. I watch her squeeze into a self that can't be denied. While the reveal may be unintentional, the self-consciousness—and the gradual shedding of it—works spectacularly on camera, bringing the film to life. It took me ten years to out myself again, to feel that aliveness rush in, and to name it as such.

Sight Unseen

Now, reviewing the footage is like staring into the eyes of a ghost. It is both me, and not. He is both there and gone. Spectral. Present.

I WATCH *The Blair Witch Project* at least once a year. With so many found-footage knockoffs being released at an increasingly rapid rate, it feels appropriate—like an homage of sorts—to return to the OG, the blueprint of effective camcorder terror-making. Of course, Heather, Josh, and Mike are all alive. But the witch is too. I imagine her, trapped in that wood, waiting to ensnare naive hikers for trekking too close. Or not trapped at all, but choosing to remain there, where mythology can't touch. It almost seems utopian, to exist perpetually unbothered, and to vanquish all who attempt to ruin it. To never be found and thus to never be held accountable for appearances. Listen. If you were to ask me to my face, I'd lie and tell you, of course she's the villain of the story. But here, on this page, I'll say it: The Blair Witch is no monster. The woods are not a trap. And if this were my film, there'd be no camera left for anyone else to find.

Bad Hombre

SARAH FONSECA

Is That You? / ¿Eres tú, papá?

THE LAST TIME I saw my father, the muscles of his forearm were firm, rolling together like waves approaching the Malecón; impact was inevitable. Like the seawall, I'd been designed to withstand the hits. Seven years later, I can still recall the size of his arms—*compact but capable*—and form—*tawny, hairless, branded with my name*—with ease. It was January when Amaurys held me against the abrading blue gingham couch where I'd once been his calypso companion, wriggling and clenching his shoulders like an iguana while Harry Belafonte's buoyant voice unraveled from a record's threads.

He pressed his forearm against my trachea. Aloud, he contemplated whether or not to break my neck.

It was not the first time that Amaurys's shouts had blown the baby hairs back from my brow, that his spittle met my iris, that his hands purpled another fun new part of my body. It was, however, the first time I gave as good as I got. I became the iguana girl a final time, slithering beneath him until my hands and feet were freed from his weight. I kneed and kicked him anywhere contact could be made. Freshly painted an iridescent pink, my nails broke flesh around his cheekbones. The fingers that dug into his eyelids were decades in the making. I wanted to puncture the tissue irreparably; no more sight, no more blinking, no more familial entanglement or obligation.

We had bonded over being physical creatures—a provincial laborer and his tomboy daughter—over his want of a son and my predisposition for being a prodigious stand-in. Our conflict arose with pubescence, with me beginning to do what physical, funny little women like me do: *other funny little women.*

Yet that night, when my father called me a "dyke bitch," he would be the only one bleeding.

I'VE SPENT AN inordinate amount of my adulthood scouring for a way to explain my wary love for this proverbial badman; an endeavor that has become all the more perilous as the country into which I was born, the United States, begins to take its own patriarchs to task in inchmeal. In my drippy adolescence, I was not above the floods of hormonal girls who took to Sylvia Plath's paternal opprobria like doctrine. I too could mouth the embittered stanzas in "Daddy" from memory: *Every woman adores a Fascist . . .*

But my father is not a Weinstein or a Himmler. Born on the cusp of the Cuban Revolution, he remains comically far from either. Amaurys is a penniless boy from Sagua de Tánamo in Holguín, the fourth-largest municipality in the country, born to a strict Black mother and a philandering mulatto father. Only later would he become a difficult monster; a character that, only recently, I have been unable to identify in creature features, slashers, or go-to psychological thrillers. A badman, and especially one the color of copper, is just a bad man; a "bad *hombre*," as our forty-fifth president famously put it.

It was not through the movies that I became unsurprised a fellow who has spent his life fighting very explicit adversaries—the sugarcane fields of Fidel Castro's labor programs, the fatal waters of the Atlantic Ocean, ICE *and* the Bureau of Prisons in the most successful American prison riot of the twentieth century—would, absent a significant tangible enemy for the first time in his life, turn his fists toward his family. But then, *¿Eres tú, papá? (Is That You?)* was placed into a projector, affirming what I'd known all along.

In the 2010s, Cuban expatriate Rudy Riverón Sánchez devised an affrighting fable of the bad hombre, one that did not reduce weary Caribbean masculinity to a beastly beige archetype. In turn, it illustrates this *patria*-informed need for domestic dominance, obedience, and control to wonderfully terrifying effect. This sophisticated characterization is made all the more remarkable by *¿Eres tú, papá?*'s provenance: as of today, it remains the only psychological horror film to have ever been made in Cuba.

In Sánchez's knowing hands, we are carried inside a characteristic concrete building that a provincial Cuban family of three calls home. The sundial moves glacially for domineering father Eduardo (Osvaldo Doimeadiós), enraptured *marimacha* daughter Lili (Gabriela Ramos), and compliant wife Alina (Lynn Cruz). It is tempting to presume, in these first scenes where a perspiring and lurching Eduardo dictates domestic affairs, that the film's women will be the primary sufferers. But American horror, with its Final Girls and dumb jocks, is written in a different tongue, one where traditional gender roles are abided by, even when they're scorned.

¿Eres tú, papá? has a fourth main character: Cuba. The film's viscous pace is an enduring, recognizable trope of the country itself. For decades, Americans, owned by Wall Street in some fashion or another, have found escapist fantasy in this 771-mile-long island just south of Key West, where free market economic doctrine seemingly does not exist; and yet, allegedly, there is clean air and world-class health care that still eludes the most developed of countries. Outsiders, realizing that many of Cuba's eleven million natives dwell in remarkable poverty, instead appreciate this languor. Though cash-poor, the country owns the clock's riches. In the imaginations of Americans—who, unable to meet our homeland's impossibly high productivity standards, yearn for a new day to be added to the week so they might finally catch up with it all—Cuba becomes a crescent-shaped utopia. Or at least a faultless holiday destination.

Obviously, this sensational view is different from the reality experienced by those confined to this island trapped between the past and the future. Sánchez meets us within the slow pace, where the highlights of any calendar day are dawn and dusk, and where bodies—though bursting forth with smiles, songs, and spells—bear labor's tolls. Eduardo, hirsute in an undershirt, is crowned in glistening sweat throughout. Alina, the domestic, grows more bruised and rope-burned as the film wears on. In a nation where citizens repress closely guarded fantasies of defection, the scent of stagnation—fecund, ripe, overpowering—is omnipresent. I am reminded of a piece of Associated Press reportage on the country where the author, a veritable outsider, attempted to describe the cryptic nature of Cuba's slow ho-hum: *The days still pass slowly under an enervating sun. After a half-century of Communism, they see time frozen in the facades of crumbling colonial mansions, the chrome of 1950s automobiles, and the face of a stopped airport clock.*

Yet Sánchez does it better—and with far fewer words.

In this family's modest abode, we begin to witness the most minute assertions of power. Eduardo anticipates dinner. Eduardo anticipates sex, and forces it on Alina with equally carnal and rote motions. Domestic violence is not sensationalized but treated as retrograde; beatings are simply something that occur when the sun hangs in the sky a certain way. Without devotion to the culture's languid pace, viewers would not be as unsettled by the hairline cracks in *¿Eres tú, papá?*'s family portrait: Alina does not eat with the family. Alina's ankles are bound together with twine to prevent her from fleeing. Alina, when disobedient, receives beatings at Eduardo's hand. Thirteen-year-old Lili, equine and lean without a curve to her name, observes it all, but continues her scrapbooking in airtight silence.

Americans still possessing an unwavering faith in law and order are likely to become motive-obsessed while watching *¿Eres tú, papá?* As though a testament to how ingratiated law enforcers are to American entertainment, it is most unusual to immerse into an hours-long film rife with illicit activity without a single policeman, district attorney, or probation officer ever appearing on-screen. It is only normal that culturally unaware spectators ask, and in some instances demand: *Why?*

The answer is in the soil of this place where our characters stand in espadrilles; it is in its necessary uniformity; it is in coveting the manifold power of the esteemed dictator, and performing the role in the domestic microcosm. "I'm doing what I think is best for my family," Eduardo tells Alina in the possessive as he fondles the twine around her ankles, his work-chapped fingers enacting a tenderness that will never be afforded to the rest of her. Though an athletic teenager and constant observer, Lili does not rise to end or deescalate her mother's captivity and torture. Alina's weeps simply continue seeping through her bedroom walls come twilight. Lili might be a quarter of Eduardo's size but something powerfully devastating looms just beneath the pimply surface.

When awakened by the symphony of clanging pans, shattering glasses, and my own mother's sobs in childhood, I would fall asleep when all was quiet again, yearning for the day I would be either big or brave enough to take on my father without earning two helpings of the after-dinner fists my mother received. My own hands remained bound. In the years preceding adulthood, my parents would divorce and reunite several times over; my father would be taken away in cuffs by provincial policemen. All the while, my mother's file at the local sheriff's office would continue to swell with instant photographs of her cuts and bruises.

When I try to recall the physical details of the beatings, my memory immediately soils itself; I am guilty of shielding myself with cinematic synecdoche. Rather than the hue of jaundiced bruises near my mother's sharp cheekbones or the specific pitches of raised voices a room away, all I can see is a scene that could be pawned from any detective neo-noir: a stack of Polaroids is cut and fanned out in two symmetrical rows across an interrogation room table. The photos' subject is identifiable as a woman, and possesses my mother's Clairol-blond hair. But I can't distinguish much else.

I am the one in the hot seat. A detective points to a photo. I nod.

Suturing this extended inventory of batterings into a single picture affords me more control over it. I do not seek to expel it. Rather, I try to embrace the collection as just another page in my family album. That such images were captured, and that I often tagged along for these encounters between Lois and detectives, seems to suffice as enough cognitive proof of violence. My reasoning for not recalling the specifics of the wounds my mother received from my father remains the simplest part of writing about them. The truth of the matter is that Verhoeven and De Palma's films pale in comparison to whatever my mother endured. *The movies are easier.*

Lili, still possessing the hope of the naive, also restructures her familial memories. She cuts fashionably adorned torsos from magazines and heads from a prized family portrait, affixing them to one another in her scrapbook. What she lacks in language, she makes up for with these images: Lili simply wants to feel like the part of a pleasant, vibrant unit. It's a desire that is as foiled by her parents as it is the political regime that prevents Eduardo from fruitfully working as a self-employed cobbler, unbeholden from state services; when *padre* is to blame, *patria* is never far behind.

I owe much to my brain for telling me "no" to cobbling dreams that are neatly compatible with the American vision of family; for denying me access to what is admittedly mine to claim. I have to accept the limits of being human; of being diasporic and thus conceding I will never know everything. At some point, recollection would have been too much for me to handle. It might very well still be too much. There is loss in the exercise, but also gain: *beauty*. If every atrocity that has befallen me over thirty-two years can be recollected as a film, there is a point. As with Lili's cutting and pasting, the jump-cuts, reverse shots, and close-ups all comprise the best bandage I can muster.

¿Eres tú, papá?'s domestic violence is only just the beginning of Alina's troubles. Being regularly beaten inevitably precipitates her shutdown, in turn furthering Lili's bond with her father in her mother's

emotional "absence." The daughter's paternal affinity, already reinforced by their shared movements, intensifies. While her father keeps Alina at home, ankles laced together and door locked from the outside, he takes her to baseball games and on shoe repair ventures on the back of his motorbike. With her lanky arms threaded around his chest, Lili speeds toward an adulthood where she will be the one to call the shots; just like daddy.

Fathers, as I know them, are a double-edged sword of queer girlhood. They generally possess the most authority within a household, in turn oscillating between the role of the righteous liberator and the autocratic warden. We—the girls—are frequently given allowances for miens and behaviors that spit in the face of every maxim of what we *should* be, should those kinetic pleasures be aligned with the patriarch's own pastimes. We get to wear pants and we get to play ball. This is especially true of girls whose existences are marked by remote poverty; when no one influential ever pauses to think of our families' existences, propriety's stakes are lower, for fathers and daughters alike. To a proletariat father, the scrappy girl becomes an emblem of pride that reassures him that his bloodline will resiliently soldier on, with or without upward mobility, with or without citizenship. For a ripple in time, we tomboys are treated as trash's frenetic, fun-loving aristocracy. But the fun ends, as ¿Eres tú, papá? illustrates, with puberty.

After a long day of work in the city, father and daughter return home on two wheels. Eduardo, a heavy drinker, takes swigs from a bottle of rum while driving until he begins to nod off at the handlebars. Lili, alarmed by his swerving, wakes him up and keeps him awake the rest of the way home by tirelessly yelling and clapping her hands. It's a macabre moment of codependency that twists the Daddy's Little Helper axiom that frequently appears on onesies: the father finds himself cared for absent his wife's cold judgment; the daughter finds herself enormously useful.

Bad Hombre

I do not recall whether The Worm, the intentionally perilous swerve across lanes that my father would perform in his truck to elicit delight from me and admonishment from my mother, came before or after he gave me my first driving lesson, or after my he offered me my first taste of Schlitz from the open can pinned between his denim thighs as he drove. All I know is that the triad of events occurred well before I was thirteen, in a muffler-less vehicle that was barreling down the half-dirt, half-gravel on which we lived. And despite not appreciating the way beer smelled like mildewed bales of hay after the rain, I loved every second of it. It would not be until much later, and quite recently, that I realized these events constituted some mild strain of abuse; the breaks could have gone out, as they often did on our thirdhand vehicles, their weary engines and manual windows forever lubricated with our elbow grease; I could have very well soared, so seldom seat belted, straight through the windshield in an Icarian effort to fly.

My father sculpted me into someone who must continually remind herself to be fearful, to clinically access an emotion for which I lack the innate cues. I became too much of a girl, which is to say: too boyish within. When gender is not a site of trauma at the beginning of life, one is permitted a bravado most women are denied. I would grow into the sort of woman my father would want killed. In many ways, it is still forgivable. My mother, you see, hated driving.

Despite the plethora of reasons to take Eduardo out, his death is indirectly caused by a child's white lie. When the patriarch discovers that Lili has desecrated the lone family photo in her scrapbook, she quickly manufactures a greater sin: her mother has been trying to escape with the help of Carlos (Jorge Enrique Caballero), Eduardo's tenderhearted assistant who resides in a rotting shack near their home. Carlos, under the illusion that Eduardo needs him to accompany him to meet a shoe leather dealer, uneasily tags along. As night falls, they stand in silence for the proprietor in a field perimetered by plantain trees, nature's alarmed trills and chirps achieving new heights.

¿Eres tú, papá? is certainly a ghost story, and Cuba Past is one of the specters that frequently appears on-screen as these two men wait for a visitor who will never show. The trees surround Eduardo and Carlos, their spliced leaves grinning in befanged taunt, hearkening back to the pre-Revolution days of Chiquita and banana republicdom. Capitalist exploitation of the nation long reigned, and was defeated. Men like Eduardo and Carlos once toiled under these very leaves for scant remuneration. Now, their own hands tied by a communist government that is only just beginning to trust its citizens, they continue to eke out a living. An inquiry persists in the cicada's trills around these two emasculated men: *Was it worth it? Was it worth it? Was it worth it?*

While taking a piss in the banana trees, Carlos discovers that Eduardo has tied Alina to one of them. Realization dawns; he's being ambushed by his boss. A scuffle ensues, culminating in Carlos fatally stabbing Eduardo with a shard of glass, avenging Alina once and for all. With the surviving wife's help, Carlos discards the corpse and the motorbike near the body of water trailing Eduardo's daily route; an intellectually sound choice of fabricated death locales for a drunkard who can barely maintain a lane.

Lili, however, is not inclined to let Eduardo go gently. Before she cuts the twine from her mother's ankles that next morning, she demands, "*¿Dónde está mi papá?*" Like her father, she uses the possessive to emphasize the bonds that matter most. An earnest attempt is made by both mother and daughter to reconnect, but the old wounds are too deep to heal. Lili cannot open her heart to the woman over whom her father presided skeptically; Alina cannot open her own to the girl who bears such a likeness to her own greatest tyrant. The tension hangs in the air like humidity before a tropical storm. As the mother gradually accepts that Eduardo is gone for good, Alina becomes herself again and begins a close friendship with Carlos. Meanwhile, Lili, all the more hell-bent on finding her father, becomes something else entirely: the Cuban girl's response to *El Cuco*, an entirely new road-ambling monster.

Bad Hombre

In the scenes leading up to Eduardo's demise by Carlos's fistful of glass, Sánchez takes great pains to stress the uncanny similarity between Eduardo and Lili; theirs is one that transcends mere genomic inheritance. When attending a baseball game, they wear matching brown and yellow outfits: his with an *E* on the chest, hers with an *L*. Both take their meals ravenously, with little attention to table manners, their hands pulling tender, newly slaughtered pork away from bone. That *¿Eres tú, papá?* was solely cast with Cuban nationals only serves to benefit the film, particularly its core dynamic. The burden of *patria* is the burden of *padre*, and the burden of *padre* becomes the burden of mija. It is vital to illustrate, even if it is lost on Western spectators. Eduardo and Lili both possess the eyes of a child, deep and brown, through which they have both witnessed great horrors. There is a stillness to the two relatives that feels foreboding; it's the stance of someone prepared for battle, though one years in the past. *New Yorker* contributor Robin Wright once defined this Cuban je ne sais quoi as "cranky melancholia," a world-weariness from which the country's youth are not exempt. "Rhetoric is still defiant," Wright wrote, "but public zealotry has atrophied. The graffiti of rebellion, once vibrant, has faded." After Eduardo vanishes, Lili—in a unique moment of sentiment—pours some of her father's rum into her soda can, offers his memory a toast, and takes an unpleasant swig. Rum, like cigars, once meant something in Cuba; now it's just the drink of choice for the self-medicating. This patriarchal sadness took on personal meaning for me when I learned that Osvaldo Doimeadiós, like my own father, is a son of Holguín.

With the exception of Spanish fluency, I was permitted my father's affects and effects. I had snakeskin cowboy boots identical to his, in miniature. Then came wheat-colored work boots with steel toes. A leather tool belt, designed to fit a twenty-inch waist, soon followed. After one of my parents' divorces and Amaurys's ephemeral domestic departures, I found a pair of threadbare Hanes boxer briefs in an overstuffed dresser drawer. I was a pirate, staking fierce claim over the battleship gray vestment, entirely indifferent to my mother's wishes, if she even had any. The elastic waistband, loose around my own waist, rose above my own trousers. I grew into a teenager, bloated yet starving. Significant acts took place in those underpants; Oedipal and homoerotic thoughts alike were had.

All those years later, my father's raggedy clothing item continually made its way back into my mother's hamper, and back to me, washed and folded. We never spoke of it.

Not long after Eduardo's disappearance, Lili sprints up and down the roads leading to their home, calling for him. Emotionally and physically extinguished, she collapses and is rescued by an elderly woman. Caridad (Eslinda Núñez) tosses the girl on her mule cart and takes her to her home, where she nourishes Lili back to health and affords her the wonders of necromantic Santería. Before returning the girl to her own home, Caridad aids Lili in beginning a ritual that will bring Eduardo back, as well. The spell, like so many others in this religious practice inherited from the island's once enslaved, involves chickens and eggs. But it is *faith*, she tells the girl, that is the primary ingredient.

The supernatural deliverables, however, arrive with the darkest of twists. Lili, bestowed with a name meaning "purity," is on the cusp of relinquishing it. Anything for *padre*. Anything for *patria*. Her civility atrophies entirely upon return. Lili begins to threaten Alina with Eduardo's inevitable second coming. She occupies his reliable rocking chair with the authority of a dictator, all the while hearing her father's voice reverberate from the yolk of an egg. When Carlos gives Lili a puppy for her fourteenth birthday, Lili traps it inside a pressure cooker. "We only accept gifts from the family," she reasons as the others rescue the dog from her unpredictable grasp. When her mother expresses an interest in visiting Caridad for counsel, Lili torches her home, the Santería practitioner howling in agony from inside. Finally, she does away with Carlos, her primary interloping adversary.

I LEARNED THAT my father was deported from the United States in 2016, nearly a year after the federal plane carrying him back to a country he never envisioned returning to thirty-five years later departed Miami International Airport. The news arrived through a Facebook message from a woman I've never met: his second ex-wife, also American. Scrambling, I took my first passport photo at a drug store and found an incontestable loophole to gain entrance to Cuba without, I'd hoped, repatriation.

One doesn't realize how large an island is until she finally, years on, thinks to examine its legend. Amaurys was supposedly living and working on a farm in Camagüey, a rural municipality a six-hour car ride from La Habana. There would be no other way of reaching him than through physical movement across a national border.

In a letter to his second wife sent ahead of my trip, Amaurys had written, in his unwaveringly delicate penmanship: *Tell Miguel and David that I love then and that ICE deport me to Cuba, I'm with my family and everyone ask me for then and you, it is beautiful in here no body closse they door and children play on the street is not to many auto mobil alot o horse wagon and fruit every where is like another world Cuba secund Lenguage is Inglesh the money is no of to much valiu is 24 Cuban peso per Dollar American everywhere I wish you came and see all the man of my family work in construction so a house is very ship in here come and visit get your Passport and visit my family, they want you to come*

Miguel and David are my younger half-brothers, though I remain the only Fonseca progeny to have held down a construction job. Through his omission of my memory—understandable given the palpable loneliness and despair that warranted the clever international marketing pitch—my father had given me a gift: release. I would be free to find him on my own terms. The futility of my inaugural search did not wound me nearly as much as it could have. He did not expect, or possibly even desire, me to locate him.

As Eduardo continues to ethereally communicate with Lili,

she becomes the brute with the boot, reenacting her father's greatest offenses against Alina. Her mother is re-bound, this time to her marriage bed, and beaten with a dripping wet towel. During my own beatings, my father would inform me that, when he was a child, it was commonplace to soak belts in water for maximum impact—a detail that, in adulthood, I've delighted in sharing with friends with an affinity for sadomasochism; this innovative beating that got away from me really shouldn't go to waste.

Lili's fatal mistakes are the singular qualities that keep viewers inured to her, perhaps in the hope that she will come to her senses. But she does not understand mortality and its fine thresholds as her father did. Lili, unlike Eduardo or Fidel, lacks the expertise to keep someone alive so that they may continue begging for death. A novice in such punishments, she forgets to give Alina—bound by her wrists, ankles, and jaw—water until it is too late; it is the great irony that water, so pure, surrounding Cuba on all sides, has killed so many of the country's heretics.

The part of Lili not yet colonized by Eduardo's spirit is bereft at her mother's death. Staring into the bathroom mirror after the tragedy, she notices her father's razor on the counter, waiting for her.

Horror is intentionally constructed to be unsettling; the characters often follow suit en masse, thwarting conversations about queer visibility in the genre tradition; how can I possibly reduce a character, masterfully sketched with the explicit intent of disturbing and provoking, to a binary "good" or "bad" representation? Had ¿Eres tú, papá? received adequate attention upon its release in the United States in 2018, queer and trans film critics would certainly have been drawn to this final scene where Lili—through this uniquely Cuban blend of birthright, trauma, and magic—becomes a man: Eduardo, the impoverished being upon whom Sánchez has bestowed, in total earnestness, a name meaning "wealthy guardian."

Lili does not go gently. Yet she does not take her father's razor to her wrists to join her family in the afterlife; *this* is not that sort of God-fearing country. Today, Santería practitioners in Cuba outnumber colonialism's vestigial Catholics eight to one. Instead, the fourteen-year-old brings the razor to her crown, shaving her head in verisimilitude to Eduardo's. Wearing her father's baseball jersey emblazoned with an *E*, she crawls into bed with her dead mother, cradles her in her arms, and weeps.

It is possible that Lili could be embraced as a trans character, though doing so would require accounting for her illustrious roster of murders through frank self-interrogation: At which disparate points in one's transition did they become a monster and cause others harm, the reasons warranted or not? It's a question that I, a girl in perpetuity, cannot answer; though I remain enthralled by the possibilities of those readings. They will not compete with but elide my own, forming a rich tapestry of narratives where gender transgression results in one, rather than being a victim of their own circumstance, fighting for what they want most in life.

The same goes for such experiences with being a cisgender outlier in general. When I look in the mirror, I see a triangular body with far more veins and sinew than is typical, a broad face with a furrowed brow that seems incensed to many white people, and breasts that still refuse to blossom. I see several dark hairs on my upper lip that inspire me to pick up a razor, not unlike Lili. Some of these phenotypic anecdotes are genetic, but much of me looks this way because I am my father's daughter, and he kept me in motion with him—rolling under cars to drain stagnant oil, holding his nails between my teeth when he lacked a free hand, climbing trees in the spirit of boyish competition—when a great many American fathers were content to let their children remain indoors with the Saturday morning cartoons. At some point, absent a father, I decided to remain in this very peculiar sort of motion. Like *¿Eres tú, papá?*'s tagline warns, sometimes, *it runs in the family*.

Black Body Snatchers

SAMUEL AUTMAN

Get Out

SEATED AT MY desk at the *Salt Lake Tribune*, my foot tapped and palms moistened at the thought that Utah's fourteenth governor was outside in his limousine, waiting to see me. In January 1993, I was twenty-six years old and, as a new *Tribune* reporter, had snagged an interview with Michael Leavitt Jr., the governor's namesake and sixteen-year-old son, without his office knowing it, a move that left them unnerved.

"He just wants to talk to you," the governor's press secretary had assured me on the phone moments earlier.

My thoughts raced. What did the governor want? Would he try to coerce me out of writing my story? What would he say, or do—or have done to me? Could a journalist actually be killed in Utah? In the movies, the Black guy should know not to get into a vehicle with an unknown white man, even—or perhaps, especially—if he's the governor, right? At six-foot-four and over 200 pounds, they'd have a hard time stuffing my body in a trunk, at least.

I considered simply not going down there, but the risk of his office never again answering my calls was too great. I grabbed my reporter's notebook, slid my coat on, walked downstairs, and pushed open the door to the cold winter wind. A long town car waited. A man in a dark suit and tie flung open the passenger's door. Braced for a verbal lashing, I climbed into the back seat.

Black Body Snatchers

IT'S UNSURPRISING THAT, twenty-four years later, *Get Out*, a horror movie written and directed by a cishet Black man in 2017, claps back to the racial horrors I experienced in the 1990s in Salt Lake City, Utah. As a Black, gay journalist in one of the nation's whitest cities, I was two moving targets for the social violence often aimed at outsiders. *Get Out*'s theme of navigating unwelcoming spaces is, in the heart and mind of this queer and Black man, the perfect lens.

The film opens with a tall, lean Black man cradling a smartphone as he navigates a dimly lit upscale neighborhood. He notices a white car following him. To get away, he crosses the street. He then sees the car parked, empty, a door open. From behind, a man in a black helmet grabs, subdues, and stuffs him in the trunk, delivering a message most Black people have been conditioned to know: *Black bodies aren't safe anywhere in America*. That opening blends horror and satire, setting a tone for a film unlike any that most of us had ever seen. Peele captures the unbearableness of being Black and existing in spaces that center whites. Ironically, the film premiered thirty-two miles away at the Sundance Film Festival in Park City. Organizers keep the ten-day festival anchored in a ski resort town in January, which appeals to white die-hard film lovers willing to traverse ice and snow to get there. Park City in January looks more like Austria than America. Perhaps without even realizing, Peele had landed the perfect setting to debut his blistering debut disguised as a horror movie. Years later, we'll learn that Daniel Kaluuya, the film's Black star and eventual Academy Award nominee for Best Actor, was somehow left off the invite list for the premiere.

MY TREPIDATION evaporated when Howdy Doody in a suit extended his right hand to me. "Welcome to Utah," Governor Leavitt said. His Beehive State pride beamed. Born in Cedar City, southern Utah, he'd spent most of his life living in the same state. Leavitt was especially proud of Utah's reputation for family values (code-speak for

Mormonism). He asked for my first impressions of his beloved state. Gazing out of the window at downtown's old and new architecture, I gave him the answer he expected: "It's really beautiful here."

Salt Lake City is indeed a stunning place, especially in snowdrifts. Encased by the Wasatch Mountains, it's hard to find a spot in the city that doesn't have a resplendent mountain view. They soothe and reassure. The streets are always clean, with little or no trash anywhere, so different from St. Louis, where I grew up. What most people notice about the city are its wide streets. Folklore tells that Brigham Young wanted to be able to lock arms with all twenty-seven of his wives and turn around in the streets with them. Locals referred to Salt Lake City and Utah generally as Zion or heavenly destination for the faithful. I call it all Mormon Land.

Ten minutes in, the small talk ceased.

"Samuel, please don't hurt my family," Leavitt said, worry carved into his face.

"Sir, you have nothing to worry about. This is going to be a harmless feature. Trust me, no one's going to be hurt. In fact, your office will call and thank me when you see it in the paper."

The assumption I'd commit journalistic violence against a teenage boy stunned me. In his mind, I was an instrument of Utah's leftist newspaper plotting against his family. Leavitt had just been elected into office, so everything was new to him. He had fabricated it in his own "sunken place," which, according to *Get Out*'s mythos, is an interior dimension where silence renders people unable to name what's oppressing them. The man from whom I expected a tongue-lashing turned out to be a father whimpering to protect his son. I felt shitty.

For about twenty minutes, we rode around downtown as I tried to calm him. The more I talked, the less he seemed convinced. Could he not accept my words because they fell from Black lips? Race was never off the table for me. "I promised my wife I'd protect our family," he kept saying, his eyes periodically watering. My editor, I explained, thought we'd do a cute story about the two Michael Leavitts living in the governor's mansion, that simple.

Finally, the limousine returned to the *Tribune* building. Leavitt seemed slightly relieved, but he was still wracked with concern. The editors wanted something whimsical, but the Leavitts fully anticipated a cruel hit-piece. I extended my right hand as we bid one another farewell. My Black body unfolded itself from the backseat, relieved to have made it out safely.

Three days later, as I had predicted, the governor's office called, thanking me for "a wonderful story." Their imagined horror movie proved to be a hologram, a fable of their own creation. Here's the delicious irony: like the friendly white people on beautiful land in *Get Out*, this Republican, Mormon governor was capable of doing far more damage to my Black, queer body than I could ever to him or his family. Over the next three and a half years, my position as a journalist gave me a bird's-eye view of the culture wars, Utah style.

As the *Salt Lake Tribune*'s first Black reporter, navigating Utah's cultural landscape where most didn't look like me, it always struck me that something that I couldn't name was undergirding people's responses to me. I had graduated from the University of Missouri's top-rated journalism program and felt called to a life beyond the regional *Tulsa World*. As I applied for positions at brand-name newspapers, the feedback was clear: I needed to up my writing game. Being Black was always the wild card hidden in the deck.

I see clear traces of myself in Chris, *Get Out*'s protagonist, an up-and-coming Black photographer whose craft for documenting his environs will be instrumental in unlocking and surviving the conspiracy that surrounds him. Like Chris, I grew up anchored in a Black community hearing contradictory messages: on one hand, we were told by Dr. King to "look to a day when people will not be judged by the color of their skin but by the content of their character," and on the other, cautioned about the dangers of losing our authentic selves.

"You'd better be careful hanging out with all of those white people," my mother would say. That's not unlike Rod, Chris's friend and the film's comic relief, asking Chris why he planned on meeting his white girlfriend's parents. Chris puts it less eloquently, of course—"What? Does she lick your balls or somethin'?"—but it's a warning all the same.

The White Girlfriend, appropriately named Rose, can barely wait for Chris to meet her parents. Her father, Dean, is a neurosurgeon, and her mother, Missy, a psychiatrist who uses hypnotherapy in her home office. When Chris asks if Rose's parents know she's dating a Black man, her response is auspicious: "My dad would've legit voted for Obama a third time if he could've." Rose displays a disarming adoration toward Chris, the perfect white seductress for a plot he cannot yet see. The Armitages represent an idealized white family, wealthy, living on a sprawling property in upstate New York. Both appear so immediately embracive of their daughter's new man. The only family member sending off hostile vibes is the younger brother, Jeremy—but, it's explained, he simply drinks too much.

My seducers were Tiffany, Jonathan, and Bethany, relatively new *Tribune* staffers who had taken reporting positions there from other states. During my October 1992 interview, the editor handed them the company credit card and they took me to an Italian restaurant, where we sat outside under the stars in a neighborhood called Sugarhouse. At least two bottles of red wine disappeared as they shared battle stories about life in Utah as non-Mormon journalists. They were the kinds of reporters I aspired to be, their stories frequently landing on the front page. As Rose is for Chris, they were attractive, charming white women I met as I ascended to bigger and better things. It wasn't lost on me that, under different circumstances, I would have never crossed paths with them. They were people I admired and respected immediately, but, in that kind of setting, whiteness is the unspoken, invisible element, visible only to those with eyes for it. Though all these years later they would certainly say race was never discussed that night, I don't even have to debate the memory, as I never had the luxury of forgetting my Blackness.

During that week of interviews, another editor asked me point-blank: "Are you *sure* you want to move out here with all these white people?" I appreciated his directness but I was already the *Tulsa World*'s sole Black reporter. He was pointing to the demographics of the state, which at the time had a Black population of fewer than one percent. I underestimated the perceptivity of his question. In Oklahoma, I took seeing other Black people on the streets for granted. In Utah, I instinctively wanted to hug them, but settled for exchanging The Black Nod we use in predominantly white spaces.

Though when I accepted the job several weeks later I never had any delusions that I would ever be anything but a Black man, his warning quickly proved prophetic. During my first week on the job, I was having lunch with three new colleagues at a *Tribune* hangout when a white waitress got salty with me. When arriving with our food, she cut a stern look in my direction.

"Sir, could you move that saucer out of the way so I can sit your clam chowder down."

"Yes, ma'am," I said, doing as she asked.

"Thank you, sir," she snapped. "That's mighty white of you."

My new colleagues were stunned and perplexed by her response to me, but I received it with little impact. The comment, strange in its content but explicit in its intention, became a signpost marking the first of many awkward exchanges and looks I'd endure over the next three and a half years. Once, at the end of a speech I was covering at the University of Utah, someone told me I could start breaking the chairs and tables down. Another time, a convenience store clerk in Provo called the police on me; the only explanation I heard from his end of the call was, "He's in here."

My favorite recurring question was, "Do you play for the Utah Jazz?"

My favorite response: "No, I don't play any instruments."

THE PINNACLE OF *Get Out*'s masterful blend of white liberal micro-aggression and sinister subtext occurs when Rose's parents host an annual party for their "like-minded" friends, nearly all of whom are tripping over themselves to corner Chris and lavish him with back-handed compliments (among them, a tired Tiger Woods name-drop.)

"The pendulum has swung back again, hasn't it?" a man shrieks. "Black is in fashion!"

Lisa, an elegant older brunette, squeezes Chris's bicep in an all too familiar way, as if she is shopping for a field slave on an auction block. "So, it is true," she asks. "Is it better?"

Rose cackles at the sexual innuendo. Chris nearly chokes on his drink. The questions and curiosity about his experiences as a Black man are relentless. Looking across the crowd, Chris feels some relief when he finally spots another Black man (at least one who isn't the help). As Chris approaches the man, he realizes he's Andre, someone he grew up with, but who now stands before him dressed in a suit too conservative and muted for his youthful body, his voice and mannerisms decidedly white. Andre, we also realize, is the man who was snatched at the beginning of the film. A puzzle piece falls into place for us, the viewer, while Chris's suspicions and confusion grow.

Get Out's most understated moments happen between Black characters, notably between Chris and Georgina, the Armitages' housekeeper. Like Andre, she speaks and carries herself as though performing whiteness. In a deeply unsettling scene, Georgina apologizes to Chris for moving his phone. "How rude of me to have touched your belongings without asking."

"Naw, it's cool," Chris assures her. "I was just confused."

Their conversation is objectively strange, but, as an interaction between Black characters, it's mind-blowing. Chris relaxes into a more urban dialect when he speaks to Georgina, but Georgina folds her arms and enunciates every word like she's being interviewed to work for an all-white corporation.

"All I know is sometimes if it's too many white people I get nervous," Chris says, as if testing her, pushing her to agree.

Georgina pauses, leaned her head forward, and begins to cry-laugh, robotically, a clear reference to the short-circuiting fembots of 1975's *The Stepford Wives*. "No, no, no, no, no, no no," Georgina insists, shaking her head. "Aren't you something? That's not my experience. Not at all. The Armitages are so good to us. They treat us like family."

They treat us like family. The phrase echoes back to the way some house slaves spoke of their masters and the way some Black housekeepers spoke, too. Peele's commentary here is particularly shrewd. Georgina's manner also critiques a segment of Black people referred to as Oreos (Black on the outside, white on the inside), more recently replaced with BINO (Black in Name Only); in other words, race traitors.

A BLACK WOMAN who had been living in Utah since the early 1980s was hired at the *Tribune* as a night desk copy editor. Over the years, her disdain for me grew. "You're too cozy with these white people, Sam." (Curiously, she came to Salt Lake before me and stayed long after I'd gone.) She also quite memorably bristled upon learning I was gay. "Baby, you're smart, good-looking, and *you're gay?* What a fucking waste." Hostility from another Black body was the last thing I wanted to deal with. Whatever familiarity we had with each other quickly dissolved.

LEGAL THEORIST Kimberlé Crenshaw had planted the seed for intersectional thinking—how race, gender, and class were factors in the lives of people of color, women particularly. The only intersection I was aware of at the time was 200 South and Main Street, near the old *Tribune* building. Queerness was incidental in my mind, for

I could control neither my skin color nor my attraction to men, but navigating Utah in the 1990s felt like a doubly clandestine existence. Because Mormon Land is always at least twenty years behind the rest of the nation, stepping into any of its gay bars—The Sun, Bricks, The Trapp—felt like what I imagined the gay social scene to be in the 1970s, smoky and verboten.

Get Out astutely captures the perpetual awkwardness of an intersectional life. The Armitages, it turns out, are part of the Order of the Coagula, a cult designed to hunt, kidnap, brainwash, and trade places with healthy, youthful Black people. Black body snatchers. Soon it becomes clear that Georgina, the gardener, and Andre all had their Black bodies harvested, their brains replaced with those of white people whose bodies were failing them. This is Rose and her family's secret plan for Chris. While fumbling around in a closet, Chris finds a cache of photos showing Rose posing with eight different Black lovers, Georgina among them, all of whom she brought home for harvesting.

The film doesn't shy away from its warning about what can happen to Black people who ingratiate themselves to white people. We are not only risking our identities but our whole selves. Given the Mormon church's sketchy ideas and theology on the origins of Black skin, its secretive rituals and sacred underwear, comparing it to the Order of the Coagula hardly seems a stretch. In the Book of Mormon, 2 Nephi 5:21, it states Black skin is cursed after "the Lord God did cause a skin of blackness to come upon them." It goes on to declare whites are "exceedingly fair and delightsome." Coupled with the church's refusal to allow the descendants of African heritage to hold the priesthood from 1849 until 1978, Mormonism becomes wedded to a racist theology and history. Given the specificity of 2 Nephi 5:21, it becomes impossible to understand how any Black person could willingly join the Church of Latter-day Saints. Unless, of course, they've been body snatched.

AND THEN, the body snatchers came for me.

One day, outside my apartment—I lived on 200 South 1300 East, which means two blocks south and thirteen blocks east of the church headquarters, because absolutely everything in Utah exists in relation to Mormonism—I found myself confronted with two attractive, *Brady Bunch*–squeaky young women who identified themselves as LDS missionaries.

"May we have a few minutes of your time, Brother Sam?" asked Sister Thurman, a blond woman with shoulder-length hair and glasses, squeezing her Book of Mormon. Sister Thurman did that thing many Americans do when they hear my name: they assume the right to assign me a nickname, to edit, to cut me down. *Brother Sam.* I winced internally at the sound of it.

If there's a more zealous human being on earth than a Mormon missionary knocking on doors in Salt Lake City, I haven't met them. After politely allowing them to outline the tenets of their faith—Sister Thurman referred to note cards—for close to fifteen minutes, I finally let out an exasperated sigh. "Can you quit looking down at that and speak to me from what's in your own heart?"

"Excuse me?" Sister Thurman asked, startled.

"Don't you know what you believe without having to read that script?"

She was quiet for a second. "What would you like to know about our church?"

"What I really want to know is why I would subscribe to a philosophy that says I am cursed because of the color of my skin."

Sister Thurman paused. "Well, it says in the Book of Mormon that the Lord did darken both the heart and skin of the wicked."

"Precisely. So why would I, a Black man, want to join *that?*" My voice rose. I'd show her wicked. "What does your church hold for me?"

"I can see that you have an argumentative spirit. We're going to have to leave," she said, exchanging a glance with her partner.

My horns grew. The gay, dark-skinned demon in me was ready for a scripture rumble. "You still haven't answered my question. What was your name again?" I knew her name.

The women closed their books and hurried away from my apartment. They promised to pray for my soul. I thanked them for coming by.

IN THE END, it is a Black man who comes to Chris's rescue. Rod, his suspicions confirmed and warnings validated, appears just in the nick of time, preventing Chris from strangling the life from Rose.

In the end, a Black man came to my rescue, too: the late Gregory B. Freeman, a friend, mentor, and columnist for the *St. Louis Post-Dispatch*, called to tell me of an opening. I applied, got it, and got out.

Portions of this essay appeared in "A Dash of Pepper in the Snow," in The Chalk Circle: Prizewinning Intercultural Essays, Wyatt-MacKenzie Publishing, 2012.

Long Nights in the Dark

RICHARD SCOTT LARSON

Halloween

JOHN CARPENTER'S *HALLOWEEN* opens with the postcoital murder of a half-naked adolescent girl at the hands of her younger brother, Michael Myers. He has just witnessed his sister's seduction of a beautiful young man while spying on them through a window on Halloween night. What follows is a dreamlike first-person sequence that ends with the viewer looking through the eyeholes of a mask. As his sister's lover bounds down the stairs and out the door, casually pulling on a striped T-shirt over a perfectly toned chest and torso, Michael seemingly takes the young man's place, retracing his steps up the stairs and into the bedroom where his sister sits topless at a vanity table. He notices that the bed behind her is unmade, the sheets ruffled, evidence of an exchange that Michael doesn't yet understand but for which he intuitively believes she must be punished.

The revelation of heterosexual desire seems to have triggered the onset of a latent evil inside Michael's young body. This evil finds its mode of expression in the shiny blade of a kitchen knife, the first iteration of what will become his weapon of choice. After donning a clownish mask that had been discarded on the floor by the departed lover, Michael hacks his screaming sister to shreds before enacting his own postclimax exit down the staircase and out the front door. Outside the house, he encounters his parents emerging from the family car, and his father calls out to him by name as he approaches the street. But rather than relieve his son of the bloodied knife, Michael's father first removes the mask. The imperative in this scene isn't immediately to disarm the costumed Michael Myers of a murder weapon; rather, it's to reveal him, to show his face.

The opening of *Halloween* is a coming-out story.

I WAS MAYBE ten years old when my father took me to the video store during one of the weekends when I was staying with him at the old house where we had all lived before the divorce, and we came home with a VHS copy of *Halloween*. I remember wandering the aisles alone while my father waited in the car, nursing one of the beers that he brought with him for even the shortest of drives. I inspected every film in the store before finally settling on *Halloween*, charmed by the haunting simplicity of the cover image of a vicious jack-o'-lantern seemingly gripping the exaggeratedly angled blade of a knife, the fire inside the pumpkin visible only through the carved-out holes of its eyes.

I was reminded of the horror paperbacks that lined the shelves of my mother's bookcase. Their covers featured eyes glowing in perfect darkness, or headlights in the distance on an otherwise empty street, or a dark house on a hilltop beneath a stormy sky with just the uppermost attic window glowing bright, as if to say that the only person inside was to be kept hidden upstairs, perpetually out of sight. By then I had already read most of those novels, shuttling them in my backpack to and from school and then from one parent's house to the other, and I already knew that what interested me in the world was also what scared me: the unexplainable, the supernatural, characters suffering random violence at the hands of strangers.

I instantly became obsessed with *Halloween*. The dread-inducing and methodically paced score became the soundtrack to my own life, and I would hum its provocative notes as I walked or cycled through the streets and sidewalks of a small town that was to me a direct facsimile of Haddonfield, Illinois, where the future victims of Michael Myers sauntered home from school clutching textbooks and discussing their plans for the night. I could see myself in the universe of *Halloween*, recognizing its contours for the shape my own life had taken. I grew up a few hours south of fictional Haddonfield in the suburbs of St. Louis, Missouri, but when Laurie Strode—the film's protagonist and Michael's primary obsession, his victims almost always being the people closest to her—peered out the window onto sidewalks filled with trick-or-treaters, she might as well have been looking out onto my street, my sidewalk, my house next door.

I was entranced by the way *Halloween*'s villain moved so slowly and ploddingly, knife in hand and mask firmly attached to his face, and yet always still managed to catch up with the young people who would eventually become his victims. As if the act of being deliberate about his choices was enough for him to get exactly what he wanted. After Michael's escape from the asylum where he's presumably been housed for the fifteen long years since his sister's murder, he's now returned home to Haddonfield, the scene of the original crime, and the camera in Carpenter's film adopts not only the pace of Michael's defining lope but also the nature of his perspective. Many of the exterior shots are framed as if viewed not by an audience but by a bystander—someone watching unnoticed, just off to the side of its characters' immediate focus, waiting for the perfect time to strike. The film teaches a voyeuristic way of being in the world, a way of looking without being seen. I recall my first furtive glances at other boys in the locker room after gym class and longing for the safety of something like Michael's mask, the ability to hide a desire that I knew would be made plain by a quick glance in the direction of my gaze.

I WATCHED *Halloween* countless times after that first viewing with my father, always in the dark, always aware that I was coming closer and closer to unearthing something locked up within myself. Sometimes I would rewind and start the film over immediately from the beginning after delighting once more in the revelation of Michael's uncanny escape after having been presumably vanquished. I recognized something in the expression of existential anguish settling onto Laurie's young face as she realizes that she's been consigned to a lifetime of looking over her shoulder for the bogeyman.

The reason I was able to watch the film so frequently was because my father never returned it to the video store. The tape and its plastic box remained at the house, the small label on the otherwise blank container revealing only the name of the film, the year of its release, and its genre: *horror*, a word that would come to imply a kind of comfort for me throughout my childhood and adolescence, an increasingly necessary escape from the real.

I finally stopped watching *Halloween* on a continuous loop when I stopped going inside my father's house during the mandatory visits after the divorce. The film remained on the other side of a doorway through which I had come to dread entering. My father was an all-day drinker by then, his eyes always glassy and far away, empty cans littering every surface of the kitchen, the carpet in the hallway perpetually soiled. He would pass out and wake up and start drinking again, cases of beer at a time, like it was some kind of race to get it all down. My mother would drop me off outside his house on Saturday mornings and I would wait for her to drive away before storing the cooler containing my lunch in the backseat of his car, always left unlocked in a neighborhood like the one we lived in, and then I would play with the neighborhood kids until dusk, when my mother would pick me up again. And by then I saw the streets of my old neighborhood through Carpenter's lens—danger lurking behind every hedgerow, the possibility of the bogeyman stepping out onto the sidewalk in front of me and the knowledge that he would catch me no matter how fast I ran.

No one knew where I was. Anything could have happened.

I WAS AFRAID of being a teenager long before I became one. What I knew or at least expected of adolescence was that it would involve performing desire in the form of pursuing girls and trying to lure them into dark corners. The heavy petting I had seen in movies always took place in closets. I didn't yet have a name for what I was, but I knew that it was derogatory. Schoolyard jeers portrayed queerness as a weakness, an affliction, some kind of monstrosity. I watched with a barely containable resentment as the girls flirted openly with the most alluring of the boys in the hallways of my large public middle school, all of their bodies having sprung suddenly from awkward childhood into something resembling beauty, and I didn't understand yet that I hated these girls because I wanted to *be* them, or at least to hold the power that they held over the boys chasing them, pawing at them, trying to claim them. I didn't understand yet that what I wanted was to be claimed by those boys in exactly that same way.

In one of my last memories of my father, we met in a public park, the old house having been lost to foreclosure, and he tried to talk to me about girls. I was twelve years old and a girl named Sarah had recently pursued me at school, leaving notes in my locker and then, in a brave show of vulnerability, asking me to a school dance. I accepted because I was afraid of what would happen if I turned her down, failing to play the part I'd been assigned. But the night of the dance came and I pretended to be sick and I avoided her afterward at school in the most cringeworthy, obvious ways. She never asked me out again after that, and we eventually became just two young people who would pass each other in the hallway with maybe a smile, maybe a small wave, the confusion and hurt in the wake of what had happened never exhumed or made right.

But I couldn't tell my father about any of that. Instead, I invented a crush and invented a failed pursuit of this imaginary crush, invented an explanation for why I spent all of my time alone.

WATCHING *HALLOWEEN* was the first time that I knowingly witnessed a blatant representation of human sexuality—in this case, heterosexual human sexuality, the kind of buzzing horniness most explicit in representations of adolescence on film and television—and what I saw confirmed to me that I was not welcome there. There's a scene in the second half of *Halloween* in which Laurie's friend, Lynda, welcomes who she believes is her boyfriend, Bob, back into the bedroom in which they've just finished having sex. She slowly reveals her naked breasts to him from behind a bedsheet, the camera's gaze sliding down her body in imitation of Bob's own, until she is fully revealed, smiling seductively as if she knows that she is giving Bob exactly what he wants. She understands his desire, and she knows how to satisfy it. But she doesn't know that the man she thinks is her boyfriend is actually Michael Myers in disguise. She doesn't know that he has just stabbed Bob to death after rushing out at him from a closet, and that what he desires is something different entirely.

I understood that I should want to look too—that what Lynda expected Bob to gawk at was something that I was also expected to gawk at—but I ended up identifying more with Michael Myers than with these young, doomed characters who would shortly succumb to the actualization of a desire that does not match their own. The experience of adolescence as a closeted queer boy is one of constantly attempting to imitate the expression of a desire that you do not feel. Identification with a bogeyman, then, shouldn't be so surprising when you imagine the bogeyman as unfit for society, his true nature having been rejected and deemed horrific.

And Michael as Bob is not only wearing the familiar mask now ubiquitously associated with his character in the *Halloween* franchise—he's also wearing a white sheet covering his entire body, with Bob's glasses resting delicately where his own eyes are. The imitation is deliberate and well-imagined. Michael is pretending to be a straight man—a straight, sexualized man—in order to make possible the expression of his true desire, a pursuit far more deviant than the enactment of a heterosexual coupling. He is wearing a mask over a mask. And he seems so cartoonish in this moment, his desire to conceal himself having reached the level of self-parody. How silly it looks to hide in plain sight.

THE SECOND TIME Michael Myers is unmasked in *Halloween* — after his father removes his mask in the film's opening sequence — is by Laurie Strode herself. She has just risen from the hallway floor where she had been recovering from the shock of what she believed to be her final encounter with Michael, having stabbed him with his own knife and believing him to be dead, when he suddenly rises from the floor behind her. He begins to walk toward Laurie just as she steps out onto the landing, and she is alone in the frame for only a moment — thinking she is safe — before Michael catches her from behind and turns her around to face him, his hands at her throat. He begins to choke her.

Laurie's panicked astonishment is palpable as she thrashes about within his grip, and in the commotion, we think she's grappling for his throat, perhaps trying to weaken his hold on her. But then we see that she's instead trying to remove his mask, as if she intuitively recognizes the source of his power. To disarm him, she must reveal him. And I remember the horrified expression on his face when it was finally displayed on-screen — ugly and confused, blinking in the sudden light, all of the threat he had previously posed dissolving in his sudden nakedness. He releases Laurie in the effort to conceal himself, fumbling desperately with the cheap plastic, and I remember hating the look of him without the mask. My body seized with an urgent, almost unbearable need for him to put it back on. I didn't want to see him like that.

EARLY IN THE summer in which I would later turn thirteen years old, my mother took me on a weeklong vacation to Florida with the man she had been dating for several years. The sprawling seaside resort was magical to me—it was the first time I had seen the ocean, and now we could see it out of almost every window—and I often explored the grounds while my mother and her boyfriend were upstairs in the rented room, sleeping off the effects of morning poolside cocktails. I would get myself lost and then make a game of finding my way back to our building again, one of several identical towers in the complex, mapping the space between them as lizards scurried across the sun-scorched path at my feet. One afternoon, I was swimming alone in the shallow end of the pool when a man waded toward me. He said he'd been watching me, that I looked lonely, like I could use some company. His chest hair was thick and his arms looked strong. He had large teeth that revealed themselves when he smiled. He suggested that we play a game.

The game we played was that I would swim between his legs, straddled wide at first, with the goal of not touching him at all as I swam through, and each time I did, he would narrow his stance further, closing the gap, making it more and more difficult for me to pass without our skin touching. I thought I was winning the game because I kept angling my body just so, and I would get through each time without my own legs rubbing against his. But then I went down again and saw that he had pulled himself out of his swimming shorts, his cock now lolling in the water above me.

I knew that he wanted me to touch it, to willfully or even accidentally lose the game. It was clear what he wanted to provide for me, and what I would be expected to provide in exchange. I wondered later, after the fear and confusion and disgust with myself had dulled to a gnawing sense of dread, what I had done to show him that I might have wanted it. Had he seen me watching the older boys in the pool whose bodies were already lined with smooth, curved muscles snaking down their arms and torsos, loose swim shorts hanging just below the stark tan lines on their waists, clinging tightly to their bodies as they pulled themselves up the ladder out of the pool? Had he known how badly I wanted to be with them, to wrestle with them in the water and allow them to hold my head under until my lungs were bursting, but that I was too afraid to approach them, too afraid that if I got too close, they would recognize what I really desired from them?

I swam away and hurried up the ladder, running all the way back to the room without bothering to gather my things. I pounded frantically on the door until my mother let me in, complaining about how much noise I was making. But the man from the pool had followed me. He knocked on the door shortly after I came inside, and when she opened it for him, he asked my mother whether I wanted to come back down and continue the game we had started. I imagined him walking slowly up from the pool while I scrambled toward safety, thinking that he could get what he wanted just by asking—by showing up and telling me exactly what was going to happen next, whether I liked it or not.

I remember shaking my head vigorously, refusing to even look up at him in the doorway from where I'd burrowed into the cushions of the cheap couch, and my mother eventually turned him away, perhaps baffled by the exchange, expecting me to have chosen a different kind of friend. But even after he was gone, I knew he had taken something from me. What I had thought was only a secret desire had actually been visible on my body all along to those who knew how to look. I had never really been wearing a mask at all.

MY FATHER DIED while we were in Florida. We didn't find out until we got back home, because no one had wanted to interrupt our vacation. I was in my mother's bedroom unpacking when she answered the phone next to the mirror at her vanity table.

The last time I'd used that telephone was when I'd hung up on my father just before our trip. He was slurring his words and I angrily accused him of being drunk yet again. Our last conversation. When my mom told me that he was gone, I thought at first that he had died from a sudden relapse of the cancer he had suffered through a few years before, during which time we would visit him in the hospital, a dimly lit room full of the various machines to which he had been attached. But the truth was that he had drank himself to death. He had been driving home from a bar. He was often drunk when he drove, beer cans nestled between his legs and at his feet; sometimes he'd pull over to vomit out the open window. He had pulled over to the side of the road this time, too, crawled out, and waited for his heart to stop.

I became a teenager one month after my father's funeral. I entered adolescence during a summer in which I didn't sleep, simply waited up every night in darkness, thinking that if I succumbed to sleep then I'd succumb to death. I watched endless horror movies on the small television above my bed in an effort to keep myself awake, and I became acquainted with other villains aside from Michael Myers, each with his own particular desire and his own particular method of enacting its consummation. I was giving myself an education in what to expect from the world, or in how I expected the world to eventually receive me, and those long nights alone in the dark were spent paralyzed at the threshold of a reckoning I couldn't yet imagine.

My father had been there, too, and he'd seen his way through to the end. Maybe that final night wasn't the darkest he had ever known, but it was the last of a series of dark nights, the end of a long pursuit by his own relentless bogeyman. Because in his story, he was the one being chased.

I FINALLY RECORDED *Halloween* onto a blank tape from a late-night television broadcast after searching in vain for the old video-store copy in the boxes in my father's basement. I watched it over and over again that summer, renewing my obsession with seeing the world through Michael's eyes. I was struck for the first time by the final moments of Carpenter's film. Following the revelation that Michael Myers has indeed escaped into the night largely unscathed, the camera lingers on images of interior domestic spaces now made fraught by Michael's various intrusions into their presumed realms of safety, as if he's perhaps still there, lying in wait behind the couch or the curtains, appearing suddenly at the top of a dark staircase. And the final shots of the film are static images of the Haddonfield houses where the murders and attacks were committed, as if to show us that what seems innocuous on the outside can in fact contain deadly secrets. The lights are all off, and we can't see in through the windows, but we know what might be lurking just beyond those seemingly inviting front doors.

By the end of *Halloween*, earlier representations of the suburban landscape as benign and knowable are rendered shortsighted, and the film asks us to gauge our expectations about these domestic spaces against the knowledge we now have about what they might contain. I would lie awake in bed the summer after my father's death and picture what my house looked like from the outside, a modest two-story in a row of small houses in a quiet neighborhood where young children often played in the street until dusk. Mine was the only upstairs bedroom window that faced out onto the street, and I often wondered whether it was obvious from the outside that someone like me was living there.

In the early morning hours, long before dawn but after the house had fallen asleep around me, the windows would be dark and the horrors on the television would be muted and I would allow myself the pleasure of my own touch. And just before I came, the man from the pool would always resurface like some kind of secret companion in my mind. I fantasized relentlessly about what might have happened if I hadn't run away that day, hadn't come up for air but instead had done everything I imagined he might have offered.

I follow him to an empty room at the resort, photographs of seashells in cheap frames on the wall, a painting of an endless horizon at sunset hung at a slight tilt above the unmade bed. He turns off the lights, draws the curtains, and steps toward me in the dark. I am already hard when he grabs me by the shoulders, throws me over to the bed, and scrambles toward me, his body heavy on top of mine as he tugs my wet swim shorts down to my ankles.

I wasn't twelve years old anymore. He wasn't doing anything wrong. After all, I had been begging for it. Everyone had seen.

This essay originally appeared, in slightly different form, as "What Halloween Taught Me About Queerness," in Electric Literature, October 31, 2017.

On Beauty and Necrosis

SACHIKO RAGOSTA

Eyes Without a Face

THOUGH THE MIRRORS throughout the house have been painted black to hide her reflection, the distorted glimpses Christiane catches of herself in knife blades and varnished wood are enough to convince her of her own monstrosity. A story of bodily rebellion, *Eyes Without a Face* follows Christiane as her father, Dr. Génessier, attempts again and again to cover her scarred-up face with a pretty new one. Dr. Génessier insists his daughter wears a pale mask between failed facial transplants. Carved to a French beauty ideal, the mask is stiff and impermeable except for two eyeholes and a small, unmoving slit between plump, bowed lips. Even with this mask, Christiane spends her days hiding away in her room. Smothering her face with a pillow, she declares, "My face frightens me. My mask frightens me even more."

MASKS ARE A familiar motif for many queer people. Faces cut to a doll-like perfection with holes to see but barely enough of an opening to breathe. I passed my youth with my best mask forward. In elementary school, I sat with the boys during lunch, a cargo shorts–wearing, mixed-race tomboy who listened to Green Day and played Pokémon on the bus. With the sprouting of an excess upon my chest came a new pressure to perform, to act as something that my body signified to the rest of the world. I began to shave my legs and wear dresses and bras just like the other presumed girls, at least the ones who were considered cool. Puberty makes us vulnerable in the changing chaos of our bodies, leaving us confused and groping about for some model, some mirror. For queerness in central Virginia, there was none. Without queer reflected back at me, I didn't know I could be anything but that long, blond-haired mannequin that came in all shapes and sizes, a fun home of white femininity. It wasn't just the lack of a physical reflection but also the lack of expansive futures. That mannequin was destined for marriage and two-and-a-half kids.

As I grew older, a new form of masking was required of me, flagging my steady march toward a singular future. As girls and boys began to date, I found myself searching for this new cover-up, a flesh-made rendering of my normalcy. Queers use the term *beard* to describe this kind of union formed to hide the identity of one or both individuals. My beards were not consciously chosen in this way. I confused an internalized overvaluation of boys' validation as a reflection of my sexuality, as me liking boys back. Though some part of me recognized the all-nighters and spontaneous ice cream dates I shared with close girlfriends was an intimacy deeper and more authentic than the prom pictures and fifteen minutes of lunch I shared with high school boyfriends so everyone else knew we were dating.

AFTER THE FIRST failed transplant, Christiane wastes away in a far corner of the mansion while her father's assistant scours the streets of Paris for the poachable faces of beautiful, blond-haired, blue-eyed women. Her father has faked her death, falsely identifying the body from which he extracted the last face as Christiane's, so that no one, not even her fiancé, Jacques, expects her to materialize outside the mansion.

The next victim is Edna Grüber, a Swiss girl with that archetypal curved nose and bright eyes. It doesn't matter whether she looks like Christiane once did. Christiane's faked death makes her a blank slate, her revival not dependent upon an accurate restoration of her face. The only requirement is that she be beautiful by the standard her father has set. Before the transplant, Christiane sneaks into the basement where Edna is strapped to an operating table. Christiane removes her mask before approaching Edna's unconscious body. Edna eases into consciousness as Christiane's fingers explore her face, the camera focusing with her to reveal the mountain ranges of raised scar tissue on Christiane's face. Edna screams as Christiane slowly backs away, her face relaxed, almost smug, her eyes unwavering from her future reflection.

MY EDNA WAS a tall artist with twinkly brown eyes and eyelashes that created the illusion of permanent mascara. His was the first face I reached for with that twisted smile after having seen my own reflection unmasked, my queerness clear and unambiguous. My Edna was the first person to whom I said the words "I'm bisexual"—the best approximation I could come up with at the time, the words that were available to me in the murky disentangling of what was mine and what was borrowed. My Edna, just as the Edna in the film, had opened his eyes to see some version of that scarred-up face. Though unlike Edna, he did not scream in horror. At least, not at first. Instead, he asked if he could watch me have sex with a woman.

WITH EDNA'S FACE successfully sewn onto Christiane, she sits at the dinner table with her father and the assistant. They praise Christiane's beauty, telling her, "You're more beautiful than ever. There is something angelic about you now." Christiane rejects these comments. Her eyes float around, uncertain. She says that while her reflection looks like her, she feels like she's looking at someone "from the Beyond." This borrowed face, though beautiful, has morphed her into something more distant, more alien than what is beneath.

After dinner, Dr. Génessier remarks that Christiane's face looks flushed. The assistant flags an awareness of what has just begun, a slow rejection of Edna's facial tissue. A chronology of Christiane's head-shots follows. Something guilty in her eyes as her skin slowly changes colors, bubbles and droops. As these images appear on the screen, Dr. Génessier explains the natural projection of necrosis, the death of flesh that does not belong.

NECROSIS WAS A slow and steady process with my Edna. About a month after coming out to him, he admitted to me that he knew I could, and feared I would, fall in love with a woman. After two months of his persistent unwanted comments about my body, appraisal of a part of me I had only felt betrayed by, and claiming that he found my intelligence intimidating, I told him I worried I was "too feminist to be in a relationship with a man." I drifted into nothingness while we had sex, fixating on some detail in the room or retreating to another world within my head as he made love to a vacant body. He noticed my dissociation and read it as a rejection of him, evidence that I must be in love with someone else. While I wasn't, I persuaded him to open up our relationship, plowing through his insistence that he only wanted to be with me. I knew this would bring our end. I knew the mask had bubbled, drooped and turned gray, no longer capable of hiding the extent to which I could not fit in a cishet relationship.

It took some time to stop seeing myself as the monster of that relationship. My scars: an insatiable appetite for novelty, a belief in nonpossessive love, and constant critiques of his rigidly gendered behavior. To my Edna: a refusal to be happy, a refusal to love him with the same ferocity with which he loved the mask we had cocreated.

COMING INTO MY queerness was an agreement to no longer borrow someone else's skin to hide myself. In my first queer relationship, my partner at the time went straight for the mask I'd worn the longest:

right out of the womb, I was swaddled in a cisgender assumption. They taped my chest for the first time in the bathroom of my childhood home, rearranging the architecture of my flesh under the stretch of KT tape they had bought for me at the pharmacy. As I considered my reflection in the very place my mask was bestowed upon me, I gasped through conflicted tears, both relieved at the clarity with which I could make out my chest and overwhelmingly aware of the curve of my hips against its flatness.

The second time I taped my chest was for a gender-blurring photo-shoot with a good friend of mine and my partner, Ale, who was just beginning to understand their own transness. Though our relationship was still discovering itself, we shared intimately as friends. Ale and I met at an indie music festival and spent the months after singing drunken R&B covers, wing-personing each other at queer parties, and finding ourselves more and more often alone together by the end of the night, discussing identity and art. Ale had seen me topless. They had shaved my head in a friend's bathroom, shirt and bra abandoned on the lid of the toilet. Yet this night we exposed ourselves through adornment. I dabbed their lips with a vibrant red as black tape pulled back a piece of the mask I wasn't entirely sure they understood as such. The three of us posed together topless. Our arms draped around each other, bare bodies glowing beneath pink and blue lights.

I slept in my tape that night and woke to a voice message from Ale, shining into the next day with the invincibility of someone who has been held unmasked and lived to tell the tale. They told me they had connected with a part of their self they hadn't seen in a while. After taking a selfie of my own unmasked shine, I peeled off the tape to relieve myself of the tugging at the center of my chest. Though I worked gently, the tape took with it strips of skin that had blistered under the pressure. The hot water of the shower burned the tender patches, tingling more of me back to life.

MASKS AND DISSOCIATION go hand in hand. Christiane describes her reflection as someone, something from the Beyond, a disconnect between herself and the skin she's been sewn into. Some part of me got swapped, lost in the Beyond to maintain the facade necessary to be here. Pain opened up a portal. I knew from my relationship to body modifications, tattoos and piercings, that there was something about pain that resituated me back into my skin, like chiropractic for the psyche. Yet, the experience of this pain, the rawness of my chest after being tugged into a configuration that felt more like me, came with a sense of clarity. Pain not as a temporary adjustment but as a stretching into the me I had forgotten in the years my reflection was nowhere to be seen. When I got out of the shower, I looked lovingly at my foggy reflection, serous fluid glowing over my ruptured skin.

BEFORE DIRECTING *Eyes Without a Face*, Georges Franju largely made documentary films uncovering the horrors of industrialism in France. *The Blood of Beasts*, perhaps his most famous documentary, offers an exclusive look into a slaughterhouse in Paris, revealing the gore behind the pristinely packaged. The jump from documentary to horror is not such a big one. Documentary acts as a kind of unmasking, picking at the seams of what the viewer thinks they know to reveal some hidden truth, a monster hiding in plain sight. In horror, the monster is often explicitly identified from the beginning, though only later do the true horrors reveal themselves. The monster provides a humbling contrast to the monstrosity found in human form. In some cases, we may come to realize that the real monster is not who we thought at all but some third party responsible for our misdirected projection of monstrosity.

The documentary work that Franju does in *Eyes Without a Face* exposes the cruelty of Dr. Génessier who, by faking his daughter's death, hiding her reflection, and insisting she only return to society once her face is sufficiently beautiful, strips her of her humanity. He reduces her to her ability to fit into hegemonic standards of beauty, disinterested in the other parts of her that remain unmarred. In this way, *Eyes Without a Face* can be read as a subversion of the stories that paint trans people as masked murders (see: *Dressed to Kill, Psycho, The Silence of the Lambs, Sleepaway Camp*, etc.)—tricksters hiding some imagined biological truth. Trans people are reduced to our ability to fit some imagined but collectively reinforced standards of gender. The extent to which we meet these standards, however, does nothing to guarantee our safety, even more so for trans people of color as these standards are carved out of whiteness. Those who "pass" are either treated as the token of desirable (read: palatable) transness or accused of betrayal when they don't introduce themselves with a declaration of their transness; those who do not "pass" are attacked for the transgression of some imagined gender code of conduct; and those whose transness is not adequately visually flagged are delegitimized, deemed "not trans enough." Dr. Génessier serves as the police of this imagined gender code of conduct in *Eyes Without a Face*, the paternalistic enforcer of a single merit of belonging.

Transness is not a masking but rather an unmasking, a stripping of a performance expected of us by way of biological essentialism. For some trans people, this process of unmasking may require physical changes. Some may identify with this notion of the death of a past self. For others these changes are not necessary. They may feel as if they were never masked at all or that no physical representation accurately approximates their truth. Unmasking can be a delicate process as a nonbinary person because of its diversity of expression. Androgyny, for example (and not in any way synonymous with nonbinary), doesn't look a certain way, though gender is ingrained in society such that liberal readings are applied to everyone, sprinkling gender on everything from haircuts to careers to alcoholic beverages. In this way, presentation, when considered for the purposes of legibility, feels futile. I can wear oversize button-down shirts that drape on a bound chest, slouch my shoulders and trim my hair short to avoid being read as "cishet woman" at the very least. But I am more fluid, more expansive than an identity built off of what I am not.

As long as I am subjected to this unconsented reading of my body, I will desire nothing more than facelessness. I think of Christiane, whose father insists she wears the mask around the house so she gets used to it rather than taking it upon himself to accept and celebrate her face as is. It is violent to ask trans people to mask ourselves so it is easier for others to "understand" us, and this is not understanding at all. An effort to understand trans people looks like giving us space to tell our own stories to outnumber the stories that highlight trans tragedy and monstrosity, so that we may see many versions of ourselves reflected in the world. The power in a reflection is not in the simple fact of seeing a physical replication of ourselves but of knowing that there is more of us beyond that. That we are both here and there, expanding past the signifiers of our bodies.

THE TITLE, *Eyes Without a Face*, begs the question: Is a face of scars not still a face? Dr. Génessier constructs this false notion of facelessness by painting the mirrors black and insisting upon a face transplant to cover his own inability to accept Christiane's face as is. To call Christiane faceless is to ignore that her face is a healed wound. Some of us are the scars of society, the admission of a wounded world. We break open publicly, a tearing of ourselves both literal, via the physical assault of marginalized people, and figurative, in the untethering of ourselves from the narratives we were born into. Our breaking bears evidence to the liquidity and resilience of the human form, a fluidity that some experiences never melt into. To be queer is to be a wound. We wear our hearts on our sleeves because there is a warrant for the public declaration of who we love. Transness, in all of its forms, is a declaration of a love of ourselves, a prioritization of our authenticity over fulfillment of some expectation.

I have heard many trans people share this story: of parents taking personally the discovery that the mask they provided is not truly their child. They grieve the loss of the mask as if it were human. When I shaved my head, I felt like my mother was eulogizing a daughter she never had. She told me my hair was one of my "most beautiful qualities." The kind of beauty she grieved was a beauty that is unobtrusive. I accept this grievance not as a rejection of me but as an expression of the pain brought about by severance from the illusion of understanding things the way they are, a response to witnessing my body being torn out of the narrative she called home.

Dr. Génessier protects himself from this severance in his pursuit of some, any, symmetrical blue-eyed face. Why is it that we find symmetrical faces more beautiful? The neatness of these faces in no way reflects the lumps and edges of life itself. Perhaps we are soothed by symmetry, the false promise of cohesion. We desire neatness in a messy world. We make ourselves complicit in the murder of authenticity when we look to others' bodies to be that coherence for us. To surround ourselves with a single notion of beauty is to avoid building resilience within our powerlessness. We instead develop a dependence upon this kind of cohesion to mask our own fragility, to protect us from our deep and utter lack of control.

AFTER THE REJECTION of Edna's face, Christiane calls her fiancé, Jacques, managing to say only his name. This single word is enough to send him spiraling into an investigation, certain that it was Christiane. This act of reaching out while presumed to be dead catapults the series of events that will set her free and kill her father. This freedom, from the mansion and from her father, eliminates her chance at a face transplant that could allow her to start anew with Jacques. The possibility of this performance, of ever returning to society with a new identity, has ended. She will live her life scars forward.

My chest, without bearing a gender, knows the misanthropy born out of misgendering as much as I do. My chest had just about accepted a life doomed to mistreatment, being pinched, nibbled, and cupped like boobs. With enough focus, I learned to ward off dissociation to be able to feel something through the numbing misinterpretation of my body. A phantom pleasure offers itself a reward for my impressive performance.

WE HAD BEEN together for just over a year the first time Ale placed a palm at the center of my chest, perfectly between those incomprehensible flaps of excess, and applied a pressure both soft and firm. As their fingers stretched out from my sternum, the weight of their hand invited oxygen into the previously tensed corners of my chest. This hand, the reach of this touch, reminding me in a moment of unexpected intimacy how to breathe like I'm really here, perfectly transplanted in a buzzing bag of cells.

My relationship with my chest is at a stalemate. In my head, I smile as fantasy traces the path for that shiny scalpel, sculpts an ideal me, a collage made from that distorted presence in the mirror and archived google image results from the search "top surgery." The palms of my hands flatten my chest only partially, pushing flesh outward, making a greater landing for the hand that once touched something deeper in me. As I consider that image, I know I will continue to feel imprecise in physical form when expression of my authenticity puts my safety at risk and does nothing to guarantee I will stop being perceived along a binary. Precision comes with more than just molding my body to a closer approximation of itself but also with feeling heard, seen and, thus, safe to be everything that my body cannot be.

Good Guys, Dolls

WILL STOCKTON

Child's Play

IT'S MARCH 2017, and my son, Hunter, accompanied by his therapist, Eric, returns home from the Anderson, South Carolina, mall with a twenty-four-inch Chucky doll, six-inch plastic knife included. Hunter is fifteen, a former foster child from the State of Texas, whom my husband, Howard, and I adopted less than six months ago. Howard and I have hired Eric as Hunter's behavior modification therapist. Hunter lies, steals, threatens others with grievous bodily harm. We want him to tell the truth, respect personal property, and disagree peaceably.

"Sorry," Eric says, pulling the time sheet out of his backpack for me to sign. "I couldn't stop him from buying that."

Eric is thirty-five, three years younger than my husband and me, and he works full-time as a high school guidance counselor. Every Tuesday, Thursday, and Sunday afternoon he shepherds Hunter into the community, fostering my son's healthy (read: *age-appropriate*, read: *sane*) interactions with other human beings. Sometimes Eric and Hunter play basketball at the Central-Clemson Recreation Center. Sometimes they eat Blizzards at Dairy Queen. Eric ostensibly uses these opportunities to monitor and correct Hunter's behaviors. But in reality, and we all know it, my son is too old for this game. At his age, after nine years in foster care, Hunter is statistically unlikely to modify his behavior.

If Hunter is a doll making his way down the assembly line, he's failed quality control and been held up for packaging.

"Let me guess," I answer. "Spencer's?" It's Hunter's favorite store. Mine, too, when I was his age. I loved the slasher movie memorabilia, the scatological knickknacks.

Eric nods, and I sign the timesheet: 3:00 p.m to 5:00 p.m. During these two hours, my son ate a pretzel, downed a Monster energy drink, and spent $50 of saved allowance on the Chucky doll he now squeezes to his chest.

HUNTER HAS, at best, a cloudy knowledge of his childhood. He doesn't want to talk about it, and when he does talk about it, he makes up stories, transforms names. He sometimes says that his mother could not take care of him, that she did not love him. But there are secrets I keep from my son because I don't want him using the Internet to contact his mother now—not when we are trying to become a family, to build a home. For instance, I don't tell Hunter that, thanks to case reports kept by Child Protective Services, I know all the reasons the state removed Hunter from his mother's custody. I don't tell him that not being able to take care of him and not loving him are two different failures. I don't tell him that his father, imprisoned when Hunter was taken into care at age five, declined to contest the termination of parental rights, unlike his mother, whose court-appointed attorney at least filed a feeble appeal.

HUNTER CLAIMS THAT he has never seen a *Child's Play* film. He rarely admits to not having done something, so I know he is telling the truth. His foster parents never let him watch horror movies. Staff at his several group homes and residential treatment centers (RTCs) would sometimes smuggle in R-rated films, and sometimes horror movies, but never any of what my son refers to as One of the Chucky Ones. Hunter therefore doesn't know that his doll, with its cracked skull and stapled polymer flesh, represents the Chucky from the last four films, not the first three; that after the serial killer Charles Lee Ray (the soul trapped in the body of a Good Guy doll) fell to his temporary death in *Child's Play 3*, chopped to bits by an amusement park motor fan, his one-time girlfriend Tiffany put him back together, bit by bit, to create the new, modern doll featured in *Bride of Chucky*, *Seed of Chucky*, *Curse of Chucky*, and *Cult of Chucky*, respectively.

Hunter says he bought the doll because he likes the name *Chucky*. I know what he means. It's onomatopoetic: *chunks* of flesh and plastic pieced together into an impossibly living being.

HUNTER ASKS IF he can watch One of the Chucky Ones, and the answer is absolutely not. My husband and I differ on this issue, but according to all the parenting literature, we must present a united front if we want to change Hunter's behavior. Howard says no R-rated movies, so I say it too, knowing adults have little control over what teenagers will watch if they're so determined.

My husband's attitude toward art is broadly Platonic: reality is good, the imitation of reality bad. Howard worries that Hunter will imitate the bad behavior he sees in R-rated movies: the obscenities, the violence. His fear is not misplaced. When Hunter, using a lighter and a disinfectant can, shoots flames across the floor of the high school bathroom, he blames a YouTube video about fire tricks. When we stop him from beating up a mall mannequin, he claims he was acting out a viral video.

If it were up to me, I wouldn't say, simply, no R-rated movies. I'm enough of a Freudian to believe that prohibition feeds desire, and that prohibiting my son from watching One of the Chucky Ones only makes him want to watch them more. At his age, I also loved horror. And I suspect that I am now somewhat better off—a happier and healthier human being—for indulging my love through books and movies, through play.

AS A TEENAGER, I consumed most horror movies in their edit-ed-for-TV versions. These movies ranged from the excellent (*The Exorcist, Rosemary's Baby, Nightmare on Elm Street*) to the execrable (*The Exorcist II: The Heretic, Phantom of the Mall: Eric's Revenge*). I watched and rewatched the first *Child's Play* trilogy downstairs in our family's bonus room on Saturday afternoons and weekend nights, hoping that my parents wouldn't open the door.

Certainly, parental censure produced a significant portion of my investment in horror. In the evangelical parlance of my childhood, my parents worried that horror movies, as well as the Stephen King, Robert McCammon, and Clive Barker books I read, "desensitized" me to carnage, sex, and sin. These books and movies, they feared, immu-nized me to evil, made me less likely to recognize and combat it. To protect my sister and me from "the culture," my parents declined to supply the house with cable TV and (as I do now) forbade the rental of R-rated movies.

Unofficially, however, my parents indulged my taste in the maca-bre. They never stopped me from reading anything except Anne Rice, whom they deemed too sexual, or from watching anything on TV except *Roseanne* and *The Simpsons*, both of which they deemed anti-thetical to family values. My parents were ambivalent disciplinarians who drew arbitrary lines around particular pop culture objects. They did their best. When, at sixteen, I began collecting R-rated Stephen King adaptations on VHS (*Pet Sematary, Carrie, The Dead Zone*), they turned a blind eye.

My love of horror has dissipated with age, with leaving home and going to college, fully escaping my Christian parents' ambivalently watchful eye and theological guidance. Suspense now interests me more than gore. I prefer human monsters—serial killers, psychopaths—to inhuman or otherworldly ones. My waning interest signals, I think, that the genre fulfilled a particularly adolescent need. It answered a teenage inquiry, unsatisfied by the Christian beliefs I inherited from my parents, about the distinction between good and evil, reality and fantasy, life and death, the limits of the body. It's also no coincidence that my investment in horror waned, in my college years, alongside my belief in God. With God went the plausibility of the supernatural, the otherworldly. Evil became more human, more material. Horror's landscape of the possible came to seem less possible, and less interesting, the more of a nonbeliever I became.

AT MY PARENTS' house in suburban Atlanta, Hunter and Chucky shut themselves inside the bonus room. Gone are the blue couch and forty-inch, cathode-ray-tube TV. The room is now filled with toys for his two new cousins, my two young nieces. The mess Hunter makes suggests that he spends most of his time in there playing with the three-story, pink, plastic dollhouse.

Standing with me in the kitchen upstairs, my mother muses, "That room gives him the opportunity he never had to be a little boy."

I joke that little boys should not play with dollhouses. But my mother knows it's not my son's poor performance of heterosexual masculinity that concerns me (I failed that test long ago). I'm concerned that playing with dolls at age fifteen signals considerable, perhaps irreparable, delay in my son's development of compassion, of empathy.

PSYCHOLOGISTS AT LEAST since Jean Piaget have theorized why children play with dolls, and why they need to play with dolls. This form of play provides a vehicle for wish fulfillment and dispute resolution. Playing with dolls helps children negotiate their relationships with other living beings.

More broadly stated, dolls are props in childhood games; and games are the primary way children determine their place within—and test the limits of—the social systems and institutions around them. Through dolls, children project themselves into the world as mother, father, dog, Snuffleupagus, soldier. Through playing with dolls, children figure out the rules that lead to success (life, happiness, friendship) and failure (death, sadness, alienation). Children act out fantasies—some pro-social, some deeply antisocial—on dolls. They reenact situations from their own lives with a difference, with different outcomes and from different vantage points. Dolls afford children the ability to learn—through role-playing, through storytelling—not only the behaviors expected of them as civilized little adults but also what it might be like to inhabit another body.

WHEN I WAS ten, our neighborhood's at-risk youth, Drew, age thirteen, showed me how to stuff a plastic army truck full of army men and Black Cat firecrackers. The explosion sent plastic shards shooting across the summer street. I lost dozens of army men that way, which was fine because I never liked army men. But I also lost Optimus Prime. Drew said I was too old to play with Transformers and killed him. I found the little bits of red- and gray-painted plastic littering Drew's front yard.

What games do Hunter and Chucky play with the dolls in that dollhouse downstairs? What aspects of my son's traumatic life do they reenact or enact differently? What desires do they satisfy? Is Hunter the good guy or the bad guy?

CARLO COLLODI'S 1883 novel *Pinocchio* tells a mythic story of childhood maturation through paternal rescue. Wishing to become a real boy, the mischievous wooden doll must first descend to the underworld, the belly of the Terrible Dogfish, and rescue his creator, the poor woodcutter Geppetto. The abundance of *Pinocchio* adaptations, the 1940 Disney film only the most famous among them, owes much to the story's archetypal structure. Real boys—which is to say, boys who will grow into men, which is to say children who will grow into adults, which is to say adults capable of living with other adults as members of a human community—must dispense with the image of their parents as invulnerable but honor them anyway. Growing up requires recognition of parental failure, but also parental resuscitation.

Child's Play murderously inverts this myth. In the world of these films, Chucky is not a mischievous-yet-essentially-good little boy. He is a Good Guy doll harboring an essentially evil soul. Charles Lee Ray wants to become a real boy *again*—and to do this he needs an *already* real boy, Andy Barclay, the only child of a single mother who works at the perfume counter at the mall. Karen Barclay has already failed her son by not buying him the Good Guy doll he wants for his birthday. And if she were a good Freudian mother, she would stop there: let Andy be sad. It's her effort to assuage her guilt by buying her son a stolen doll off a street peddler that ushers in evil.

Karen Barclay does not fail again, which is all for the worse. At the end of *Child's Play*, she rescues Andy by shooting off Chucky's appendages. Only in *Child's Play 2* do we learn that Andy is thereafter taken into state custody. His mother's stories about a murderous doll have forced the state to institutionalize her. Andy has become a foster child.

DRIVING HOME one afternoon that May, I find Hunter standing in the street outside our house. He is wearing a Chicago Bulls jersey, red skinny jeans, and construction boots. He clutches Chucky to his chest and waves at me with the knife hand.

I roll down my window and take my son's picture. I text the picture to Eric.

"For you to sell one day to CNN," I write.

BECAUSE I'M AN inconsistent disciplinarian, I invite Hunter and Chucky to watch the original *Nightmare on Elm Street*. Howard is out of town.

Officially, I want Hunter to see *Nightmare on Elm Street* because it terrified me as a child, and watching scary movies with your son seems like something fathers should do. Unofficially, I want Hunter to see *Nightmare on Elm Street* so that he knows what good parenting looks like. The Elm Street parents are notoriously absent from the film. They murder Fred Krueger in an effort to protect their kids, but thereafter wander out of their children's lives, leaving them to fight their nighttime battles alone.

As Krueger's first victim, Tina Gray, climbs the bedroom walls in her tortured sleep—thrashing, screaming, gushing blood—I look over at Chucky and my son seated on the chaise lounge.

"Are you okay?" I ask. I suspect Hunter has never before seen anything like this.

He nods. "That looks fake as shit."

AN ELEMENTARY Freudian thesis: murder marks a failure in the civilizing process, a gap in one's education. "Civilization," Freud writes, "describes the whole sum of the achievements and the regulations which distinguish our lives from those of our animal ancestors and which serve two purposes—namely, to protect men against nature and to adjust their mutual relationships." Civilization, Freud continues, makes us miserable. Self-regulation demands the repression of desire. Human achievements, like rescuing our parents from the belly of the Terrible Dogfish, prove arduous, grueling. But through civilization we live as humans rather than as animals. Civilization enables human community. It constitutes human community.

By "childhood," then, let us refer to the period of civilizing education in *Homo sapiens*.

Good Guys, Dolls

As a species, our long childhood provides us with considerable time—necessary time—to gain this education. We're not born knowing not to harm one another. We learn how to protect ourselves against harm, how to adjust our mutual relationships so as not to harm ourselves and other people, as we grow up. We learn of what harm consists—and the degrees to which we and others like us can withstand it—as we mature.

ANOTHER ELEMENTARY Freudian thesis: we're all born murderers. Hopefully, we grow out of it.

LIKE MANY big brothers, I used to rip the limbs off my sister's Barbie dolls. I had my reasons: Revenge, animus. Jealousy. I liked Barbie dolls more than army men, although never as much as Transformers. I sometimes played Barbie with my sister. I was Barbie, she Ken, the family dog Barbie and Ken's car. When Hannah and I weren't being horrible to each other, we did a fine job playing house.

SOME GAMES NEED to be played. Some stopped. And sometimes it's hard to tell the difference. Watch *Child's Play* 3. Colonel Cochran, the commander at Kent Military Academy, hates the thought of his cadets playing with dolls. He orders sixteen-year-old Cadet Andy Barclay to forget these "fantasies" of psychopathic toys, paraphrasing no less an authority than Saint Paul: "When I was a child, I thought as a child. And when I became a man, I put away childish things" (1 Corinthians 13:11). It sounds easy enough, notwithstanding Andy's years in foster care, the institutionalization of his mother, and Chucky's brutal murder of his foster parents.

"At Kent," the Colonel brags, "we take bed wetters and turn them into men."

This turning requires the cadets to put away one set of games (domestic games, doll play) in exchange for another: namely, Army Man. But in his once-more-resurrected doll body, Charles Lee Ray now wants to play Hide the Soul with the young cadet Ronald Tyler. In the Academy cellar, where Tyler has absconded with his shameful toy, the incantation begins. Clouds gather as the cadets outside march with their guns around the field. Only Colonel Cochran, coming to inventory supplies for a game of Capture the Flag, interrupts the transfer: "We don't play with dolls now do we, Tyler? Dolls are for girls."

For girls or for children? Do both fall under the category of "bed wetters"? Either way, Colonel Cochran saves Tyler's life by stopping this game. Tossing Chucky in the garbage, he also sets into motion a string of gruesome campus murders.

HUNTER SAYS HE learned most of his behaviors from the other kids in RTCs. He was once a blank slate, then their student. He blames his former RTC peers when he flips over a desk and threatens to have his teacher shot; when he emails a series of threats to a student whom he mistakenly believes insulted him on Snapchat; when he tries to punch me in the face as I tackle him in the middle of the road and two police cars siren up behind us; when, during a dinner-time tantrum, he promises, "Three of us are going to sleep tonight, but only one of us will wake up!"

HUNTER ASKS ME if I believe in possession, and honestly, this is a hard question to answer. I no longer believe in demons, spirits, or souls, much less possession, so the answer is no. But he knows I don't believe and asks anyway. He wants me to play a game with him. He invites me to extend the limits of the possible in this imaginative space. So, I shake my head and say, "Maybe." If he needs me to, I will say yes.

FOSTER PARENTS ARRIVE pre-failed. That's what makes foster children's attachment to their new parents so hard. Foster children don't idealize you. They know you can't protect them.

"Are we even qualified to take care of a boy like this?" Phil Simpson asks the social worker in *Child's Play 2*. Phil and his wife, Joanne, have just learned about Andy's "fairy tale" regarding the killer doll—his way of coping, the social worker explains, with the trauma of witnessing multiple murders. Phil Simpson worries, not for the last time, that Andy may need more help than he and his wife can provide.

What Andy needs—what most traumatized children need—is someone who will listen to and believe them. Pieced back together by the Play Pals toy company in an effort to exonerate their doll in the press, Chucky returns for Andy. He sends the disbelieving Phil Simpson toppling off the basement stairs, breaking his neck. He slits Joanne Simpson's throat.

The Simpsons prove no more capable than Karen Barclay of protecting the boy from evil.

CHILDREN NEED TO believe that the world is a safe place, even if it's not. Or they need to be exposed to danger slowly, in stages, through games and play. Childhood trauma is a premature encounter with evil.

I tried to explain this thesis to Hunter when I took him to see *It* two weeks after its September 2017 opening. Stephen King's book, and the original 1990 TV miniseries, meant a lot to me as a teenager. Seven children band together to defeat, and defeat again, a murderous, alien malevolence. They win by refusing to fear this creature who feeds off terror. *It* analogized my church youth group's battles with Satan—the difference, I now understand, being that the evil in the world of *It* is real.

My psychological abstraction was lost on my son. *It* merely scared the shit out of him. He swore blood pooled up in his sink, too, and started checking the sewer grates for clowns.

IN THE KITCHEN, Eric pulls out his phone and flips to a grainy picture of his teenage self standing beside Ed and Lorraine Warren on the back porch of their house in Connecticut. Through family friends, he met these founders of the New England Society for Psychic Research, the paranormal investigators played by Patrick Wilson and Vera Farmiga in James Wan's *Conjuring* films.

"Did you see the doll?" Hunter asks, he and Chucky both peering over my shoulder. He means Annabelle, the Raggedy Ann doll the Warrens declared possessed by the ghost of Annabelle Higgins. The Warrens keep the doll encased in glass at their Occult Museum.

"I did!" Eric says, his face as lit up with excitement as my son's. "It was so creepy!"

"Do you think it's really alive?"

Eric shrugs. He doesn't know. And Hunter starts talking about how sometimes he wakes up to find Chucky asleep in the closet.

IF MY LIFE were a movie about possession, this would be the part where the worried parents seek professional medical help for their troubled child. In *The Exorcist*, Chris MacNeil takes her daughter, Regan, to the hospital following several distributing events, including the violent shaking and levitation of Regan's bed. The doctors draw the girl's blood, run an EKG, and take her temperature. Lighting a cigarette in the office hallway, the doctor then explains to Ms. MacNeil that Regan suffers from "a disturbance in the chemical-electrical activity of the brain . . . in the temporal lobe . . . up here in the lateral part of the brain." The condition is rare, but it does cause hallucinations and convulsions, or "muscular spasms."

Chris MacNeil came to the hospital for precisely such an answer, but she is not satisfied: "That was no spasm. I got on the bed. The whole bed was thumping and rising off the floor and shaking. The whole thing, with me on it."

Now the doctor must wonder if the mother hallucinates, too. "Ms. MacNeil," he tries again, "the problem with your daughter is not her bed. It's her brain."

This doctor is wrong, of course. The problem is not Regan's bed or her brain. The problem is an ancient demon from the Middle East, Pazuzu, who for some reason has traveled across the ocean and possessed the body of this girl, the daughter of a divorced actress who is shooting a film in Georgetown. Why Regan? Is demonic possession a metaphor for puberty, for the awakening of sexual knowledge, as suggested by the infamous scene in which Regan masturbates with a crucifix? Does the absence of a father—a Father, in both Freudian and Christian terms—render her vulnerable? Is possession her mother's fault for getting a divorce? Does Regan invite Pazuzu's possession through her play with the Ouija board that she finds in the closet? Does Father Merrin bring Pazuzu back to Georgetown from his archeological dig in Iraq? Is the doubting Father Karras, not Merrin or Regan, Pazuzu's real target?

The film does not answer any of these questions, only raises them. As Elis Hanson explains in "Knowing Children: Desire and Interpretation in *The Exorcist*," the film's "very narrative structure is out to get us," forcing us "to wonder why the devil is there at all, through what psychological, sexual or moral flaw he is admitted to the film, and why there are so many unexplained mysteries." But there is no why.

HUNTER'S OBSESSION with Chucky should come as no surprise. Surely there's a part of me that, at age thirty-six, wanted a doll, one my husband wasn't so sure we needed.

"SIR," HUNTER SAID one day early in our relationship (before Eric, before Chucky) when he still called me *sir*. We were waiting at the Central-Clemson Recreation Center for his swim lesson to begin. "What if you went through my phone and found nothing but pictures of knees? Just hundreds of pictures of knees. Wouldn't that be weird?"

My son hangs onto the wall of the therapy pool, leans back and pulls his skinny legs up to his stomach. His knees break the surface of the water. "Knees."

He laughs. I laugh.

On the way home, he clarifies: "You can trust me not to take pictures of people's knees. I don't have a phone."

HOWARD AND I joke that Hunter doesn't need a therapist. He needs an exorcist. We make variations on this joke, too. Eric needs to remember his Bible and his Holy Water. We should advertise for someone who wants to babysit Rosemary's teen. When Hunter forces himself to vomit sweet potatoes all over the dining room table, I tease him and call him Regan.

HOWARD AND I hospitalized Hunter for the first time six months after he came to live with us. Manic, he tore apart his room, ripped posters off the wall and threw his books off the bookshelf. As I watched him rage from the doorway, I remembered the advice of another foster parent who suggested filming these tantrums and then watching them with your teen them later—to discuss, essentially, how crazy they look, and how such behavior will get them hospitalized or jailed. I took out my phone and started filming.

But I succeeded only in turning my son into a movie star. He threw a mason jar against the wall and, accidentally or on purpose, cut his arm with one of the shards. He yelled, "Pick up the goddamn glass, faggot!" alternately stomping around his room and flopping down on the bed. He smeared blood on the wall, his bedsheets, and the carpet. Lying on his back, he pulled his knees high over his head and farted. This tantrum continued for forty-five minutes before we drove him to Oconee Medical, where the nurse whisked him past triage and the doctor sedated him after he tried to mount the wheeled blood pressure monitor.

"Could your son be on any street drugs?" the doctor asked. He was young, clearly a resident, trying to maintain a professional demeanor in the face of an obviously possessed boy.

"Is Pazuzu a street drug?"

ANDY BARCLAY RETURNS to the *Child's Play* franchise in *Cult of Chucky*. We don't know much about him. He lives alone in a cabin in the woods. He owns numerous firearms. He has trouble dating due to all the stories about him on the Internet. "I was six," he tries in vain to explain to a woman he likes. "My babysitter was murdered, along with my teacher and my case worker, and thirty-seven other people over the years, that I'm aware of." Having blown Chucky to bits with a shotgun, he now keeps the doll's still-living head in a safe, behind his framed Kent Military Academy sweatshirt. Periodically, he takes Chucky out to torture him with an array of different devices.

It's a common trope of horror films: banish the evil only to have it return. Or disperse. In *Cult of Chucky*, Andy's efforts to contain the doll to his safe fail because Chucky transfers his soul into multiple Good Guy dolls at once. Using a voodoo spell he finds on the Internet, Chucky breaks the rule of the game that would restrain him to one body.

It Came From the Closet

HUNTER PLAYS WITH Chucky for eight months, then gives him away to the younger brother of a friend. I do not ask why, grateful to see the doll go, glad to no longer hear of Chucky's nighttime antics, hopeful that Chucky has satisfied whatever need Hunter had for him, and that the evil is gone.

This essay originally appeared, in slightly different form, as "Child's Play," in the Bennington Review, Issue 7, 2020.

The Healed Body

JUDE ELLISON S. DOYLE

In My Skin / Dans ma peau

IT WASN'T until I got pregnant that I finally saw how distant I was from my own body. This was late 2016, early 2017, and I was about to turn thirty-five, a late age for a first baby. I spent half my day reading pregnancy manuals and websites, baffled and embarrassed by their maniacally chipper tone, which seemed to be aimed not at parents of small children but at the actual children themselves: Baby is the size of a grape! A papaya! A spaghetti squash! It's all right to be nervous. But more all right to be happy! Mom (the pregnant person is always addressed, in these texts, as "Mom") is getting ready for a *big change*!

I was not *getting ready* for a big change, I was in the midst of one. My personality shifted with my hormones, giving me new tastes and interests and a terrifying ability to cry in public. I swelled and rounded, changed shirt sizes and pant sizes and shoe sizes, puffed up at the joints until I had the tree-trunk legs of a brontosaurus. In the more scientific manuals, I learned that my body had doubled its amount of blood; that the baby's cells were mingling with mine, and would stay there after I gave birth, rendering me a biological chimera; that I was growing a new organ, the placenta, and when I gave birth, I would both expel and (the manuals strongly encouraged) eat it.

The teenage edgelord in me delighted in this information. A parasite turns you into a mutant and forces you to eat your own organs; what's cooler than that? Yet, when I tried to talk to other people about how disgusting pregnancy was, I was met with baffled politeness, not only from the world at large but from pregnant women. This experience of being lost at sea in my own body, held captive to its processes, seemed to be mine alone. In fact, if the expressions on people's faces were any indication, it was mildly crazy.

Yet the more I sat with the feeling, the more it seemed to me that my body had never belonged to me. There were whole areas—my hair, my breasts—that I was keeping around primarily because they got a reaction from people. There were processes that had always felt unwelcome; as a teenager, my periods were so distressing that I once passed out in the middle of a McDonald's because I felt one coming on. I could never figure out all the little things women were supposed to *do*, how it was that they managed to look adult and female and put-together. It seemed easy, or at least manageable; a necessary life skill, like cooking dinner. I just couldn't do it. My body was something I needed to manipulate, a weird, soft machine I was never quite sure of operating correctly. I fed it like a pet, washed it like a car, exercised it . . . well, no, I didn't exercise it, because that would require getting in there and fucking around, and I spent as much time reading or drinking or otherwise getting out of my body as I could.

It never would have occurred to me to call these feelings "dysphoria." I pushed through them the same way I'd always pushed through the pangs of shame and panic I got when I tried to do girly things or present as convincingly feminine, telling myself it was just internalized misogyny or poor self-esteem. Yet it seems clear to me now that my pregnancy was the beginning of my coming-out process as a nonbinary transmasculine person. It called my body to my attention. It made me realize that I could successfully and intentionally undergo *a big change*.

Now that I'm out, my former alienation from my body seems normal. I wasn't "put together" because I was trying to put together the wrong thing. It's like I bought a coffee table at IKEA and spent thirty-five years trying to assemble a couch with the parts. Frustration was inevitable. Yet in the moment, before I knew any other name for my experiences, my only comparison was body horror—specifically, the body horror movie I loved most in the world, and have loved ever since I saw a crappy VHS copy of it in college: *In My Skin*, the 2002 independent movie by French writer-director Marina de Van.

IN MY SKIN (*Dans ma peau*) is one of those movies that frequently makes lists of the "most disturbing movies ever" or "toughest horror movies to watch." The college boyfriend I rented it with noped-out by the second act, telling me he was just too uncomfortable to keep going. I've always enjoyed the nerdy flex of watching a horror movie that is too much for some cis guy, and yet it pains me that *In My Skin* is remembered primarily as a gross-out feature. The violence here is nowhere near as graphic as the average *Saw* or *Hostel* movie. *In My Skin* is scarier than those movies precisely because it reaches the viewer on a level that soulless splatter porn can't; the injuries feel real and painful because they're grounded in a frighteningly believable portrait of one woman's self-destruction.

We open on a heroine, Esther (played by de Van, directing herself), who seems to more or less have her life together: she's got a job at an advertising firm, with a promotion in the near future; she has a boyfriend who wants to move in together; she's putting him off, but it seems clear where things are headed. It's a recognizable white, upper middle-class, postfeminist, heterosexual trajectory. It's what she's supposed to want, even if some key elements, like the boyfriend, don't excite her as much as she'd like.

One night, at a drunken party, Esther manages to rip her calf open on a piece of jagged metal in someone's yard. Due to some combination of shock and nerve damage and alcohol, Esther doesn't feel the injury, and goes through the whole night without realizing that her leg is gushing blood. She only sees what's happened when she goes to the bathroom; she gasps, and fingers the edges of her wound, and begins crying. It's not clear whether she's in pain or simply horrified by what she's seeing.

I mean to say: Esther is betrayed and traumatized to see her body shedding blood from a hole that shouldn't be there. You can see where the transmasculine viewer might connect. It is also bizarrely relatable to see how Esther tries to deal with the injury, which is, at first, by pretending she doesn't have one; she goes over to her friends and casually mentions that she might need to go to the hospital, but she wants to stop at a bar for one last drink first. The doctor who eventually stitches Esther up is baffled by her dissociation: "Are you sure it's *your* leg?" he jokes.

Esther doesn't laugh. She also doesn't answer. Esther becomes obsessed with her injury, and with the numbness that seems to be spreading out over her whole body. She begins trying to re-create the thrill of getting hurt; first pinching and picking at herself, then cutting herself, then doing several things so gross that one hesitates to spoil them, except to say that this one woman somehow becomes both the perpetrator and the victim of an entire Texas Chainsaw Massacre before the credits roll.

The gross-outs are real, but never cheap. Esther's self-harm addiction mounts slowly and realistically; the brief relief of a cutting session in the break room slowly giving way to more sessions, more extreme injuries, entire weekends spent alone in a hotel room, doing things to yourself that you have to explain later as the result of a car accident. Some scenes are uncomfortable precisely because de Van's slack-jawed, compulsive pleasure as she works on herself feels like watching someone masturbate. It's that kind of problem: an urge you can't get rid of without indulging, a gross but pressing need.

Esther's self-destruction is a symptom of alienation: from capitalism (during a business dinner, Esther has to forcibly restrain her hand from skittering around the table) or from womanhood (after one cutting session, she watches a female friend apply moisturizer, baffled by the concept of feminine self-care) or from heterosexuality (her boyfriend tries to "cure" her by fucking her while asking if she can feel him; he does not get the answer he's hoping for). Careful viewers will have noted that de Van's heroine shares a name with Esther Greenwood, the protagonist of Sylvia Plath's novel *The Bell Jar*. Like that other Esther, she self-destructs in part because meeting the expectations placed on women already feels like a kind of self-harm.

Most importantly, though, the cutting is symptomatic of Esther's alienation from Esther. She doesn't hate her body, she tells us, but she also doesn't think of it as *her*. Her self-injury is exploratory, almost clinical; she's a scientist, testing the foreign object of her flesh, trying to see what it can do. In fact, there is no part of Esther's life that is truly *hers*: her friends are not really her friends, the man she fucks isn't someone she particularly wants to be fucking, her professional success is maintained at the cost of disappearing into back rooms and wine cellars and coming apart at the seams. She takes her body apart because she is trying to get back inside it. She's not trying to kill herself. She's trying to prove she's alive.

It's dangerous, I know, to connect transmasculinity or gender dysphoria with a movie about female self-mutilation. The idea that transmasculine people are self-harming "women" is currently one of the main talking points TERFs (trans-exclusionary radical feminists) use to try to argue us out of existence.

As I write this, the number one book result on Amazon for "trans men" is a book called *Irreversible Damage*. The title is splashed across the page in big, bloodred letters, with a subtitle promising to expose the "Transgender Craze That's Seducing Our Daughters" in the same tone 1950s horror movie posters used to advertise a "Terrifying Monster of the Ages!" or some "Students Made Victims of Terror-Beast!" Beneath the titles, there's an illustration of a little girl, or possibly a baby doll, who is still alive and conscious despite the gigantic, red-rimmed, perfectly circular hole scooped out of her stomach.

The message is clear: transmasculinity is body horror. The average trans boy, according to *Irreversible Damage* author Abigail Shrier, is "psychologically alienated from her [sic] own body, and headed toward medical self-harm;"[1] she predicts that medical transition will leave such a boy "angry, regretful, maimed, and sterile."[2] Give or take a "sterile," he sounds very much like Esther from *In My Skin*.

Other TERFs have resorted to putting transmasculine bodies on display, hoping that the supposed freakishness of top surgery scars or testosterone-squared jawlines will scare the public away from supporting us. Photographer Laura Dodsworth has published an entire series of seminude portraits of "detransitioners," women who formerly identified as transmasculine. Dodsworth was inspired, she says, by the horror she feels when she thinks about trans men's bodies: "For me, the idea of having my breasts, ovaries, and womb removed, and then wanting them back, creates a feeling so unnerving that I cannot occupy it for long."[3]

She can, however, ask other people to occupy it in front of her while she takes pictures. It's not clear whether Dodsworth informed her subjects that she would accompany the photos of their naked bodies with commentary on how scary and disgusting they are; nor is it clear how Dodsworth's "unnerved" feeling is different from the pleasurable disgust carnival-goers feel at freak shows.

First things first: The posttransition body is not a mutilated body. It's a healed body. Transition is not a symptom of psychological distress but a means to cure it. That "unnerving" feeling Dodsworth imagines— the horror of looking down at a body you don't recognize, one which

1. Abigail Shrier, "Gender Activists Are Trying to Cancel My Book; Why Is Silicon Valley Helping Them?" *Pittsburgh Post-Gazette*, November 24, 2020, https://www.post-gazette.com/opinion/2020/11/22/Gender-activists-Silicon-Valley-Transgender-LGBTQ/stories/202011220021.
2. Shrier, "Gender Activists."
3. Laura Dodsworth, "The Detransitioners," *Medium*, August 18, 2020, https://medium.com/@barereality/the-detransitioners-72a4e01a10f9.

can't do what you want or need it to do—is already felt by many people who are uncomfortable in their assigned genders, and it is spectacularly cruel for someone to use her own imaginary dysphoria as an excuse to deny transpeople treatment for theirs.

Yet the rubbernecking dread transphobic "feminists" have for trans bodies—Shrier, or Dodsworth, or J. K. Rowling, for whom trans boys are merely psychologically damaged and self-hating "girls" who've succumbed to the "allure of escaping womanhood"[4]—is not unfamiliar to me as a horror fan. Whether these women know it are not, they're talking about transpeople in the same way that sexist men have historically talked about the bodies of cis women.

The body horror genre is deeply rooted in cis men's fear of femininity, and considers cis female bodies to be inherently freakish, flawed, and deformed. In particular, body horror often focuses an obsessive disgust on cis women's reproductive cycle, either in a sideways fashion—like the exceptionally vaginal face-hugger in *Alien*, or that franchise's many chest-bursting images of "childbirth"—or directly, as in David Lynch's *Eraserhead*, where a woman's fertility dooms her man to a life of tending the foul horror she's produced. Body horror king David Cronenberg spent much of the '80s explaining why he was scared of vaginas. There was the pulsating external uterus of *The Brood*, where a (cis) woman's capacity to reproduce without a man led to countless hammer-based murders, or the "mutant women" of *Dead Ringers*, with their insatiable sexual needs and triple-headed Cerberus vaginas. Both movies feature a woman chewing through an umbilical cord with her teeth, I guess because no one told Cronenberg about the placenta thing.

This is how horror is used by the dominant culture: to justify fear and violence toward the Other, the Alien, the Mutant—and in a patriarchy,

4. J. K. Rowling, "J. K. Rowling Writes About Her Reasons for Speaking Out on Sex and Gender Issues," JKRowling.com, June 10, 2020, https://www.jkrowling.com/opinions/j-k-rowling-writes-about-her-reasons-for-speaking-out-on-sex-and-gender-issues/.

that title will always belong primarily to people who aren't white cis men. Whether it's David Cronenberg's umbilical phobia, Laura Dodsworth's close-ups of top-surgery scars, or the countless ways that cis-directed comedies and slasher movies have trained us to fear the bodies of trans women, horror is always located outside, in the marginalized person, in the body that doesn't look like the person behind the camera.

I'm not interested in this type of horror, to put it mildly. Yet I still describe my own experiences in terms of body horror, because I am my own person to describe. I still hold out hope for body horror stories told by marginalized people, stories that are not about demonizing or destroying the Other but confronting the least comfortable parts of yourself. (It's significant that when David Cronenberg discovered male anal penetration in the '90s—*Naked Lunch*, *eXistenZ*—his gross-outs were improved.) There is a difference between feeling uncomfortable with your own body and having others proclaim how uncomfortable they are with you, between the horror felt by a person and the horror caused by a monster. Few movies understand this as well as *In My Skin*.

Marina de Van spends a lot of time naked in her own movie. Esther is perpetually taking clothes off, putting them on, hanging out at home in her underwear, taking showers. The camera encourages us to study her body in detail; here are her hands, here are her legs, here's the odd fold of skin gathered at her right hip. The nudity has a strange dissociative effect, like catching your reflection unexpectedly in a mirror—de Van is both the object of our gaze and the subject directing it, somehow behind the camera and in front of it at the same time. All this serves a very practical purpose: de Van wants us to understand the architecture of Esther's body before she destroys it. She's laying out the parameters of the crime scene, giving us a tour of the house before she tears it down.

These points were missed by the film's early (and nearly all male) critics, who invariably took the sight of a woman's body on screen as an invitation to rate her looks: "Ms. de Van, who resembles a feral, gap-toothed version of the young Leslie Caron, is at once beautiful and ugly,"[5] runs a representative assessment from Stephen Holden's *New York Times* review. Dennis Lim at the *Village Voice* praised her "arresting screen presence" while also calling her "pale, flared-nostriled, and gap-toothed."[6] There are just so many more interesting things you could say about Marina de Van's teeth in this movie—like, for instance, the fact that she uses them to eat her own leg like a chicken wing. Even in a movie about how women's bodies are treated like meat, these men can't help but leave three-star Yelp reviews for hers.

Cis men seemed incapable of understanding that a woman's body could be put on screen for reasons other than objectification. We're not meant to want Esther—we're meant to *be* her. The movie is effective precisely because de Van blurs the boundaries between inside and outside, self and other, person and object, audience and action; when viewers of *In My Skin* scream or flinch at some gruesome injury, it's because we're so connected to Esther's body that it feels like we are being injured. In the moment, as he squirms and averts his eyes from the bloody screen, the cis male viewer of *In My Skin* has become the very thing he's spent his whole life trying not to resemble: a woman.

It's that invitation to occupy the marginalized and monstrous body, to feel what it feels, that makes *In My Skin* unique. The power to make our oppressors share our perspective, to make them see the world as we see it—to bring them inside our skin, as de Van puts it—is one of the most potent tools any storyteller has. *In My Skin* is not an overtly feminist movie, but it makes the still-radical assumption that we will be able to identify with a woman enough to take her suffering as seriously as our own.

5. Stephen Holden, "Desperately Trying to Relate to Her Body by Cutting It," *New York Times*, November 7, 2003, https://www.nytimes.com/2003/11/07/movies/film-review-desperately-trying-to-relate-to-her-body-by-cutting-it.html.

6. Dennis Lim, "Into the Cut," *Village Voice*, November 4, 2003, https://www.villagevoice.com/2003/11/04/into-the-cut/.

It worked. I'm not a woman. I feel my own pain, and Esther's, when I watch this movie. What I relate to is not the cutting, though; the TERFs are wrong on that. What I relate to is the suffering the cutting is intended to relieve. It's the baffled sense of being locked out of your own body; unable to connect with the person that is supposed to be you. Esther's desperate need to get back inside herself, to have even one moment of being fully present in her own life, is something I've felt many times. It's something I stopped feeling only when I transitioned.

I got so used to pushing past discomfort in the first thirty-five years of my life. I maintained my disconnected body in a manner that pleased others, gritted my teeth through periods and pregnancy, suppressed the flashes of anguish and shame and self-disgust that arose at predictable moments, but for no reason I could name. It's only now, when the discomfort has lifted somewhat, that I realize I was hurting myself every day of my life. The injury was there. I just didn't let myself feel it. I covered it up, mopped up the blood, went out and asked if anyone wanted to grab a beer.

When we cannot put ourselves together, we tear ourselves apart. This is true no matter who we are, no matter what reason we have for not fitting into the lives we're given. Esther never explains why she needs to destroy herself, yet the answer is always right there in front of us. Why does any animal chew its own leg off? Because it's trapped.

Notes On *Sleepaway Camp*

VIET DINH

Sleepaway Camp

In fond memory of Susan Sontag, a doer.

1. So, we begin with *Sleepaway Camp*, as we must, at the end: a freeze-frame of the main character, Angela, by a lakeshore. She holds a guttural growl in her throat, an animalistic gurgle. Her face, in close-up, has twisted into a rictus equal parts glee and rage. This is clearly an homage to the ending of Truffaut's *The 400 Blows*, though Jean-Pierre Léaud was never fully nude, holding a knife, blood streaked down his torso.

2. I had heard about this scene before I'd seen the film. It was the first thing people mentioned. *Angela was a boy all along!* But this pre-knowledge didn't spoil the film. Instead, it made me more eager to see it. In my younger days, before I grasped the complex interplay of sexuality and gender, I thought I should have been a girl, since I liked boys, and only girls liked boys. I was sometimes mistaken for a girl, and, rather than correct the mistake, I pitched my voice higher, as to not embarrass the other party.

3. *The actress who played Angela was really a boy! No, the penis was prosthetic! I heard she underwent a sex change operation after the film!* This was the '80s. We didn't have the language back then. *Sleepaway Camp*

was simply the reductio ad absurdum of its siblings—*Psycho*, *Dressed to Kill*, *The Silence of the Lambs*—in which the murderer play-acts a different gender.

4. More than twenty years after the release of *Sleepaway Camp*, the director, Robert Hiltzik, revealed that the Angela at the end of the film was played by a college student, wearing a "potato chip-thin" mask of dental acrylic molded from the face of the actress who played Angela. As Sontag writes, "Camp is the triumph of the epicene style. (The convertibility of 'man' and 'woman,' 'person' and 'thing.')." *Sleepaway Camp* is the nexus of the netherworld, an in-between place for those who are in-between.

5. I attended my first camp between sixth and seventh grade. I had been elected vice president of the class, and my school sponsored the trip to Leadership Camp. (My parents, ever frugal, would never have paid.) But what can you teach a seventh grader about anything? I learned the excitement of being unmoored from my parents for a week. I learned how to sleep in bunks with complete strangers, how to listen to their nighttime breathing and burping, the confusing smell creeping from our pores and feet that left other animals baffled.

6. When we, ferried by school bus, arrived at camp, one counselor said, "You know the *Friday the 13th* movies were filmed here." It was a blatant lie, and I knew it; our camp in Colorado looked nothing like the New Jersey woods. But by 1987, we'd already surpassed the camp slasher saturation point. As far as we knew, every summer camp was a murderous playground.

7. Examples of death from the *Sleepaway Camp* oeuvre:
   scalded with boiling water
   mobbed by hornets
   drowned in a leech-infested outhouse
   garroted with a guitar string
   exploded firecracker up the nose
   smashed by a Mack truck
   misplaced lawnmower
   dropped from a flagpole

8. Such creative deaths! Our malleable bodies are subject to an infinite number of injuries. Slasher films have always competed to portray the most realistic and gruesome arterial spray, but *Sleepaway Camp* goes for the outrageous. If *The Silence of the Lambs* offers violence that sips a glass of chianti, *Sleepaway Camp* rips into a bag of Franzia with its teeth.

9. Sontag writes, "The hallmark of Camp is the spirit of extravagance. Camp is a woman walking around in a dress made of three million feathers." Camp is also a preteen getting a hot curling iron jabbed into her vagina.

10. Let us then praise Judy, she of the off-set ponytail and Long Island accent. Judy exemplifies what Sontag calls an "instant character": "a state of continual incandescence—a person being one, very intense thing." In Judy's case, a bitch. She chews the scenery so thoroughly that her line deliveries come with splinters: "She's a real carpenter's dream: flat as a board and needs a screw!" Obviously, she was not reaching for Final Girl status.

11. (Fascinating aside #1: Jane Krakowski auditioned for the role of Judy.)

12. In *Men, Women, and Chainsaws*, Carol Clover suggests some identifying characteristics of a Final Girl: she must be virginal or sexually unavailable. She presents as feminine, but during the final conflict with the killer, she displays masculine traits. She takes the power of observation—formerly reserved for the killer and his point-of-view shots—for herself. She outwits. She survives.

13. Here's what I observed at Leadership Camp: if I looked at the row behind me on the bleachers, I could see up another boy's shorts; during basketball practice, a jump shot could mean a shirt riding up, a brief flash of an underwear waistband. I learned how to stay silent, how to cover my mouth with both hands so that nothing could escape. Not a whimper, not a sigh. Even if a rat ran under the bed, I would not pee my pants. I would stay safe.

14. *Sleepaway Camp* doesn't feature a traditional Final Girl. The closest possibility is Susie, the kindhearted counselor who doesn't get more than five minutes of screen time. We're left with the possibility that Angela—with her intense stares, her literal embodiment of masculine traits—serves as both Final Girl and killer.

15. Who among us doesn't aspire to be a Final Girl? Who doesn't want to emerge—bloodied, triumphant—into the sunlight? But in the Manichean worldview of slasher movies, gays and lesbians represent a threat to conventional normality and thus can only be victims—or killers.

16. *Sleepaway Camp* doesn't shy away from killing off prepubescents ("Baldies," as Artie, the pedophile camp cook, calls them), which meant that, at Leadership Camp, I'd be the first to go. I was willowy, weak, and wore glasses. My body was pale and hairless. I couldn't do a lay-up to save my life.

17. (Fascinating aside #2: The actor who played Artie's second-in-command was James Earl Jones's father.)

18. But who am I kidding? Slasher films almost never feature Asians. This "invisibility" becomes a protective cloak: we are neither "killer" nor "victim"; neither "saved" nor "slaughtered." If I needed to, I could slip, undetected, between worlds: between child and adult, black and white. I was the perpetual vice president, lurking in the shadows of those higher in the chain of command.

19. I would have to wait until *Sleepaway Camp III: Teenage Wasteland* to see an Asian. (By contrast, it took the *Friday the 13th* series eight sequels before it had its first Asian. And she was strangled—*strangled!*—by Jason.) More surprisingly, however—there were two Asians, one of each gender. The female was busty and showed her tits, but the male was nothing like how Asian men were usually portrayed. Instead of being an awkward nerd, Greg had an air of California cool about him. He reminded me of my cousins in California, who seemed to have it all: Z Cavaricci pants, Oakley sunglasses, short sleeve button-ups with angular, neon-colored prints—peak '80s, before I realized that '80s style was terrible.

20. "So many of the objects prized by Camp taste," Sontag writes, "are old-fashioned, out of date, démodé. It's not a love of the old as such. It's simply that the process of aging or deterioration provides the necessary detachment—or arouses a necessary sympathy."

21. As a child, while my parents shopped at an Asian grocery store on Federal Boulevard—Little Saigon, as it's known in Denver—I went to the video store next door. It stocked Chinese soap operas, period dramas with martial arts action, and *Paris by Night* (a Vietnamese musical extravaganza) bootlegs. But I lingered in the small horror section, trying to decipher each tape cover, each promising a cornucopia of terrors. I knew better than to ask my parents if I could rent one. They didn't object to the content but rather the cost of rental. I contented myself on whatever movies, edited and broken-up-for-commercial-breaks, were broadcast on *Friday Night Frights*, which showed at 11 p.m. after *Nightline*. With the sound turned down on the television, I braced myself on the corner of my mother's waterbed.

22. The VHS cover of *Sleepaway Camp* features a bloody knife rising out of the water, impaling a sneaker. The back cover doesn't offer stills of the film, unlike other horror movies; instead, it depicts an epistle, handwritten in achingly perfect cursive. "Get me out of here right away!" the letter exhorts, as if adults have ever saved anyone's life in a slasher film. The letter ends with "Wait a minute, I think I hear someone coming up b—." An ink streak. Blood splatter.

23. Harry Benshoff suggests that slasher movies might reflect the growing paranoia around AIDS. "The modern horror films' focus on visceral gore and bodily fluids," he writes, "neatly dovetails into AIDS hysteria . . . even when the monster queer is a lesbian rather than a gay man."

24. Slashers invert traditional horror movie morality. Horror, according to philosopher Noël Carroll, must have a "monster," a being that transgresses the laws of nature, that has violated the body's corporeal form, that has breached the void between life and death, that has divided itself from sanity. Monsters are meant to be feared, reviled, or even possibly pitied—because they are never meant *to be*.

25. Slashers, by contrast, make the victims the transgressors. Consider the oft-stated "rules" for surviving a slasher film: no sex, no drugs, no wandering off alone. What are these rules if not conservative morality? What is the killer if not a brutal enforcer of this morality?

26. In elementary school, a female acquaintance and I were on the swings during lunch. I liked to go high, feel the whoosh of air, the vertiginous sense that mimicked flight, and, at the highest point before my body's pendulum drew me back, jump. The girl next to me went first and missed the landing, landing flat on her ass in the gravel, her dressing hiking up her legs. "Are you looking at my panties?" she called to me. I was still swinging. I shook my head. I was not looking. But I had seen them, and had been seen.

27. Even then, I knew my attraction to boys. In the first grade, I held hands with other boys, thinking nothing of it, until a second grader told me that it was weird and that I shouldn't. He didn't call me a *faggot*—that word was still blissfully distant—but he did call me *gay*. I thought, *Of course I'm happy!* having been fooled by "Deck the Halls." But when I went to the library and looked up gay in the dictionary, I found the definition, which led me to look up *homosexuality*, which in turn led me to understand my own aberrance.

28. Being gay is like knowing the ending of *Sleepaway Camp*. You know it's coming, it's been there all along, waiting for you, and you can't help but stare at the penis.

29. *Sleepaway Camp* prominently features male nudity and almost no female nudity. Examples, excluding various short-shorts, cutoff T-shirts, and flesh-adhering jeans, include:

   14:15—prominent gym shorts bulge
   23:30—face in butt prank
   31:50—skinny-dipping off a pier
   34:10—crotch-grab through underwear
   34:40—cock outline in tighty-whities
   1:18:55—reclining nude from behind

30. (Fascinating aside #3: The actor who plays Billy, the crotch-grabber at 34:10, is now a renowned fashion designer.)

31. The original DVD release of the *Sleepaway Camp* trilogy ham-handedly edits its skinny-dipping scene. Normally, the violence and gore get discreetly trimmed, but in this case, eight pasty-white boy asses got cut. Originally, Robert Hiltzik, the director, had worried about getting an X rating. "If I had gotten an X," he said, "I would have had to contemplate changing the ending, which is something I didn't want to do."

32. The summer before I was to attend grad school, I presented a paper at the Lambda Rising Queer Studies Conference in Boulder, Colorado. Titled "They Don't Call It 'Camp' for Nothing: Subversive Morality in *Sleepaway Camp*," I argued that the film presents a homosexual version

of Laura Mulvey's "male gaze," which lingers on male bodies and, for the most part, ignores female ones.

33. This gay male gaze disappears in the sequels, which feature tits-and-ass aplenty. At a recent 24-hour horror movie marathon sponsored by Exhumed Films, I grew annoyed by the guys behind me, who felt the need to verbally announce, "Boobies!" every time a pair appeared on-screen.

34. (Fascinating aside #4: In the sequels, the actress who plays Angela, who has purportedly undergone a sex-change operation, is Bruce Springsteen's sister.)

35. As I delivered my presentation, I fast-forwarded through the film, a VHS bootleg. I had printed out my notes, a jumble of feminist film theory, queer theory, and Continental philosophy, time-coded to correspond with certain scenes. The audience seemed amused that I had put this much effort into this piece of pop culture detritus. This was something I loved, and I wanted other people to understand why I loved it.

36. Sontag: "Camp taste identifies with what it is enjoying. People who share this feeling are not laughing at the thing they label as 'a camp,' they're enjoying it. Camp is a *tender* feeling."

37. After my presentation, an audience member posed the question: Even if this movie was subversively queer-positive, why shouldn't we view it as transphobic? I didn't have an answer then; I still struggle with

it. But the issue of transphobia, while important, might also be beside the point. While horror movies provide many things, moral instruction isn't usually one of them. As Sontag says, "Camp is a solvent of morality. It neutralizes moral indignation, sponsors playfulness."

38. A more rational response: both trans and queer identities are innate. With Angela, being trans has been forced onto her, as opposed to something she adopts for herself. In a 2011 interview, Hiltzik says, "There are definitely gender conflicts going on with Angela. Starting at an early age, she was exposed to multiple sexualities—her father was gay. Then she was thrust into a gender transformation—whether she wanted it or not."

39. Angela's gender transformation comes at the hands of her flighty, divorced Aunt Martha, the subject of plenty of online speculation. Because of her garish makeup and exaggerated line delivery, some people have suggested that Aunt Martha, herself, is transsexual. (*Look at those mannish hands*, they say.) One outlandish theory posits that Aunt Martha is Lenny, the male lover of Angela's father, John, in drag.

40. But Aunt Martha's presence allows the film to make a case for same-sex marriage. Since there was no legal gay marriage in 1983, after John's death, presumably Lenny had no legal rights and could not have gotten custody of Peter. Without those protections, Peter was thus given to his disturbed aunt, who wanted nothing more than a little girl.

41. (Fascinating aside #5: The actor who plays the young Peter is the older brother of Mike "The Situation" Sorrentino from *Jersey Shore*.)

42. I don't think Hiltzik originally set out to direct a pro-gay slasher. After all, the queer and transgender elements are meant to shock the audience. But given the other sexual deviations in the film—including pedophilia and gerontophilia—homosexuality seems tame by comparison. Indeed, as Sontag points out, "the pure examples of Camp are unintentional; they are dead serious."

43. The audience wants to root for Angela. Unlike other slashers, Angela doesn't serve as an arbiter of morality, but rather fights against bullying and homophobia. "If you think about it," Hiltzik says, "she is a champion for the abused."

44. After Leadership Camp, I started cursing. Not a lot, but enough for my friends to keep a running total. Perhaps this was the start of rage—the realization that the world wasn't how I wanted to be, that it wasn't how it should have been—and that I didn't have to accept it. But, at the time, I had no idea how difficult would be for anger to hit its correct target.

45. In Benjamin Moser's biography of Sontag, he describes a moment when she berates the inventor of the birth control pill after he praises "Notes on Camp": "She has no interest in discussing that essay and never will. He should never have brought it up. He is behind the times, intellectually dead. Hasn't he ever read any of her other works? Doesn't he keep up?"

46. Why does Angela hatchet those kiddie campers, leaving nothing but thick red splotches on the downy innards of their sleeping bags? On the

surface, it seems to be retribution for throwing sand on her, but that feels disproportionate. The real answer: when anger starts to burn, it quickly burns out of control. Angela is the representative of queer rage, a fire that consumes all before it.

47. One theory for the appeal of horror films is that they provide catharsis, a safe place where the audience can relieve themselves of pent-up fears and anxieties, perhaps even anger. As Sontag says, "We are better able to enjoy a fantasy as fantasy when it is not our own."

48. Paul and Angela's budding relationship is, after all, a depiction of young gay love, with all its attendant confusions and pain. During their first moment of intimacy, Angela has a flashback to her father and Lenny in a scene that's meant to convey conflicting emotions about her sexuality. The two men, in soft focus, lounge in bed, shirtless. They're against a black background, almost as though they're floating in outer space. As the soundtrack and camera swirl ominously, dissolves of a young Peter pointing at a young Angela foreshadow the two characters merging.

49. It's possible this was the first homosexual relationship I saw depicted in mass media. I started watching *Dynasty* after the Moldavian Massacre, which had killed off one-half of a gay couple. I never got into *Soap*. I'd never seen tenderness and intimacy between two men before, even though I craved it. As actor Dan Tursi said in an interview, "[The other actor] and I really worked on that scene . . . and played it like a love scene no matter what the gender."

50. The promotion of camp taste, particularly by homosexuals, is "self-serving," Sontag writes. "Homosexuals have pinned their integration into society on promoting the aesthetic sense." And there, in *Sleepaway Camp*, I found myself: a swirl of gender confusion; the first stirrings of desire; the nexus of rage and confusion; and, perhaps, the hope of love.

51. So, we end with *Sleepaway Camp*, as we must, at the beginning: summertime, a boat, two children, their father. The father's lover stands on shore, in striped trunks. It takes us a moment to understand that this scene is of familial bliss. It tastes unfamiliar to the tongue, ephemeral, like the smell of ice on the breeze. This is before the speedboat, before the screaming, before the stupid teenagers. It's summer. We are still alive.

Artist's Note

AS A FAN of horror movies (from as far back as the '70s, when my dad introduced me to classics like *Psycho*, *The Exorcist*, and *The Fog*), I was so excited when Joe asked me to participate in the making of *It Came from the Closet*. As I read through the collection, I found myself drawn to the personal, emotional stories of queer openings that accompanied these musings on film. For each section of the anthology, I unearthed specific visual moments from the individual essays and collaged them together in a single image, as though they were scenes from a film, in homage to the horror movie posters of the '70s and '80s that were such a visceral part of my childhood. I hope I've done some justice to the very intimate reflections that make up this book and to the ever-expanding stories that we as queer people have to tell.

—Bishakh Som
Brooklyn, NY

About the Contributors

SAMUEL AUTMAN writes at the intersections of identity, place, and pop culture. His essays have appeared in *Kept Secret: The Half-Truth in Nonfiction, The Best of Brevity: Twenty Groundbreaking Years of Flash Nonfiction, The Chalk Circle: Intercultural Prizewinning Essays, The St. Louis Anthology, Sweeter Voices Still: An LGBTQ Anthology from Middle America*, and numerous literary magazines. He teaches creative writing at DePauw University. www.samuelautman.com

JEN CORRIGAN is a prose writer who lives in Iowa. Their writing has appeared in *Prairie Schooner, Catapult, Literary Hub, Salon*, and elsewhere. They are currently working on a novel.

VIET DINH was born in Vietnam and grew up in Colorado. He attended Johns Hopkins University and the University of Houston and currently teaches at the University of Delaware. He has received fellowships from the National Endowment for the Arts and the Delaware Division of the Arts, as well as two O. Henry Awards and the Alice Hoffman Prize for Fiction from *Ploughshares*. His stories have appeared in *Zoetrope: All-Story, Witness, Fence, Five Points, Chicago Review, Threepenny Review*, and *Best American Nonrequired Reading* 2017. His debut novel, *After Disasters*, a finalist for the PEN/Faulkner Prize, was released in 2016. He is still wary of summer camps.

JUDE ELLISON S. DOYLE is the author of *Trainwreck: The Women We Love to Hate, Mock, and Fear . . . and Why* (Melville House, 2016) and *Dead Blondes and Bad Mothers: Monstrosity, Patriarchy, and the Fear*

of Female Power (Melville House, 2019), the latter being named one of *Kirkus Reviews*'s Best Non-Fiction Books of 2019. *Maw*, his horror comic series from BOOM! Studios, debuted in September 2021.

RYAN DZELZKALNS has poems appearing with *Assaracus*, *DIAGRAM*, *The Offing*, the *Shanghai Literary Review*, *Tin House*, and others. He received an MFA from New York University and a BA from Macalester College, where he was awarded the Wendy Parrish Poetry Prize. He was recently a Fulbright scholar in Tokyo, where he still lives. www.RyanDz.com

SARAH FONSECA is a self-taught writer from the Georgia foothills who lives in New York City. Her fiction and cinema writing have appeared in *Bosie*, *Evergreen Review*, *Leste Magazine*, the *Los Angeles Review of Books*, Museum of the Moving Image's *Reverse Shot*, and others. She is a coeditor of *The New Lesbian Pulp*, forthcoming from Feminist Press.

BRUCE OWENS GRIMM is a Pushcart-nominated, queer ghost-nerd based in Chicago. He is a coeditor of *Fat and Queer: An Anthology of Queer and Trans Bodies and Lives*. His essays and reviews have appeared in *The Rumpus*, *Brevity's Nonfiction Blog*, *Sweet: A Literary Confection*, *Entropy*, *AWP's Writer's Notebook*, *Iron Horse Literary Review*, *Older Queer Voices*, *Ghost City Review*, and elsewhere. He attended the 2021 Tin House Winter Workshop as well as residencies and workshops at The Fine Arts Work Center in Provincetown, Vermont Studio Center, and the Virginia Center for the Creative Arts (VCCA) among others. @bruceowensgrimm

RICHARD SCOTT LARSON earned his MFA from New York University, and he is the recent recipient of fellowships from MacDowell and the New York Foundation for the Arts. His creative and critical work has appeared in the *Los Angeles Review of Books*, *Chicago Review of Books*, *Harvard Review*, *Colorado Review*, *Electric Literature*, and elsewhere. His writing has also been listed as notable in *The Best American Essays*, and he is an active member of the National Book Critics Circle.

JONATHAN ROBBINS LEON identifies as a queer author of memoir and fiction. His work has been published by Flame Tree Press, Dark Moon Digest, and Distant Shore Publishing. He regards himself as a Shirley Jackson enthusiast and decent Bette Davis impersonator. He and his husband Nick are caretakers of a haunted house and fathers to a super villain.

TUCKER LIEBERMAN is the author of very trans nonfiction books—*Painting Dragons*, *Bad Fire*, and *Ten Past Noon*—and a bilingual poetry collection, *Enkidu Is Dead and Not Dead / Enkidu está muerto y no lo está*. Among the anthologies to which he has contributed, Lambda Literary has recognized *Balancing on the Mechitza* (2011 winner), *Letters For My Brothers* (2012 finalist), and *Trans-Galactic Bike Ride* (2021 finalist). Tucker is frightened by pumpkin spice lattes, which is not to say he would never drink one, since things that are frightening are sometimes good. Previously, he worked for a decade for an investment company, and this was mostly not scary. Originally from Boston, he now haunts Bogotá, Colombia, with his husband, Arturo Serrano, where they scheme about how to publish their novels. www.tuckerlieberman.com

ZEFYR LISOWSKI is a trans and queer writer, artist, three-time Pushcart nominee, and North Carolinian currently living in NYC. She's a Poetry Coeditor for *Apogee* and the author of *Blood Box*, winner of the Black River Editor's Choice Award from Black Lawrence Press and released in fall 2019; she's also the author of the microchap *Wolf Inventory* (Ghost City Press, 2018) and a 2019 Tin House Summer Workshop Fellow. Zefyr's work has appeared in *Literary Hub*, *Nat. Brut.*, *Muzzle*

Magazine, and *DIAGRAM*, among many other places. She's also received support from Sundress Academy for the Arts, McGill University, the New York Live Ideas Fest, the Blue Mountain Center for the Arts, and the 2019 CUNY Graduate Center Adjunct Incubator Grant.

KIRSTY LOGAN's latest book is *Now She is Witch* (Harvill Secker, 2023), a queer medieval witch revenge quest. Forthcoming is *The Unfamiliar* (Virago, 2023), a memoir of queer pregnancy and parenthood. She is also the author of two novels, three story collections, two chapbooks, a short memoir, a 10-hour audio play for Audible, and several collaborative projects with musicians and visual artists. Her books have won the Lambda, Polari, Saboteur, Scott and Gavin Wallace awards. Her work has been optioned for TV, adapted for stage, recorded for radio and podcasts, exhibited in galleries and distributed from a vintage Wurlitzer cigarette machine.

CARMEN MARIA MACHADO is the author of the short story collection *Her Body and Other Parties*, which was a finalist for the National Book Award, and the best-selling memoir *In the Dream House*. She is a Guggenheim Fellow and the Abrams Artist-in-Residence at the University of Pennsylvania.

LAURA MAW is a writer of essays and arts criticism. Her work has been published in the *New Statesman*, the *White Review*, the *Los Angeles Review of Books*, *Hazlitt*, *Electric Literature*, and *Literary Hub*, among others.

CARROW NARBY is a hobbyist writer based on the north shore of Massachusetts. Their essays and fiction have appeared in *Bitch*, *The Toast*, *The Establishment*, *PodCastle*, and *Glittership*. They also contributed a piece of fabricated scholarship to *The Anthology of Babel*, published in 2020 by Punctum Books.

About the Contributors

SACHIKO RAGOSTA (they/them) is a Bay Area–based speculative fiction writer, sexual and reproductive health researcher, and sex educator. As a nonbinary, mixed-race, second generation Japanese American writer, they use fiction to examine the resilience and resolve born out of nonbelonging. They are the author of the chapbook *The Mythology of Blood and Boyhood*, available on their website sachikor.com, and are currently working with Intergalactic Gaysians, a group of Queer and Trans Asian and Pacific Islander (QTAPI) writers, to publish an anthology of QTAPI speculative fiction.

SUMIKO SAULSON is an award-winning author of Afrosurrealist and multicultural sci-fi and horror. Ze is the editor of the anthologies and collections *Black Magic Women, Scry of Lust, Black Celebration,* and *Wickedly Abled.* Ze is the winner of the 2016 HWA StokerCon Scholarship from Hell, 2017 BCC Voice Reframing the Other contest, 2017 Mixy Award, and the 2018 AWW Afrosurrealist Writer Award, and is a 2020 HWA Diversity Grant recipient. Ze has an AA in English from Berkeley City College and writes a column called *Writing While Black* for the *San Francisco BayView,* a national Black newspaper. Ze is the host of the SOMA Leather and LGBT Cultural District's Erotic Storytelling Hour and Social Media Manager at the Horror Writers Association.

PRINCE SHAKUR is an award-winning queer Jamaican American writer, organizer, and podcast host living in Columbus, Ohio. His journalism and nonfiction have appeared in *Teen Vogue, Vice, Level,* and more on social movements, black resilience in the face of iconography, and queer culture. His memoir *When They Tell You to Be Good* is forthcoming from Tin House Books.

BISHAKH SOM is an Indian American trans femme visual artist and author. Her work has appeared in the *New Yorker, Autostraddle, We're Still Here, Beyond, vol. 2, The Strumpet*, the *Boston Review, Black Warrior Review, Vice*, the *Brooklyn Rail, Buzzfeed, Ink Brick*, the *Huffington Post, The Graphic Canon vol. 3*, and *Little Nemo: Dream Another Dream*. She received the Xeric grant in 2003 for her comics collection Angel. Her graphic novel *Apsara Engine* (Feminist Press) is the winner of a 2021 L.A. Times Book Prize for Best Graphic Novel and a 2021 Lambda Literary Award winner for Best LGBTQ Comics. Her graphic memoir *Spellbound* (Street Noise Books) was also a 2021 Lambda Literary Award finalist.

WILL STOCKTON teaches English in Clemson, South Carolina. His essays have appeared in *Hotel America, Broad Street*, and *Bennington Review*.

GRANT SUTTON writes and practices acupuncture in New Orleans, Louisiana.

TOSHA R. TAYLOR is a lecturer in Languages, Literature, and Writing at Manhattanville College in New York. Her academic research predominantly concerns abjection and extreme violence and sexuality in horror media, as does her creative work. Recently published works include studies of horror memes, post-object fandoms, women's horror filmmaking, queer horror, and performative masculinity in rock music. She holds a PhD from Loughborough University.

S. TRIMBLE is a writer and teacher from Toronto, Ontario. She's written on pop culture for *The ROM Magazine* and *Bitch Media*, and her book on visions of the end times, *Undead Ends: Stories of Apocalypse*, is available from Rutgers University Press. Trimble teaches courses on pop culture and writing at the University of Toronto's Women and Gender Studies Institute. She's a puppy parent, NBA nerd, and fan of all things monstrous and ghostly.

About the Contributors

STEFFAN TRIPLETT is a poet and essayist from Joplin, Missouri. His essays have appeared in *Electric Literature, Longreads, Literary Hub, Vulture,* and *Iowa Review.* Steffan's work has been anthologized in *Nepantla: An Anthology Dedicated to Queer Poets of Color* (Nightboat, 2018), *Revisiting the Elegy in the Black Lives Matter Era* (Routledge, 2019), and *Sweeter Voices Still: An LGBTQ Anthology from Middle America* (Belt Publishing, 2021). Steffan has been a fellow for Callaloo and Lambda Literary and is a VONA/Voices alumnus. He currently teaches at the University of Pittsburgh where he is the interim Assistant Director for the Center for African American Poetry and Poetics.

ADDIE TSAI (any/all) is a queer nonbinary artist and writer of color. They collaborated with Dominic Walsh Dance Theater on *Victor Frankenstein* and *Camille Claudel,* among others. Addie holds an MFA from Warren Wilson College and a PhD in Dance from Texas Woman's University. She is the author of the queer Asian young adult novel *Dear Twin. Unwieldy Creatures,* their adult queer biracial retelling of *Frankenstein,* is forthcoming from Jaded Ibis Press. They are the Fiction Coeditor at *Anomaly,* Staff Writer at *Spectrum South,* and Founding Editor & Editor in Chief at *just femme & dandy.*

SPENCER WILLIAMS is from Chula Vista, California. She is the author of the chapbook *Alien Pink* (The Atlas Review, 2017) and has work featured in *Muzzle, PANK, Apogee,* and *Bright Wall/Dark Room.* She received her MFA in creative writing at Rutgers University–Newark and is currently a PhD student in poetics at the University at Buffalo. Her film work has screened at Fotofocus Biennial and the Milwaukee LGBT Film Festival. She tweets @burritotheif.

JOE VALLESE is Clinical Associate Professor in the Expository Writing Program at New York University. His creative and pop culture writing appears in *Bomb*, *Vice*, *Backstage*, *PopMatters*, *Southeast Review*, and *North American Review*, among other publications. He has been nominated for a Pushcart Prize and named a Notable in *The Best American Essays*. He is coeditor of the anthology *What's Your Exit? A Literary Detour Through New Jersey* (Word Riot Press). He holds an MFA from NYU, and MAT and BA degrees from Bard College.

Acknowledgments

DREAMING UP AN anthology is kind of like sketching the blueprint for a house without any guarantee that you'll ever find anyone to help you build it.

My forever gratitude to the Feminist Press team, who provided a foundation more supportive than I could have hoped for: Lauren Rosemary Hook, Drew Stevens, Jisu Kim, Nadine Santoro, Lucia Brown, Isla Ng, and Rachel Page. A particularly big hug to Nick Whitney, editor extraordinaire and disciple of the Black Swan, for loving and championing this project from the start, and for so enthusiastically believing that it was *our turn*.

To the beautiful, enormously talented contributors whose experiences inhabit these pages and bring them to life: thank you for your patience and your continued labor through the sometimes arduous editorial and revision process, and for having faith when I promised we were making something truly special together. I also want to sincerely thank the dozens of other writers whose work I was unable to include; it was a privilege to receive your words.

Thanks to Veronica Esposito for the careful copyedit.

Special thanks to Bishakh Som, for so perfectly translating these essays into tableaus that tell a story all their own, and to Bráulio Amado for the queer-sexy-cool cover design.

To my generous friends, many of whom did double-duty as early ears and eyes for this project: Suzanne Richardson, Brooke Lewis, Susan Fox Rogers, Sarah Goffman, Martha Hart, Hunter McClamrock,

Lauren Vallese, Tom Cannavino, KC Serota, Kristen Keys, Matt Mazur, Carley Moore, Michael Tyrell, Gita DasBender, Raluca Albu, and Kristin Raymundo. A special shout-out to Christine Jensch at NYU, whose behind-the-scenes magic helped make this collection even fuller than I'd imagined.

Amanda Whalen, thank you for your grace and your selflessness, and for letting me tell everyone all about it.

Thank you to my father, Dominick Vallese, for bringing horror into the house; for the weekly trips to B. Dalton to buy the new R. L. Stine or the latest horror movie novelization; for reading me vintage *Tales from the Crypt* comics as bedtime stories; for making sure we never missed an opening night of a new *Elm Street*. And to my siblings, Dom, Vinny, and Monica, for always letting me watch with you, and for always knowing when to cover my eyes.

Thank you to my saintly-patient and endlessly encouraging husband, Alex Servello, who made it possible for me to disappear into the office for hours on end as I wrote, and read, and re-read, and edited myself dizzy. I'm particularly grateful that you have no poker face; when I told you about my idea for this book and your eyes lit up, I knew it was right. I'm so proud of the life and the family we've made together, and "love" has too few letters to express how I feel about you.

Finally, to my son, my Elio (*Elio, Elio*): in the early days and years of this project, I dreamed of you; in the thick of first-round edits, you dreamed soundly on my chest as I softly clicked and typed. When you're old enough one day to pluck this book from the shelf, I hope you'll shrug and wonder why a bunch of queer writers reflecting on and stepping inside of horror movies was ever such a radical idea in the first place.